The Business of Sports

The Business of Sports

Volume 2
Economic Perspectives on Sport

EDITED BY BRAD R. HUMPHREYS
AND DENNIS R. HOWARD

Praeger Perspectives

PRAEGER

Westport, Connecticut
London

Library of Congress Cataloging-in-Publication Data

The business of sports / edited by Brad R. Humphreys and Dennis R. Howard.

    p. cm.

Includes bibliographical references and index.

ISBN 978-0-275-99340-5 ((set) : alk. paper) — ISBN 978-0-275-99341-2 ((vol. 1) : alk. paper) — ISBN 978-0-275-99342-9 ((vol. 2) : alk. paper) — ISBN 978-0-275-99343-6 ((vol. 3) : alk. paper)

1. Professional sports—Economic aspects. 2. Sports—Economic aspects. 3. Sports administration. I. Humphreys, Brad R. II. Howard, Dennis Ramsay, 1945–

GV716.B89 2008

796.06′91—dc22   2008008547

British Library Cataloguing in Publication Data is available.

Library of Congress Catalog Card Number: 2008008547
ISBN: 978-0-275-99340-5 (set)
      978-0-275-99341-2 (vol. 1)
      978-0-275-99342-9 (vol. 2)
      978-0-275-99343-6 (vol. 3)

First published in 2008

Praeger Publishers, 88 Post Road West, Westport, CT 06881
An imprint of Greenwood Publishing Group, Inc.
www.praeger.com

Printed in the United States of America

The paper used in this book complies with the Permanent Paper Standard issued by the National Information Standards Organization (Z39.48–1984).

10 9 8 7 6 5 4 3 2 1

Contents

Preface

Volume 2 of *The Business of Sports* examines sport through the lens of economics. Economics is the study of how society deals with scarcity. Any society faces the problem of allocating scarce resources among competing activities. The sport industry faces the same problems. Teams and leagues face a limited amount of high-caliber talent and must decide how to allocate this talent. Any country has a limited number of markets that can support top-level sports teams and leagues must determine where to best place their franchises. Teams have limited resources to devote to paying players and must determine how to compensate their employees. Economics can bring powerful new insights into these issues, and many more important issues faced by the sports business.

One of the most important issues facing any professional sports organization is how to structure the competition in a way that produces the most exciting outcome on the field or court. Several years ago, economists noticed an interesting similarity in the way corporations structure their promotion and compensation schemes and the way the sports event organizers structure their competitions. Both face similar problems in terms of their ability to monitor effort and their desire to induce maximum effort on the part of all participants/employees. Economic models of this setting have come to be called "tournament theory." Since this observation, economists have frequently used sports outcomes to test the predictions of tournament theory; the lessons from this research have broad applicability on the ballfield and in the boardroom. Bernd Frick and Rob Simmons survey the tournament theory literature, explore the link between corporate personnel management practice and sports events, and explain the interesting conclusions that emerge from this literature and what they mean for organizers of sporting events.

In addition to the question of how to structure the competition, sports leagues also face the issue of how the ownership of teams should be structured. This issue is more complex in sports leagues than in other business settings because of the jointly produced nature of the product produced by sports leagues. Nike does not need Adidas to produce and sell running shoes. In fact, Nike would prefer to take as much of Adidas' market share as possible, and if Adidas ceased to exist Nike would make more profits. But the same thing cannot be said of the New York Yankees and the Boston Red Sox. Although the Yankees would like to beat the Red Sox as often as possible on the field, they could not produce and sell a valuable product without the Red Sox. If the Red Sox ceased to exist, the Yankees would be far less profitable. This is the paradox of competition in sports leagues. A number of interesting business models have been developed to address the unique incentives present in sports leagues. One emerging approach is the "single-entity ownership" model that is used by Major League Soccer in North America. In a single-entity ownership league all teams are owned by one corporate entity. Although single-entity leagues are well equipped to address some of the incentive problems inherent in sports leagues, the legal status of single-entity sports leagues has often run afoul of antitrust laws in the United States, because these laws were not intended to apply to industries where the individual firms jointly produce output. Bradley Ruskin and Jon Oram discuss single-entity sports leagues and recount the evolution of antitrust law as applied to these leagues.

One of the most important allocation problems facing sports leagues is how to distribute the limited number of wins that are available in any season. The allocation of wins, commonly called "competitive balance" by sports fans, is fundamentally an economic problem. If leagues do not allocate wins in an appropriate way, fans will lose interest in the league's product and the league will cease to be a viable business venture. Economists have paid a great deal of attention to this allocation problem over the past twenty years and Brian Soebbing summarizes what economists have to say about competitive balance.

Although sports leagues grow in size over time through expansion, every sports league is a monopoly, and economics teaches us that monopolies make profits by restricting the amount of output produced. In practical terms, this means that there will be fewer teams in any sports league than society would like to have at any given time. There will always be more viable markets for sports teams than there are teams. Franchise moves are a fact of life in North American professional sports leagues. Daniel Rascher applies the economist's toolbox of analytical techniques to the topic of franchise moves in professional sports leagues. Rascher assesses the past history of franchise moves in the United States and Canada, and provides interesting insights into why your favorite local team may be playing in another city half way across the continent in a few years.

Because they are businesses, the competition among professional sports teams extends beyond the ballfield and into the boardroom. The sports pages, and business pages, are filled with stories about how much various sports teams are worth, in dollar terms. And because sports teams are valuable assets, they are frequently bought and sold in the open market just like any other commodity. Mitchell Ziets and David Haber address the interesting question of how much professional sports teams are worth. Unlike many other corporations that have shares traded on stock exchanges, professional sports teams in North America are privately held businesses with no publicly traded shares. This leads to some difficulties when determining the financial value of sports teams, the focus of the chapter by Ziets and Haber.

Sports teams and leagues are not the only organizations that face the fundamental economic problem of the allocation of scarce resources to infinite wants and needs. Federal, state, and local governments face the same problem: government has a limited ability to raise tax revenues and an unlimited set of taxpayer demands to satisfy. Interestingly, professional sports teams and leagues are recipients of government handouts. Much of the money spent on new and renovated professional sports facilities over the past few decades in the United States and Canada has come from state and local government subsidies. It is not uncommon for a new professional sports facility in the United States to be built entirely with government funds. Because our government does not have access to unlimited funds, subsidies for professional sports facility construction demands careful attention. Xia Feng provides a thorough and critical analysis of the economic justification for government subsidization of sports facility construction. Feng points out that the most common justification for these subsidies, the economic impact of sports on urban economies, has surprisingly little support in terms of credible empirical evidence.

Professional athletes earn salaries far greater than the average worker. While some observers decry these salaries as examples of where modern societies have gone wrong, a number of the chapters in these volumes point out that the modern professional sports franchise is an extremely profitable commercial enterprise. Economists have been studying the issue of pay and performance in the workplace for decades. Bernd Frick and Rob Simmons summarize the economics of pay and performance in professional sports. This lively and insightful discussion of how salaries are determined provides an interesting perspective on the huge salaries earned by twenty-first-century athletes.

The rising salaries of professional athletes have not escaped the attention of the owners of sports teams and the officials in sports leagues. Surely no reader will be surprised by this observation. But readers unfamiliar with the economic history of professional sports leagues in North America may be surprised to learn that "out of control" salaries were a major concern of the owners of professional baseball teams almost from the moment that the National League was formed almost one hundred and thirty years ago. From the perspective of professional sports team owners, athletes have always been overpaid. Michael Leeds examines the ways in which professional sports leagues have tried to rein in the growth of athletes' salaries, the reasons why salary caps never seem to be effective, and the consequences of these events.

The sports business has a number of interesting features that distinguish it from other industries. One of these features is the important nonmarket benefits generated by sports businesses. When a Wall Street brokerage house pulls off a successful IPO, or a merger and acquisitions lawyer seals a multi-billion-dollar merger deal, the average Jane in the street has little reason to celebrate, despite the large economic impact of these events. But when the local professional sports team wins a key playoff game, the entire city, even casual fans who did not attend the game or watch it on TV, celebrates and experiences an enhanced sense of civic pride. From an economic perspective, the intangible benefits generated by sport are called nontraded goods, because you can't buy a dozen World Series championships at the corner store. Even though these benefits are intangible, they are still important. Moreover, these intangible benefits may explain why local governments continue to subsidize professional sports facility construction despite the lack of economic impact from these facilities. Can intangible benefits from sport justify the large public subsidies for new stadium and arena construction? How valuable are these intangible benefits, in terms of dollars and cents? In the past few years, economists have begun to address these questions. Bruce Johnson surveys the emerging economic research on valuing the intangible benefits generated by sports and explains why this research is vitally important in the public debate over stadium subsidies.

Speaking of the public debate on subsidies for the construction of sports facilities, just how much of taxpayers' dollars actually go to the construction of palatial new stadiums and arenas? A careful examination of newspaper and broadcast media coverage often reveals a number of different, conflicting reports of the total cost to the taxpayer of that shiny new arena downtown. Andrew Zimbalist and Judith Grant Long recently took a very close look at the nitty-gritty details of new stadium and arena construction deals and assessed just how much these projects actually cost taxpayers. Their provocative conclusion: a lot more than sports team owners would have you think.

In the final chapter of volume 2, John Fizel describes the interesting economics of salary arbitration in Major League Baseball. MLB team owners implemented salary arbitration as a cost containment mechanism, to rein in those spiraling salaries paid to athletes. But a funny thing happened on the way to cost containment: even though salary arbitration was designed to hold down salaries, and even though owners win the majority of arbitration hearings, salary arbitration in baseball has been very beneficial for baseball players. Fizel's chapter explains why this interesting and surprising outcome occurred.

ACKNOWLEDGMENTS

A project on the scale of *The Business of Sport* is a huge undertaking. From inception to publication, it has taken a long time and a lot of work—more than either of us realized when we first took on this project. We could not have completed it without the help of many people, all of whom deserve our deepest thanks and appreciation. First and foremost, we thank each and every one of our contributing authors. We have been blessed to work with such a talented group, and we gratefully acknowledge the contributions of all of these hard-working individuals.

We also got a tremendous amount of editorial support from the staff at Praeger Publishers/Greenwood Press. Praeger is an excellent, professional, well-run publishing house, and the efforts of the editors there have made significant contributions to the project. We thank all of the Praeger/Greenwood editorial staff members who assisted us in the completion of *The Business of Sport* for their help. We also thank Jane Ruseski, Brian Soebbing, Dan "Professor Puck" Mason, Tiffany Richardson, Angela Ronk, Jill Gurke, Amie Cowie, Craig Depken, Andy Zimbalist, Rick Zuber, and Paul Swangard for their help, support, and valuable input. We couldn't have done this without you.

One

The Allocation of Rewards in Athletic Contests

Bernd Frick and Rob Simmons

Like most top-tier games in professional basketball, baseball, and soccer, high-level competitions in individualistic sports, such as the tennis tournaments of Wimbledon and Flushing Meadows, the golf tournaments of Augusta and St. Andrews, as well as the marathons of New York and London, attract not only thousands of spectators, but also a TV audience of millions of fans. Moreover, these (and other) individualistic sports have recently received increased attention from economists trying to test a number of hypotheses that can be derived from "tournament theory" or—as a synonym—"contest theory." In this chapter we first provide a brief description of the development of prize-money levels and structures in professional golf, tennis, and distance running, and athletes' incomes over the last years. We then summarize the basic insights and the core predictions of tournament/contest theory and review the available literature on the incentive effects of tournament pay systems in athletic contests. Finally, we raise some of the questions that have not yet been answered and should, therefore, be dealt with in future research.

THE DEVELOPMENT OF PRIZE-MONEY LEVELS AND STRUCTURES

The top events in tennis, golf, and—to a much lesser extent—distance running offer considerable purses to the successful contestants. Moreover, all three sports are organized like a pyramid, with different categories of tournaments for the top athletes, as well as less-talented/less-successful players and developing talent.

The Association of Tennis Professionals (ATP) tour calendar for 2007 includes sixty-three different tournaments with considerable variation in the prize purses they offered, from $332,000 to $3.7 million.[1] Nine of these tournaments belong to the Masters Series, offering between $2.5 million and $3.2 million each. This series is crowned by the Masters Cup, to which the eight highest-ranked players in the preceding year are invited. The prize purse of this tournament currently stands at $3.7 million. The remaining fifty-three tournaments belong to the International Series, nine of which have Gold status due to the higher prize money they offer (more than $1 million). The most prestigious tournaments, however, are the four Grand Slam events (Melbourne, London, Paris, New York) organized by the International Tennis Federation (ITF). In 2007 the total prize purses offered by these four tournaments varied between $15 million and $23 million.

In these latter tournaments, the winners of the two singles competitions, for example, receive between $800,000 and $1 million while the runner-up is paid approximately 50 percent of that amount (see Figure 1.1). In the tournaments offering lower purses, the distribution of the prize money is slightly different, with the winner receiving a larger share of the pie. Players failing to qualify for the ATP events in 2007 could compete in one of the 174 different "challenger tournaments" offering considerably lower prize

FIGURE 1.1

Prize Money Levels and Structures in the Grand Slam Tennis Tournaments, 2007

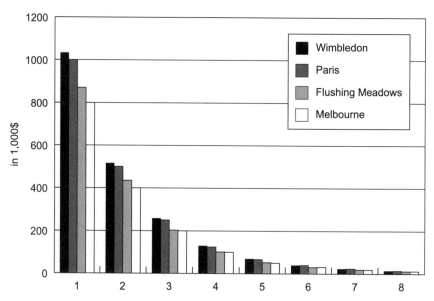

purses (ranging from $25,000 to $125,000) to try to accumulate the ranking points required to get admission to the (better-paying and more prestigious) ATP tournaments. Moreover, nearly 4,200 different "futures tournaments" are played all over the world every year, offering purses between $10,000 and $15,000.

In professional golf, the total prize purse in the most prestigious competition, the PGA Tour, reached $295 million in 2007. The purse per tournament (approximately fifty) varies between $3.5 million and $9 million with the percentage breakdown being identical regardless of the total purse. The winner of a tournament always receives 18 percent of the total purse, the runner-up is awarded 10 percent, and the player finishing third receives 6.8 percent (see Figure 1.2).[2] Thus, as in the case of tennis, we observe a highly nonlinear distribution of rewards to performance, with the top performers receiving disproportionately large shares of the money that is at stake.

Again, as in the case of tennis, in golf a "super tournament" to which the most successful players are invited at the end of the season (tour championship) links the different contests together. Moreover, there are two minor professional tours in the United States: the Champions Tour for players aged fifty and more, and the Nationwide Tour for younger and/or less successful players trying to qualify for the PGA Tour.[3] Both tours consist of slightly more than thirty tournaments offering prize purses between

FIGURE 1.2
Prize Money Distribution in the PGA Tournaments

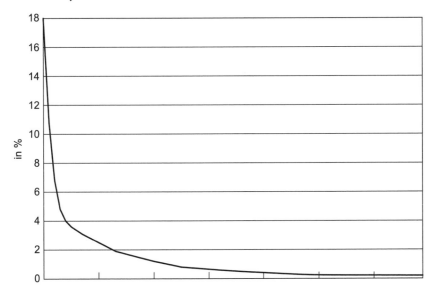

$1.6 million and $2.6 million (Champions Tour) and $.450 million and $.775 million (Nationwide Tour). Here again, the distribution of the purse is identical across all tournaments.

A quite different picture emerges if we look at the purses of the five city marathons forming the World Marathon Majors (the races in Berlin, Boston, Chicago, London, and New York).[4] Unlike the top-tier tournaments in tennis and golf, where entry is restricted to athletes who have qualified for the respective event (more on that below), participation in either of these races—as well as in other city marathons—is open. The five events, along with the Olympic Marathon and the International Association of Athletics Federations (IAAF) World Championships Marathon, serve as the qualifying races in the series. At the conclusion of each qualifying race, the top five male and female finishers are awarded points based on their finish place. At the conclusion of each two-year series, a $1-million prize purse will be split equally between the top male and female point earners, providing each champion with $500,000. The total score for each athlete in a series will consist of points earned from a maximum of four qualifying races during that two-year cycle. Athletes earn points by placing among the top five in qualifying races. Points are allocated following each race as follows: First place results in twenty-five points, second place fifteen points, third place ten points, fourth place five points, and fifth place one point. Points from a maximum of four qualifying races will be scored. If an athlete earns points in more than four events, the athlete's best four finishes will be scored.

It appears from Figure 1.3 that the winner usually receives twice the amount that goes to the runner-up, while the second-place finisher receives about 30 percent more than the person finishing in third place. Unlike tennis and golf tournaments, the number of athletes who receive a share of the purse varies considerably in long-distance running. In Chicago only the top five finishers are paid, while in Boston the top fifteen are paid (the remaining three races are somewhere between these two extremes). Moreover, in the case of distance-running events, the prize purse is usually considerably enhanced by performance-related bonuses. If athletes break certain barriers (such as two hours and ten minutes for men or two hours and thirty minutes for women) or run a new course or even a world record, they can considerably increase their revenues (see Table 1.1).

Obviously, bonus payments are not correlated with the prize purse or the amount of money that can be earned by the winner, but are related to the difficulty of the course. The men's two most recent world records have been set in Berlin, suggesting that Berlin is the fastest of the five courses. New York, on the other hand, is clearly the most difficult one.

FIGURE 1.3
Prize Money Levels in the World Marathon Majors, 2006–2007

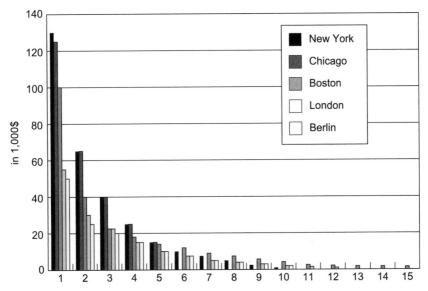

TABLE 1.1
Bonus Payments in Major City Marathons (Men)

Required Performance	Berlin	Boston	Chicago	London	New York
Sub 2:10:00	4,000[a]	—	7,500	3,000	25,000
Sub 2:08:30	10,000	—	15,000	15,000	40,000
Sub 2:07:30	20,000	—	30,000	25,000[b]	70,000
Sub 2:06:30	40,000	—	55,000	—	—
Course record	n.d.	25,000	200,000	25,000	60,000
World record	65,000	50,000	300,000	125,000	n.d.

[a]Required time: 2:09:30.
[b]Required time: 2:08:00.
Notes: — = No bonus available; n.d. = bonus not disclosed.

These differences in total prize purses and prize distributions translate into different annual and lifetime earnings of the respective groups of athletes. Table 1.2 reveals that the annual as well as the career earnings of golf and tennis players are about twenty times higher than those of long-distance runners who, in general, earn more than most other track-and-field athletes (with the notable exception of sprinters).[5] This finding holds irrespective of whether one looks at number one, number ten, or number fifty on the respective earnings list.

TABLE 1.2
Top Earners in Selected Individual Sports

Overall Money Rank	Sport / Gender			
	2006 Earnings[a]		Career Earnings	
	Name	Amount	Name	Amount
	Road Running / Women[b]			
1	Berhane Adere	237,500	Paula Radcliffe	1,842,835
10	Meseret Defar	126,000	Susan Chepkemei	768,095
50	Nataliya Volguina	29,165	Nuta Olaru	292,175
	Road Running / Men[b]			
1	Robert Cheruiyot	266,000	Haile Gebrselassie	2,343,883
10	Daniel Njenga	80,000	Moses Tanui	553,395
50	Evans Cheruiyot	29,820	Sammy Korir	275,070
	Tennis / Women[c]			
1	Justine Henin	4,204,810	Steffi Graf	21,895,277
10	Patty Schnyder	883,685	Kim Clijsters	14,764,295
50	Iveta Benesova	251,563	Nathalie Dechy	3,514,709
	Tennis /Men[c]			
1	Roger Federer	8,343,835	Pete Sampras	43,280,489
10	Jonas Bjorkman	1,221,485	Lleyton Hewitt	17,215,012
50	Nicolas Kiefer	456,005	Thomas Johansson	6,535,842
	Golf / Women[c]			
1	Lorena Ochoa	2,592,872	Annika Sorenstam	20,641,936
10	Pat Hurst	1,128,662	Christie Kerr	7,752,263
50	Nancy Scranton	274,304	Janice Moodie	3,066,135
	Golf / Men[c]			
1	Tiger Woods	9,941,563	Tiger Woods	65,712,324
10	Brett Wetterich	3,023,185	Kenny Perry	20,335,031
50	Richard S. Johnson	1,555,376	Shigeki Maruyama	12,241,561

[a]Annual earnings in nominal US$.
[b]Complete through August 2007.
[c]Complete through December 2006.
Sources: www.rrm.com, www.pgatour.com, www.lpga.com, www.tennisessentials.com, www.tennis.bravehost.com, www.nascar.com

It is, of course, quite likely that the figures presented in Table 1.2 underestimate the earnings of the distance runners because their "incomes ... are generally a mysterious mix of shoe-contract money and appearance fees, which for the top performers can total far more than $1 million a year. Yet in a marketplace in which celebrity is often measured by salary, these invisible niches have no promotional value."[6] However, since the endorsement contracts signed by the top golf and tennis players (remember the multimillion and multiyear contracts of Tiger Woods and the Williams sisters with Nike) are generally much higher than the ones granted to distance runners, the figures presented above grossly underestimate the earnings differentials between the three groups of individual athletes.

ATHLETIC CONTESTS AS RANK-ORDER TOURNAMENTS

Athletic contests, such as golf tournaments and long-distance foot races, are invariably rank-ordered because most of the social interest and value of these events lies in ascertaining the best contestant. The contests themselves represent a test of abilities and motivations among the individual participants; the common and binding rules of the game allow relative evaluations. Athletes entering a particular contest choose their effort levels and other actions (such as their strategies) to optimize against the efforts of opponents, given the rules of the game and the costs and rewards of winning.[7]

From an economic point of view, the structure of athletic contests can be described as follows: First, prizes are fixed in advance and are—with the exception of performance-related bonuses in marathon races—independent of absolute performance. This means that the winner receives the first prize not for being good, but for being (slightly) better than the runner-up. The amount of money that goes to the winner is not affected by the amount by which he or she beats the runner-up. Even if both athletes do extremely well, neither the total prize money nor its distribution will be affected. Second, the level of effort with which each athlete expends to win the contest entered depends on the size of the (potential) prize. This implies that the larger the spread between the winner's and the loser's prize, the higher the effort exerted by both athletes. Thus, prize structures are designed to induce individual contestants to put forth more effort, which in turn increases the interest of sports fans in that competition (with the likely consequence that the organizer's profits increase, too). This does not mean, however, that contest organizers should implement a winner-take-all tournament, because there clearly is a limit to spread. Although additional spread induces more effort, the average prize money must be high enough to attract athletes to enter the event in the first place.

Athletes typically receive feedback during the competition about their relative positions. Since final payoffs usually depend only on rank order and not on absolute performance, contestants will adjust their behavior in response to that intermediate information: A golfer who, on the last day of a tournament, knows that he is ten strokes behind the leader has less incentive to put forth effort that a player who is just one stroke behind. Similarly, a marathon runner who is informed by his coach at km 30 that he is two minutes behind the leader is less likely to speed up than a runner who is just twenty seconds behind. Moreover, if athletes can choose between "risky" and "safe" strategies, they are likely to alter their choice of strategy in response to intermediate information, that is, a tennis player who is three points behind in the final set of a match is likely to play with more risk by, for example, serving harder. Thus, in a tournament the leader has an incentive to pursue a "safe" strategy while the trailer usually pursues a "risky" strategy.[8]

Apart from the "incentive function" described above, athletic contests also serve a "sorting function." By having a pyramidal structure of events it is possible to let individuals compete with one another and then have winners compete with other winners to get admission to the top-tier tournaments where higher prize purses are at stake. In the end, such a structure is equivalent to a multiple-round elimination tournament. Both systems try to ensure that only the most able competitors make it to the final round or the final contest.[9] Summarizing, the function of minor tournaments is not only to identify particularly able athletes but also to avoid "contamination" of the professional elite. This is important insofar as, for example, the prize money that is being paid to a first-round loser in a Grand Slam tournament often exceeds the amount of money he can earn in a minor tournament. Moreover, as the number of contestants increases, the individual's probability of winning decreases. Since with too many participants, each contestant is discouraged to put forth effort, free and open entry is generally not the optimal participation policy.

Thus, organizers of top events usually try to limit the number of entries. In tennis, for example, 96 of the 128 spots at a Grand Slam tournament are filled according to the current world ranking, with the remaining 32 slots filled by players who have to qualify immediately before the tournament in an elimination round. In golf entry to most PGA tournaments is limited to 144 or 156 players with a few tournaments restricting entry much more severely. Again, the rationing device is a player's past performance. The highest-priority category consist of golfers who have either won a tournament in the recent past or who finished among the top 125 money winners in the previous years. The middle category consists of players who were among the top 15 money winners on the PGA's minor-league golf tour or finished among the top 35 at the annual PGA qualifying tournament before the start of the season. The lowest-priority category consists of players who do not qualify for either one of the first two groups. While golfers in the first category have guaranteed slots in any tournament they wish to enter, players from the second category are occasionally denied access by the rationing rule. Finally, players from the third category are most of the time not admitted to a tournament they wish to enter.[10] In distance running, access to a particular race is usually not restricted by eligibility or performance but by the local organizer's willingness to pay for an athlete's travel costs and accommodation. Since the organizers of the more renowned races have an incentive to assemble the best athletes, recent top performers have a much higher probability of being invited, that is, the selection procedure is in the end quite similar to the one described above for golf and tennis.

Effort usually suffers when heterogeneous athletes compete against each other.[11] Effort has the largest effect on changing the probability of winning when the contestants are of similar ability. If ability differs among contestants, then both the talented and the less talented tend to restrict their effort. To maintain high levels of effort it is important to group athletes so that they are evenly matched with those against which they will directly compete. Another possibility is to implement handicap rules that compensate the weaker athletes' disadvantage or to offer additional rewards to the weaker athletes.[12] Thus, heterogeneity is another reason not to implement a winner-take-all prize money structure: In order to motivate weaker athletes to put forth effort, prizes for the runner-up, the third finisher, and so on, are clearly warranted.[13]

The asymmetric prize structure in a single athletic contest is very often supplemented by a "super contest" that links together the single events. The option value of competing in that latter contest provides additional motivation to athletes to perform well in the individual tournaments they enter over the course of a season. When the athlete reaches the final round, there is no longer any option value, that is, winning the super contest is the end of the story. Therefore, the prize money in that final contest is usually particularly high. The three individualistic sports that are of particular interest in this chapter have all introduced such a super contest—the Tour Championship in golf, the Masters Cup in tennis and the World Marathon Majors in distance running.

The research discussed in the previous section can be summarized under three different headings: (1) the impact of prizes and prize spreads on incentives to perform; (2) the impact of the structure of the contest on the individual athlete's strategic behavior; and (3) the different responses of risk-loving and risk-averse athletes to tournament incentive systems. In the next section, we review the existing evidence on the earnings of athletes in individual sports in light of these factors.

TOURNAMENT INCENTIVES AND ATHLETIC PERFORMANCE: A REVIEW OF THE EVIDENCE

In an extensive survey of labor markets in professional (team) sports, Lawrence Kahn concluded that "some of the most intriguing evidence on the links from incentives to performance comes from sports … like golf and marathon running."[14] In these sports it is possible to collect data on individual performance and to relate that data to the prize money offered in individual tournaments. Here, we review the existing evidence about the prize structure and earnings from professional golf, tennis, distance running, and selected other individual sports.

Sorting versus Motivation: What Explains Athletes' Behavior?

Golf

Ronald Ehrenberg and Michael Bognanno were the first to analyze the prize money-performance relationship examining the scores in American and European PGA golf tournaments.[15] Their first important finding is that scores are lower, indicating that effort is higher, when the prize purse is higher. Second, they looked at the impact of a player's position after the third day on his or her performance on the last day of the tournament. The prediction is that players who are trailing one or more of their opponents very closely have a larger incentive to perform well as the marginal returns to effort are higher. This prediction is again strongly supported by the data. Finally, since the prize spread decreases with order of finish (the differences between two adjacent ranks get smaller; see Figure 1.2) effort is expected to be higher (and scores lower) in the final round when a player has a higher standing at the beginning of this round. Again, this prediction is strongly confirmed by the data.[16] Focusing on the sorting effects of tournaments, Ehrenberg and Bognanno also showed that exempt players (those who are allowed to enter any tournament they wish to play) are more likely than nonexempt players to enter tournaments that offer particularly high prize money.[17]

This latter finding is extended to yet another aspect: In a recent study Thomas Rhoads found that players' annual entry decisions change as their exemption status changes; players enjoying a lengthy exemption status enter significantly fewer events per year compared to players whose exemption status is about to expire.[18] Todd McFall, Charles Knoeber, and Walter Thurman examined the incentive effects of a "grand prize" by comparing player performance on the PGA tour before and after the introduction of the season-ending Tour Championship.[19] They found considerable changes, particularly in the behavior of the most successful players: Since entry into the final tournament is restricted to those thirty players who win the most money during the regular season, players who win early in the year face incentives to try harder and perform better than they otherwise would (and the reverse for those who lose early). Toward the end of the season, when those who have won early are assured of a spot in the finals, they will try less hard compared to those still competing for a spot (those around the "cut-off-rank" on the money list).

Tennis

Using data from the semifinals and the finals of men's and women's major tennis tournaments played in the years 1990–2002 and 2002–2004, respectively, Uwe Sunde on the one hand and Thierry Lallemand, Robert Plasman, and Francois Rycx on the other hand try to separate the incentive effects of prize money from the impact of *ex ante* heterogeneity in players' abilities.[20] Both studies find that the incentive effect on effort resulting from playing a final, where the prize to be won is about twice as high as the prize for winning the semifinal, is positive and statistically highly significant. Thus, women and men seem to react to prize incentives in a very similar way. The remaining results for men and women, however, are completely different: While for women uneven contests lead favorites to win more games and underdogs to perform more poorly, the exact opposite seems to be true for men.

These results, although incompatible at first sight, can easily be reconciled: If the difference in the number of games won by the favorite and the underdog increases with the difference in the individual players' ranking position, it is the "capability aspect" of heterogeneity that dominates. If, on the other hand, the difference in the number of games won by the favorite and the underdog decreases as the difference in the ranking positions increases, the incentive aspect of heterogeneity seems to dominate. Surprising as they may be, these results certainly do not suggest that men and women behave differently in a highly competitive environment (more on that below). A plausible interpretation is that the heterogeneity measures used in the two studies— the absolute difference in the ranking points of the contestants—more accurately reflects heterogeneity in the abilities of women than in those of men.

Douglas Coate and Donijo Robbins analyzed the long-run effect of prize money on player careers by looking, first, at the number of tournaments played per year and, second, the timing of retirement.[21] They used a sample of some 240 male and 220 female tennis players who attained a singles ranking in the top fifty at least once on their respective tours between 1979 and 1994 and found that a $50,000 reduction in real tournament earnings increases the probability of retiring in the following year by 15 percent. Moreover, the higher the prize money a player has won in the previous season, the more tournaments she enters in the current season. Obviously, both findings are in line with the incentive story outlined above.[22]

Distance Running

Michael Maloney and Robert McCormick use data from 115 foot races ranging in distance from one mile to full marathon that were held in the southeastern United States between 1987 and 1991.[23] They find that both the average prize paid and the prize spread have the predicted negative and statistically significant influence on finish times: Doubling the average prize leads to a fall in average times by about 2 percent and doubling the prize spread leads to a fall in average times by about 4 percent. They interpret their findings to be consistent with the "sorting hypothesis" as well as the "incentive hypothesis." Using data from 135 different races ranging in distance from 5k to full marathon Jim Lynch and Jeffrey Zax also confirmed the hypothesis that times are faster in races offering higher prize money. However, when controlling for runner ability by including a measure of the athletes' recent race history in the regression, the incentive effects of the prize level and spread completely disappear.[24] The authors therefore attribute the impact of prize spread to the sorting effects of tournaments rather than the incentive effects.

Bernd Frick, as well as Bernd Frick and Rainer Klaeren, used data from fifty-seven different city marathons run worldwide between 1983 and 1995 and involving much larger prize money (around $135,000 per race in 1993 dollars).[25] They found that (a) doubling the average prize reduces average times by 1 percent; (b) doubling the spread improves average times by 2 percent; (c) doubling bonus payments improves average finish times by about .75 percent. Moreover, an increase in prize fund, spread, and bonus payments also increases the closeness of the race (measured as the time difference between the winner and the next four finishers). Finally, race times are decreasing in the number of "in the money" ranks (i.e., the number of prizes). Thus, all the characteristics of the prize fund seem to influence the elite runners' performance in the way predicted by tournament theory. However, when controlling for the endogeneity of the prize purse as well as for runner abilities, Bernd Frick and Joachim Prinz find that the prize purse becomes insignificant while the spread variables retain their statistical significance.[26] This seems to suggest that the selection effect of tournament pay systems dominates the incentive effect.

Horse Racing

Sue Fernie and David Metcalf analyzed the influence of alternative remuneration systems on the performance of a sample of British jockeys. They found that replacing incentive contracts by noncontingent retainer payments introduces moral hazard into a payment system that had proved to be very successful at overcoming such behavior: Jockeys who signed contracts that guaranteed them a fixed instead of a variable income showed a dramatically deteriorating performance.[27] Not surprisingly, therefore, none of these contracts was renewed—with the interesting consequence that most of the jockeys returned to their previous performance levels once they were paid strictly according to their results again. Analyzing data from Arabian horse races in the United States and Canada, Jim Lynch found that jockeys increase their efforts (lower their times) in the second half of races when the amount of prize money lost by dropping one place is greater and when there is less distance between them and their closest competitor.[28] Moreover, Jim Lynch and Jeffrey Zax showed that races with the highest prize purses attract contestants of varying ability. This contamination effect can be eliminated by increasing the prize spread, which in turn will induce contestants to self-select into tournaments based on their individual abilities.[29] Finally, Glenn Boyle, Graeme Guthrie, and Luke Gorton demonstrated that client-owned horses perform significantly better than horses owned by their trainers. Trainers have an incentive to devote more effort to horses they own themselves, but in doing so they run the risk that horses owned by clients will be transferred to other stables in the future. Thus, apart from financial incentives reputational incentives seem to be very important in this context, too.[30]

Other Individualistic Sports

Apart from foot and horse races as well as golf and tennis tournaments, a number of other individualistic sports have produced empirical studies on the prize money-performance relationship:

- Using a three-year panel from the U.S. Professional Bowlers Association Michael Bognanno found a consistently positive and generally significant influence of total prize money on bowlers' performance (as measured by the number of pins per round). This supports the main prediction of tournament theory that higher prize levels and, hence, dispersion among prizes lead to higher output. However, he also found that the percentage of prize money allocated to first place has a significantly negative influence, suggesting that greater skewness reduces the rewards to winning—a finding that presents a contradiction to the theory under test.[31]

- Brian Becker and Mark Huselid drew on two different panels from auto racing (NASCAR and the International Motor Sports Association) to study the influence of prize money differentials on both driver performance and safety. They found that the prize spread has indeed the expected incentive effects on individual performance and that these effects peak at rather high spreads and then level off. Perhaps most important is yet another finding: Driver safety is adversely affected by increasing the prize spread, suggesting that tournaments may produce "undesirable" behavior as well.[32] Peter von Allmen demonstrated that the reward structure in NASCAR is efficient because of the linearity of the reward structure of individual races that is accompanied by highly nonlinear end-of-season rewards.[33] The analysis shows that the need to maintain sponsorship exposure, combined with drivers' willingness to take risks (and the possible catastrophic result of negative outcomes of such behavior), creates a competitive environment where winner-take-all would be inefficient.[34] In a companion paper, von Allmen showed that neither in NASCAR nor in Championship Auto Racing Team (CART) do drivers respond to the possibility of increases in marginal winnings or losses.[35]

- Joachim Prinz used data from forty-four different long-distance triathlons ("Ironman" races) held in nine different locations all over the world over the period 1989–1999. Ironman contests are interesting insofar as purses are rather low compared to sports like golf and tennis (the average purse a top ten finisher takes home is slightly more than $3,000) while the training requirements by far exceed those in most other sports.[36] Nevertheless, the author found that both a higher purse and a greater spread result in faster finish times. Moreover, the smaller the difference between the prize money attached to a specific rank and the preceding rank, the slower the finish times. These findings are robust on further controls, such as athlete quality (measured by the personal records of the athletes).[37]

Summarizing, it appears that the amount of prize money offered induces considerable selection effects while the distribution of the purse induces the participants to put forth effort in an attempt to maximize their individual revenues.

Incentives, Risk-Taking and Strategic Behavior

Identifying the most able athletes by rank-order tournaments is problematic if the contestants are able to choose strategies of different risk for two reasons. First, the tournaments' outcomes are then mainly determined by luck or random components and therefore do not provide much information about the athletes' abilities. Second, athletes preferring high-risk strategies often choose low-effort levels. Since risk-taking behavior is likely to bias the results of a contest, it is of interest to explore, first, to what extent athletes make use of risky strategies and, second, whether the choice of such strategies pays off for the athlete.

Christian Grund and Oliver Gürtler studied the risk-taking behavior of head coaches in the German Bundesliga in 2003/04 by looking at the positions of players who are substituted during a match.[38] In principle, a coach can undertake a risk-neutral substitution (the player taken off the field and the player sent on the field have the same tactical position), a risk-taking substitution (a defender is replaced by either a midfielder or a forward or a midfielder by a forward), or a risk-reducing substitution (a midfielder or a forward is replaced by a defender or a forward by a midfielder). A risk-taking substitution increases the probability to score a goal, but also increases the possibility that a goal is scored against the team. As expected, the probability of risk-taking (risk-reducing) substitutions decreases (increases) with the difference in goals: Coaches replace defensive players with offensive ones when their team is behind and substitute offensive players for defensive ones when their team is ahead. However, risk-taking behavior does not pay: The increase in the probability of scoring an additional goal is more than offset by the increasing probability of conceding a (further) goal.

Studying videotapes of all middle- and long-distance races at the 1992 Olympic Games in Barcelona, David Boyd and Laura Boyd showed that in the men's races (but not in the women's) the underdogs moved first and the favorites tended to wait: While the prerace favorites (measured by prior performance) usually start out conservatively and then move up past other runners as the race develops, the underdogs tend to start quickly but see their performance and relative race position deteriorate as the event transpires. The fact that the men's races are considerably more strategic than the women's is apparently due to the fact that the talent pool is more concentrated for men than for women.[39] Not surprisingly, risky strategies pay off for the underdog only on the middle distances. The longer the race is, the less likely the underdog is to win.

A further study that deserves being mentioned in this context is the one by Stephen Bronars and Gerald Oettinger. They tested for effects of risk-taking in golf tournaments by analyzing whether players who appear to have an incentive to take (avoid) risks over the last holes of the final round are more (less) likely to shoot scores that deviate considerably from par (the "normal" result for a professional).[40] Surprisingly, their results are in accordance with tournament theory, but are not statistically significant.

Jason Abrevaya studies individual performance in ladder tournaments, using data from professional bowling competitions. He found that underdogs win more often than expected and explained this not by differing individual responses to (financial) incentives, but by "hot-hand" and "regression-to-the-mean" theories.[41] Moreover, when analyzing data from sumo wrestling, Mark Duggan and Steven Levitt were less interested in testing predictions derived from tournament theory than finding evidence for corruption. Nevertheless, they showed that wrestlers' effort apparently increases when the marginal returns to winning increase.[42] Keith Willoughby and Kent Kostiuk examined the choice between taking a single point and blanking an end in the latter stages of a curling game. It turns out that blanking an end is the better alternative, but it is usually only chosen by Americans, but not by Europeans.[43] David Laband found that tournament wins are concentrated among a small number of top players in tennis, but not in golf. He does not explain this by referring to differences in risk-taking, but by emphasizing the importance of the match-play structure of competition and the practice of seeding the top players against weaker players in the early rounds of a tennis tournament.[44]

Assuming for a moment that the card game poker is indeed a sport, a study by Yungmin Lee is quite interesting. Poker tournaments are particularly suitable to study risk-taking behavior, because risk-taking is the essential component of an individual's strategy while the problem of effort choice is trivial. Moreover, poker tournaments provide a unique opportunity to evaluate risk-taking behavior under well-defined rules in the face of high monetary incentives—something that cannot be achieved in a laboratory experiment.[45] Apart from that, players are homogenous in quality and are unlikely to make systematic mistakes in statistical calculations. Using data from twenty-seven tournaments of the World Poker Tour in 2002/03–2003/04 it was found that risk-taking behavior is completely in line with the predictions of tournament theory: Players choose the degree of risk depending on monetary incentives; that is, if a player is trailed by the nearest leader by a larger gap or leads the nearest follower by a larger gap, the player usually bets more, suggesting that risk-taking is clearly dependent on chip spread. Moreover, a larger expected gain or a smaller expected loss strengthens the incentives for risk-taking. Thus, even poker players—who are seldom considered "athletes"—behave in ways that are consistent with the behaviors found in other professional sports.

Do Male and Female Athletes Respond Differently to Incentives?

Recently, a number of primarily experimental studies have tried to answer the question whether women respond differently to competitive pressure than men. While Uri Gneezy, Muriel Niederle, and Aldo Rustichini reveal the existence of a significant gender gap in a tournament setting (men's performance increases significantly with the competitiveness of the environment but women's performance does not),[46] Henry Paarsch and Bruce Shearer reach the opposite conclusion.[47] Using data from a tree-planting company in British Columbia they found no difference in the reaction to incentives between male and female workers. The productivity differential of male planters is exclusively due to differences in ability.[48]

A closer look at the findings presented by Bernd Frick as well as Bernd Frick and Rainer Klaeren suggests that female runners respond much more than men to an increase of the prize purse as well as to changes in the prize spread. However, women seem not to respond to bonus payments (additional rewards for absolute performance). While at odds with the traditional tournament model at first sight, there is a rather simple explanation for the different behaviors of men and women: With regard to their performances, the male marathon elite is much more homogeneous than the female elite. In 1996, for example, the difference between the fastest runner of the year and number fifty on that list was 2:39 minutes in the men's field and 4:37 in the women's. Given the same number of races for men and women, this implies that members of the female elite can (and indeed do) avoid competing against each other. Such a behavior is not possible for men, who (due to the homogeneity of the competition) will always face other runners of similar strength. Given these specific conditions it is hardly surprising that bonus payments do not induce higher effort levels in the women's races.

Due to the heterogeneity among the female elite, it was (and still is) quite possible for a woman to win a marathon with a suboptimal performance, while this is entirely impossible for a male runner. While this may sound strange to most people (sports fans as well as economists), the authors present ample evidence for this proposition: The female winners of the races in their sample were on average more than six minutes slower than the actual world record (then 2:21:06), while the male winners were only about three minutes slower than the record (then 2:06:50). Moreover, in 1995 the fastest fifty times in the women's races have been clocked by forty-two different runners while forty-eight different men were needed to deliver the fifty best performances of that year. Apparently, it is rational for female elite runners to participate in more than two marathons per year and to try to finish "within the money" several times instead of running only two marathons per year (as most of the male athletes do) with the goal of winning prize money as well as a bonus for an especially noticeable performance.[49]

Danielle Paserman studied the response of male and female tennis players to competitive pressure in nine different Grand Slam tournaments played between 2005 and 2007, that is, in a setting with large monetary rewards.[50] Her major finding is that men's performance (measured by either unforced errors or winners) does not vary much depending on the importance of the point, while women's performance deteriorates significantly as points become more important. The results of a number of additional tests suggest that women play a more conservative and less aggressive strategy as points become more important, that is, men hit faster first serves as importance rises, while women hit significantly lower first serves as the stakes become higher.

SUMMARY AND IMPLICATIONS FOR FURTHER RESEARCH

Summarizing the available evidence, it appears that virtually all of the predictions of tournament theory are unequivocally supported by data from a variety of contests (footraces, golf and tennis tournaments, horse races, auto racing, triathlons, and bowling competitions).

Although monetary rewards do have the incentive and selection effects predicted by tournament theory, several qualifications seem to be warranted: First, in situations, where the abilities of the contestants differ, bonuses for absolute performance may be an adequate instrument to induce the more able athletes not to reduce their effort levels. However, if these athletes have outside options in the sense of being able to enter additional competitions, it is very likely that they will choose a less risky strategy by competing more often at a level well below their abilities.

Second, if cooperation requirements are crucial for the performance of the contestants, increasing the number of prizes awarded may be a helpful strategy because this will reduce the opportunity costs of contestants who fear that otherwise they will end up without any compensation. Thus, if it is in the interest of the organizer "to keep the field together," it may be wise to pay prizes to a larger number of contestants.[51]

Moreover, two important puzzles remain to be solved: First, a convincing separation of the incentive and the selection effects of tournaments has not been performed yet, but should be possible given the data that is available from, for example, track and field: Since the IAAF's Grand Prix Circuit consists of three different series of events with prize-money levels that differ between the series but are identical across the meetings in any one of the series (but not over time), empirical tests of the relative contribution of incentive and (self-) selection effects to explain the observed patterns of performance are now possible in a quasi-experimental setting. Second, the introduction of prize money in 1993 (in the form of a car) and the subsequent changes in the level as well as the distribution of the prize money at the IAAF's World Championships in Athletics provides yet another quasi-experimental setting to study the impact of financial rewards on the behavior of utility-maximizing agents.

NOTES

1. Depending on the size of the prize purse these tournaments admit either thirty-two or sixty-four players (sometimes players have to compete successfully in an elimination round to be admitted). Only the Grand Slam tournaments start with a field of 128 players.

2. A virtually identical structure exists, for example, in Europe with the European PGA, the Seniors Tour and the Challenge Tour. On average, these tours offer

considerably smaller purses than their U.S. counterparts: In 2007 the purses varied between €0.5m and €6.2m (European PGA), €0.19m and €1.5m (European Seniors), and €0.12m and €0.605m (Challenge Tour).

3. A large fraction of the players on the Champions Tour have been active on the PGA's main tour already and continue to play after they became eligible for the Champions Tour. However, many of the seniors have never played as professionals when they were younger.

4. According to *Spiridon*—the most popular running magazine in the German speaking countries—there are at least 1,000 city marathons in the world (most of them either in Europe or in the United States). While some of them draw up to 35,000 runners, others have less than 100 finishers.

5. "Track and field pays a lot more for sprinters than it does for top distance runners. That's not the injustice, though. If the top distance runners start griping about money, ... the women's throwers would consider killing them and burying them in shallow graves near minor European villages. And if the women's throwers start griping ... the racewalkers would have a legitimate grudge." Jeff Hollobaugh, "Equal Prize Money Is Unrealistic," *ESPN Olympic Sports*, September 30, 2003, http://espn.go.com/oly/columns/hollobaugh/1627368.html.

6. Tim Layden, "Prize Money vs. Appearance Fees," *Sports Illustrated*, July 22, 1998, http://sportsillustrated.cnn.com/features/1998/weekly/9807027/it0727/c.html. According to various press reports, sprinter Carl Lewis was able to command an appearance fee of $100,000 in the mid-1980s. The average athlete, however, will be happy already if the organizers pay her travel costs. Tyson Gay, the current 100- and 200-meter World Champion, receives $50,000 in appearance fees for his starts since he won three titles in Osaka in August 2007.

7. The following sections draw heavily from Edward P. Lazear, *Personnel Economics for Managers* (New York: John Wiley 1998), 223–257, and Sherwin Rosen, "Promotions, Elections and Other Contests," *Journal of Institutional and Theoretical Economics* 144 (1988): 73–90. For a more formal discussion of the concept see Armen A. Alchian, "Promotions, Elections and Other Contests: Comment," *Journal of Institutional and Theoretical Economics* 144 (1988): 91–93; Michael L. Bognanno, "Corporate Tournaments," *Journal of Labor Economics* 19 (2001): 290–315; Derek J. Clark and Christian Riis, "Rank-Order Tournaments and Selection," Memorandum no. 27, Department of Economics, University of Oslo, 1996; William H. Cooper, William J. Graham, and Lorraine S. Dyke, "Tournament Players," *Research in Personnel and Human Resources Management* 11 (1993): 83–132; Ronald A. Dye, "The Trouble with Tournaments," *Economic Inquiry* 22 (1984): 147–149; Jerry R. Green and Nancy L. Stokey, "A Comparison of Tournaments and Contracts," *Journal of Political Economy* 91 (1983): 349–364; Kai A. Konrad, "Strategy in Contests—An Introduction," mimeo, Social Science Research Center, Berlin, 2007; Edward P. Lazear and Sherwin Rosen, "Rank Order Tournaments as Optimal Labor Contracts," *Journal of Political Economy* 89 (1981): 841–864; Kenneth J. McLaughlin, "Aspects of Tournament Models: A Survey," *Research in Labor Economics* 9 (1988): 225–256; Benny Moldovanu and Avner Sela, "The Optimal Allocation of Prizes in Contests," *American Economic Review* 91 (2001): 542–558; Benny Moldovanu and Avner Sela, "Contest Architecture," *Journal of Economic Theory* 126 (2006): 70–97; Barry J. Nalebuff and Joseph E. Stiglitz, "Prizes and

Incentives: Towards a General Theory of Compensation and Competition," *Bell Journal of Economics* 14 (1983): 21–43; Mary O'Keefe, William K. Viscusi, and Richard J. Zeckhauser, "Economic Contests: Comparative Reward Schemes," *Journal of Labor Economics* 2 (1984): 27–56; Sherwin Rosen, "Prizes and Incentives in Elimination Tournaments," *American Economic Review* 76 (1986): 701–715. A thorough review of contest theory with particular reference to team sports is provided by Stefan Szymanski, "The Economic Design of Sporting Contests," *Journal of Economic Literature* 41 (2003): 1137–1187.

8. See Hans K. Hvide, "Tournament Rewards and Risk-Taking," *Journal of Labor Economics* 20 (2002): 877–898; Hans K. Hvide and Eirik G. Kristiansen, "Risk-Taking in Selection Contests," *Games and Economic Behavior* 42 (2003): 172–179, as well as Matthias Kräkel and Dirk Sliwka Kräkel, "Risk-Taking in Asymmetric Tournaments," *German Economic Review* 5 (2004): 103–116.

9. Fullerton and McAfee discuss a "contest selection auction" as a potential device to prevent adverse selection of less able participants into a tournament offering high prize money. See Richard L. Fullerton and Randolph P. McAfee, "Auctioning Entry into Tournaments," *Journal of Political Economy* 107 (1999): 573–605.

10. For a further description of the structure of the "professional golf circus" see Rex L. Cottle, "Economics of the Professional Golfers' Association Tour," in: *Sportometrics*, ed. Brian L. Goff and Robert D. Tollison (College Station: Texas A&M University Press, 1990), 277–291, and Stephen Shmanske, *Golfonomics* (River Edge, NJ: World Scientific Publishing, 2004), 193–210.

11. In this situation, the "underdog" may wish to sabotage the other contestants instead of putting forth more effort. In order to avoid such behavior, contestants have to be monitored. See Matthias Kräkel, "Helping and Sabotaging in Tournaments," *International Game Theory Review* 7 (2005): 211–228.

12. If it is difficult to determine the athletes' ability levels, it is advisable to repeat the competition. Take as an example a golf tournament where the contestants have to complete eighteen holes a day over a period of four days. Under these circumstances it is very unlikely that a lucky (instead of an able) athlete wins. See Oliver Gürtler, "Are 18 Holes Enough for Tiger Woods?," *Bulletin of Economic Research* 58 (2006): 267–284.

13. Stefan Szymanski and Tomasso M. Valletti, "Incentive Effects of Second Prizes," *European Journal of Political Economy*, 21 (2004): 467–481. In some individualistic sports, such as gymnastics, figure skating, and ski jumping, the athletes' ranking at the end of the competition is not only determined by their "objective performance," but also by the "subjective impression" of (impartial?) judges. Erik Zitzewitz documents a "nationalistic bias" in the evaluations of judges in figure skating. This introduces an element of luck (or "noise") into the competition which, in turn, leads to a lower level of effort. The reason is that noise reduces the value of effort by reducing the probability of winning. When luck is important, it is important to offset the decline in effort by using a larger prize spread. See Erik Zitzewitz, "Nationalism in Winter Sports Judging and Its Lessons for Organizational Decision Making," *Journal of Economics and Management Strategy* 15 (2006): 67–99.

14. See Lawrence M. Kahn, "The Sports Business as a Labor Market Laboratory," *Journal of Economic Perspectives* 14 (2000): 75–94.

15. See Ronald G. Ehrenberg and Michael L. Bognanno, "Do Tournaments Have Incentive Effects?" *Journal of Political Economy* 98 (1990): 1307–1324, and Ronald G. Ehrenberg and Michael L. Bognanno, "The Incentive Effects of Tournaments Revisited: Evidence from the European PGA Tour," *Industrial and Labor Relations Review* 43 (1990): 74–88.

16. Using data from the 1992 season, Orszag was unable to replicate these findings. He attributes this unexpected result to increased media coverage since the 1980s which might have led to increased nervousness among players, thus distorting the relationship between effort and performance. See Jonathan M. Orszag, "A New Look at Incentive Effects and Golf Tournaments," *Economics Letters* 46 (1994): 77–88.

Using data from the 2000 Ladies PGA tour, Matthews, Sommers, and Peschiera find that a higher prize purse has a negative impact on players' performance, that is, it increases (instead of decreases) the number of strokes required to complete the course. See Peter Hans Matthews, Paul M. Sommers, and Francisco J. Peschiera, "Incentives and Superstars on the LPGA Tour," *Applied Economics* 39 (2007): 87–94.

17. Using longitudinal data covering five consecutive seasons (1996–2000) with 12,700 player-tournament-observations Bronars and Oettinger confirm this result. See Stephen G. Bronars and Gerald S. Oettinger, "Effort, Risk-Taking, and Participation in Tournaments: Evidence from Professional Golf," mimeo, Department of Economics, University of Texas, 2001.

18. See Thomas A. Rhoads, "Labor Supply on the PGA Tour: The Effect of Higher Expected Earnings and Stricter Exemption Status on Annual Entry Decisions," *Journal of Sports Economics* 8 (2007): 83–98. In another recent paper, Hood shows that on the PGA tour an increase in the participation of top players leads to a significant increase in the prize purse in the following year and that a change in the purse has again a positive impact on the entry decisions of the top players. See Matthew Hood, "The Purse Is Not Enough: Modeling Professional Golfers Entry Decision," *Journal of Sports Economics* 7 (2006): 289–308.

19. See Todd A. McFall, Charles R. Knoeber, and Walter N. Thurman, "Contests, Grand Prizes, and the Hot Hand," mimeo, Department of Economics, Wake Forest University, 2006.

20. See Thierry Lallemand, Robert Plasman, and Francois Rycx, "Women and Competition in Elimination Tournaments: Evidence from Professional Tennis Data," IZA Discussion Paper no. 1843, 2005, and Uwe Sunde, "Potential, Prizes and Performance: Testing Tournament Theory with Professional Tennis Data," IZA Discussion Paper no. 947, 2003.

21. Douglas Coate and Donijo Robbins, "The Tournament Careers of Top-Ranked Men and Women Tennis Professionals: Are the Gentlemen More Committed than the Ladies?" *Journal of Labor Research* 22 (2001): 185–193.

22. Garin and von Allmen show that in Grand Slam tournaments an increase in the prize purse between two rounds induces players to put forth considerably more effort in the sense of hitting more aces and more "winners," that is, shots that cannot be returned by the opponent. See Renee Garin and Peter von Allmen, "Gender Effects in Rank Order Tournaments: The Case of Professional Tennis," mimeo, Department of Economics, Moravian College, Bethlehem, Pa., 2005.

23. See Michael T. Maloney and Robert E. McCormick, "The Response of Workers to Wages in Tournaments: Evidence from Foot Races," *Journal of Sports Economics* 1 (2000): 99–123.

24. See Jim G. Lynch and Jeffrey S. Zax, "The Rewards to Running: Prize Structure and Performance in Professional Road Racing," *Journal of Sports Economics* 1 (2000): 323–340.

25. See Bernd Frick, "Lohn und Leistung im professionellen Sport: Das Beispiel Stadt-Marathon," *Konjunkturpolitik* 44 (1998): 114–140, as well as Bernd Frick and Rainer Klaeren, "Die Anreizwirkungen leistungsabhängiger Entgelte: Theoretische Überlegungen und empirische Befunde aus dem Bereich des professionellen Sports," *Zeitschrift für Betriebswirtschaft* 67 (1997): 1117–1138.

26. Bernd Frick and Joachim Prinz, "Pay and Performance in Professional Road Running: The Case of City Marathons," *International Journal of Sports Finance* 2 (2007): 25–35.

27. Sue Fernie and David Metcalf, "It's Not What You Pay, It's the Way that You Pay It, and That's What Gets Results: Jockeys' Pay and Performance," *Labour* 13 (1999): 385–411.

28. Jim G. Lynch, "The Effort Effects of Prizes in the Second Half of Tournaments," *Journal of Economic Behavior and Organization* 57 (2005): 115–129.

29. Jim Lynch and Jeffrey S. Zax, "Prizes, Selection and Performance in Arabian Horse Racing," Working Paper no. 98-26, Department of Economics, University of Colorado at Boulder, 1998.

30. See Glenn Boyle, Graeme Guthrie, and Luke Gorton, "Whither Reputation? Dynamic Incentives in the Sport of Kings," mimeo, Victoria University of Wellington, Wellington, New Zealand, 2006.

31. See Michael L. Bognanno, "An Empirical Test of Tournament Theory," Ph.D. diss., Cornell University, Ithaca, N.Y., 1990.

32. See Brian E. Becker and Mark A. Huselid, "The Incentive Effects of Tournament Compensation Systems," *Administrative Science Quarterly* 37 (1992): 336–350.

33. Peter von Allmen, "Is the Reward System in NASCAR Efficient?" *Journal of Sports Economics* 2 (2001): 62–79.

34. Empirical evidence in support of these assumptions is provided by Craig A Depken and Dennis P. Wilson, "The Efficiency of the NASCAR Reward System: Initial Empirical Evidence," *Journal of Sports Economics* 5 (2004): 371–386.

35. See Peter von Allmen, "A Comparison of the Reward Schemes in NASCAR Winston Cup and Championship Auto Racing Team (CART) Auto Racing," mimeo, Economics and Business Department, Moravian College, Bethlehem, Pa., 2002. Moreover, Kristina Terkun and Michael T. Maloney find evidence supportive of tournament theory by using data from the motorcycle industry. See Michael T. Maloney and Kristina Terkun, "Road Warrior Booty: Prize Structures in Motorcycle Racing," *Contributions to Economic Analysis and Policy* 1 (2002): 1–16.

36. On average, professional iron(wo)men train eight hours a day approaching 35k of swimming, 1.000k of biking, and 100k of running per week.

37. See Joachim Prinz, "Performance Pay and Incentive Effects in Tournaments," M.Sc. diss., Institute of International Economics and Management, Copenhagen Business School, 1999.

38. See Christian Grund and Oliver Gürtler, "An Empirical Study on Risk-Taking in Tournaments," *Applied Economics Letters* 12 (2005): 457–461. A soccer team consists of eleven players. The players are specialized in one of the following positions: They are either goalkeeper, defender, midfielder, or forward (only one goalkeeper is allowed in the team). Up to three substitutions per team are allowed during a match.

39. See David W. Boyd and Laura A. Boyd, "Strategic Behaviour in Contests: Evidence from the 1992 Barcelona Olympic Games," *Applied Economics* 27 (1995): 1037–1043. Munasinghe, O'Flaherty and Danninger compare the development of local (high school) and world records in track and field to separate the overlapping effects of technical change (better equipment, better training methods, etc.) and globalization (increased competition) and find that the former is more important than the latter to explain the observed pattern. See Lalith Munasinghe, Brendan O'Flaherty, and Stephan Danninger, "Globalization and the Rate of Technological Progress: What Track and Field Records Show," *Journal of Political Economy* 109 (2001): 1132–1149. Moreover, Scully documents the decreasing returns to training. See Gerald W. Scully, "Diminishing Returns and the Limit of Athletic Performance," *Scottish Journal of Political Economy* 47 (2000): 456–470.

40. Bronars and Oettinger, "Effort, Risk-Taking and Participation in Tournaments."

41. See Jason Abrevaya, "Ladder Tournaments and Underdogs: Lessons from Professional Bowling," *Journal of Economic Behavior and Organization* 47 (2002): 87–101.

42. See Mark Duggan and Steven D. Levitt, "Winning Isn't Everything: Corruption in Sumo Wrestling," *American Economic Review* 92 (2002): 1594–1605.

43. See Keith A. Willoughby and Kent J. Kostiuk, "An Analysis of a Strategic Decision in the Sport of Curling," *Decision Analysis* 2 (2005): 58–63.

44. See David N. Laband, "How the Structure of Competition Influences Performance in Professional Sports: The Case of Tennis and Golf," in: *Sportometrics,* ed. Brian L. Goff and Robert D. Tollison (College Station: Texas A&M University 1990), 133–150.

45. See Yungmin Lee, "Prize and Risk-Taking Strategy in Tournaments: Evidence from Professional Poker Players," IZA Discussion Paper no. 1435, Bonn 2004.

46. See Uri Gneezy, Muriel Niederle, and Aldo Rustichini, "Performance in Competitive Environments: Gender Differences," *Quarterly Journal of Economics* 118 (2003): 1049–1074. In a laboratory setting, Niederle and Vesterlund find that twice as many men as women choose a tournament compensation system over a fixed salary. However, there seem to be no gender differences under either remuneration system. See Muriel Niederle and Lisa Vesterlund, "Do Women Shy Away from Competition? Do Men Compete Too Much?" NBER Working Paper 11474, Cambridge, Mass., 2005.

47. See Henry J. Paarsch and Bruce S. Shearer, "Do Women React Differently to Incentives? Evidence from Experimental Data and Payroll Records," *European Economic Review* 51 (2007): 1682–1707.

48. This is consistent with a finding reported that although women are more risk-averse than men, the former are no less likely to adopt a high-variance strategy in a tournament competition. See Donald Vandegrift and Paul Brown, "Gender Differences in the Use of High-Variance Strategies in Tournament Competition," *Journal of Socio-Economics* 34 (2005): 834–849.

49. In 2001 exactly eighty-eight men finished a marathon in less than 2:11 while an equal number of women were faster than 2:30. While a time of 2:10:59 is only

4.2 percent slower than the existing world record of 2:05:44, a 2:29:59 is already 8.1 percent slower than the 2001 world record of 2:18:47 (in 2003 it has been improved to 2:15:45). Also in 2001, only nineteen female, but 135 male athletes finished a marathon within 105 percent of the then-current world record. See Robert O. Deaner, "More Males Run Relatively Fast in U.S. Road Races: Further Evidence of a Sex Difference in Competitiveness," *Evolutionary Psychology* 4 (2006): 303–314, for an explanation why more men than women are running fast.

50. See M. Danielle Paserman, "Gender Differences in Performance in Competitive Environments: Evidence from Professional Tennis Players," IZA Discussion Paper no. 2834, 2007.

51. See Szymanski and Valletti, "Incentive Effects of Second Prizes," 467–481.

Two

Single-Entity Ownership in Sports Leagues and Antitrust Law

Bradley I. Ruskin and Jon H. Oram

Long the victim of antitrust challenges, sports leagues are now facing a new and more favorable playing field. For the past several decades, these organizations have steadfastly maintained that a league's internal decisions should not be subject to Section 1 of the Sherman Act, which forbids contracts or concerted action among businesses in restraint of trade, because these organizations effectively operate as single economic units, incapable of combining or conspiring with themselves. Yet for years courts have been reluctant to accept these arguments, instead viewing the members of the league in part as "competitors" both athletically and economically. (For the purposes of this chapter, the term *league* will be used to describe professional sports leagues [such as the National Football League, National Basketball Association, National Hockey League, and Women's National Basketball Association], professional sports circuits [such as the National Association for Stock Car Racing [NASCAR], Women's Tennis Association, Association of Tennis Professionals, and Professional Golf Association], and other organizations that govern or produce a particular sport.)

Courts that rejected the so-called single-entity defense typically focused on the form of the leagues, particularly the fact that such leagues are typically comprised of a number of teams, or operators, each of which is a separate legal entity. In response to these decisions, when entrepreneurs formed new leagues, they were often organized as single, centralized, limited-liability companies, so as to pass scrutiny under prior antitrust jurisprudence that emphasized the corporate form of the league as the determinative factor in Section 1 analysis.

Significantly, a recent Supreme Court opinion from outside the world of sports suggests that the justices are open to considering additional factors in determining whether a league should be viewed as a single entity. In *Texaco, Inc. v. Dagher*, the Supreme Court recognized that a legitimate joint venture can be treated as a single economic unit for certain purposes under Section 1. While the ultimate scope and impact of the *Texaco* holding will no doubt be determined by pending and future cases applying its precepts, it is likely that the single-entity arguments posed by sports leagues for the past twenty-five years will be, and should be, reexamined in light of this important decision.

SECTION 1 OF THE SHERMAN ACT AND THE SINGLE-ENTITY DEFENSE

Like most other interstate businesses, sports leagues are subject to the Sherman Antitrust Act and the regulations promulgated thereunder by the Federal Trade Commission (FTC).[1] The Sherman Act was adopted in 1890 in response to growing concerns over the concentration of economic power in large corporations and combinations of businesses. Accordingly, Section 1 of the Sherman Antitrust Act declares that "[e]very contract, combination in the form of trust or otherwise, or conspiracy, in restraint of trade or commerce among the several States, or with foreign nations, is declared to be illegal."[2]

Were Section 1 interpreted and applied literally, it would prohibit most commercial arrangements, because any contract between two entities in which one agrees to do—or not do—something can be said to restrain trade in some manner. However, courts have not applied Section 1 literally. Instead, they have recognized that the act only prohibits agreements that "unreasonably" restrain trade. The test of whether an agreement is or is not unreasonable is whether it is anticompetitive. In conducting that inquiry, courts generally divide conduct into two broad categories: (1) conduct that is evaluated under the *per se* test; and (2) conduct that is evaluated under the Rule of Reason test. Under the first category, certain types of conduct are deemed to be *per se* illegal because courts have historically determined that they are inherently anticompetitive. For example, agreements among competitors to fix prices are *per se* illegal. Agreements or actions categorized as *per se* illegal are not subject to any reasonableness test or further scrutiny: a violation of Section 1 is conclusively established.

If the action is not *per se* illegal, courts will apply the so-called Rule of Reason analysis. The Rule of Reason is essentially a balancing test that has been developed specifically in the antitrust context. When applying the Rule of Reason, the court must examine the anticompetitive effects of the conduct alleged to be a violation of Section 1 and weigh those effects against the purported business justifications and any pro-competitive effects of such conduct. Justice Louis Brandeis articulated the classic statement of the Rule of Reason in *Chicago Bd. of Trade v. United States* (1918):

> The court must ordinarily consider the facts peculiar to the business to which the restraint is applied, its condition before and after the restraint was imposed, the nature of the restraint and its effect, actual or probable. The history of the restraint, the evil believed to exist, the reason for adopting the particular remedy, the purpose or end sought to be attained, are all relevant facts.[3]

THE SINGLE-ENTITY DEFENSE TO SECTION 1 SCRUTINY

The essence of the single-entity defense is that Section 1 cannot be applied to the conduct of just one entity because the statute only prohibits *contracts, combinations,* and *conspiracies* in restraint of trade. Each of these requires concerted action by separate legal entities. By definition, a single entity is incapable of conspiracy—one cannot conspire with oneself. Likewise, a firm or corporation, whose operations and employees are considered to be a single corporate unit, cannot conspire with its employees.[4] Officers, directors, and employees within a single firm all have a broad common interest with the corporation.

> The officers of a single firm are not separate economic actors pursuing separate economic interests, so agreements among them do not bring together economic power that was previously pursuing divergent goals. Coordination within a firm is as likely to result from an effort to compete as from an effort to stifle competition.[5]

Yet, a single entity may still have divergent interests within the organization. Take, for example, General Motors. Its Oldsmobile and Cadillac divisions may have different employees, advertise separately, sell different vehicles, and at some level compete for consumers. Nonetheless, these two divisions operate within the framework of a single corporate umbrella with a broad common goal. Similarly, consider a law firm, where several attorneys join together to offer their services as a group in order to maximize profits. The attorneys—who would otherwise be competitors in the marketplace had they not formed the firm—have established a partnership with one another pursuant to a written agreement. They have agreed to work together to produce a joint product and not compete with each other. The attorneys may hold diverse viewpoints and might even disagree on firm policy. Any of them can choose to leave the firm at any point, and any of them may sue the firm under its partnership agreement. So, too, each attorney's compensation is typically determined based on both the success of the entire firm and his or her individual performance. However, none of these factors changes the fact that the firm is regarded as a single entity when it makes internal decisions.

For example, partners in a law firm make internal decisions on the fees for their services, the salaries payable to associates and staff, and partner compensation—whether according to the amount of business they generate, or on a pro rata basis, or in lockstep fashion according to seniority. None of these decisions is problematic under the antitrust laws because the firm is a single economic unit in the market despite encompassing different viewpoints and being comprised of individuals who would otherwise be competitors. Few would argue that a single law firm can be viewed as an illegal combination or conspiracy under Section 1.

Therefore, a defendant in a Section 1 challenge can avoid liability by successfully establishing that, like the law firm, it is acting as a single economic unit and, therefore, its internal decisions are exempt from Section 1 scrutiny. If a defendant can prove that it is a legitimate single entity, the alleged Section 1 action will not be *per se* illegal, nor will it be subject to Rule of Reason scrutiny, because a single entity is by definition incapable of combining or conspiring with itself.

Notably, the single-entity defense does not immunize a defendant from the antitrust laws. A company's internal decisions may still be scrutinized under Section 2 of the Sherman Act, which prohibits monopolization or attempts to monopolize any part of interstate trade or commerce.[6] So, too, its external agreements with third parties—like those of any other economic actor—must pass muster under Section 1. But a single entity's internal decisions, conduct, and agreements are properly not subject to Section 1 review.

THE SINGLE-ENTITY DEFENSE AS ARTICULATED BY SPORTS LEAGUES

Since the 1970s sports leagues have been subject to numerous antitrust challenges brought by players, owners, facilities, telecasters, licensees, consumers, and a panoply of others. The leagues often responded to these challenges by arguing that they are, in fact, single entities not capable of violating Section 1 alone. The league typically asserts that it is a single, integrated unit, which by definition is incapable of conspiracy when it makes its internal decisions. Plaintiffs, however, typically allege that the league is simply a collection of competitors that have conspired to make decisions and act jointly to artificially raise prices, reduce output, and exclude competitors.

The tension between cooperation and competition—two fundamental aspects of the formation and management of sports leagues—must be considered when applying the single-entity concept to a league. First, while a typical sports league cannot deny that it is comprised of dozens of individual teams and a management organization, those participants together, like the employees of a company, produce a single product: the professional sport or circuit itself. Each team (or participant) within the league is incapable of producing this product individually. Consider baseball. As popular as the New York Yankees are, no one would pay to watch the Yankees without an opponent. Therefore, some significant degree of cooperation is unquestionably necessary in order for the league to create its product. Accordingly, the league's management must make certain decisions that will govern the entire league in order to enable the production of the product, such as setting rules of the game, organizing team schedules, and setting equipment specifications.

Likewise, the league's member teams must be able to form and enforce agreements with one another. Without that ability, the league could not oversee or govern the actions of its individual teams, and it would be impossible for the league to organize a successful season or control the quality of its product. These arrangements do not restrain competition; in fact, they promote competition between the league's product and other sports and other entertainment offerings. The ability of the National Basketball Association (NBA), for example, to coordinate a successful season, organizing its schedule of games and securing broadcast rights, enables the NBA to compete with the National Football League (NFL), the National Hockey League (NHL), and other sports with seasons played and telecast contemporaneously, as well as other media distribution and live spectator events. As the Supreme Court noted in *NCAA v. Board of Regents* about the NCAA and league sports generally: "[W]hat the NCAA and its member institutions market in this case is competition itself—contests between competing institutions. Of course, this would be completely ineffective if there were no rules on which the competitors agreed to create and define the competition to be marketed."[7]

However, the creation and operation of a sports league also necessitates a degree of athletic competition. Competition among teams on the playing field is essential to the creation of the product. The entire league benefits by having teams that are sufficiently distinct and separate, so that when they meet, the product itself is compelling. This perceived separateness between teams can be crucial to the league's profitability and success. Indeed, if sports fans do not trust that a league's teams are legitimate competitors on the field, they will likely devalue the authenticity of the league's product.

This inescapable tension between cooperation and competition inherent in sports leagues complicates the single-entity analysis. The leagues and their proponents argue that despite the fact that member teams are separate legal entities that do compete with each other on the field, the league nonetheless ought to be considered a single economic unit for antitrust purposes because its internal decisions do not constitute of the type of collective action that Section 1 was designed to regulate.

SECTION 1 CHALLENGES TO SPORTS LEAGUES

In the early 1980s, sports leagues answered antitrust challenges, almost uniformly, with the single-entity defense. Unfortunately for the leagues, they were also, almost uniformly, unsuccessful. Though courts were receptive to the argument, ultimately they were unwilling to treat leagues' internal agreements as outside the scope of a full Rule of Reason examination under Section 1.

NFL v. NASL

In 1978 the National Football League (NFL) was engaged in a dispute with two of its team owners. Certain of the owners' family members owned interests in North American Soccer League (NASL) teams, despite a long-standing NFL policy that discouraged NFL owners or their immediate family members from having interests in competing leagues. In the face of the growing competition that certain NFL teams were facing from local NASL teams, many NFL owners, in particular, Max Winter of the Minnesota Vikings and Leonard Tose of the Philadelphia Eagles, lobbied the NFL to take action. In response, the NFL proposed an amendment to its by-laws making its policy against cross-ownership a formal ban on any NFL owner or certain of their family members owning an interest in any other major team sport.

In response, Lamar Hunt of the Kansas City Chiefs and Joe Robbie of the Miami Dolphins filed suit against the NFL, as their respective wives' ownership of NASL teams put them in violation of the league's rules. They alleged that the cross-ownership ban violated Section 1 of the Sherman Act. The NFL maintained that it was a single entity and therefore exempt from Section 1's Rule of Reason scrutiny. The trial court accepted the NFL's single-entity defense argument and held that there was no Section 1 violation.

The Second Circuit reversed on appeal and ruled that the NFL was not a single entity. The court's reasoning formed the foundation for much of the subsequent jurisprudence on the single-entity defense. The court conceded that a certain degree of cooperation is essential in order for the NFL to create its "product" of NFL football; that is, no single NFL team can produce the product without the cooperation of other teams. It also acknowledged that the success of the NFL depends on the stability of each individual team and its ability to participate in the coordinate effort to produce games. However, despite recognizing the importance of this coordination, the Second Circuit held that the fact that NFL teams conducted certain activities separately from the rest of the league demonstrated that the teams were separate entities for antitrust purposes. For example, the court cited the fact that each team was a separately owned legal entity that derived a portion of its revenue from sources such as local television and concessions. It emphasized that these local revenues were not shared with other teams and, as a result, profits vary across NFL teams. Thus, the teams were "separate economic entities engaged in a joint venture" and the league's single-entity defense failed. The court ultimately held that the cross-ownership ban failed the Rule of Reason test because its anticompetitive effects outweighed its pro-competitive justifications.[8]

The Supreme Court refused to grant the NFL's petition for certiorari. However, in a rare dissent from the Court's opinion, Justice William H. Rehnquist criticized the Second Circuit's decision and explained why the NFL should be considered a single entity for purposes of Section 1. Justice Rehnquist concluded that the NFL owners were joint venturers producing a product that "competes with other sports and other forms of entertainment in the entertainment market." In his view, although individual NFL teams competed with one another on the playing field, they were rarely competitors in the marketplace. Moreover, he viewed this interdependence as necessary to the enterprise. Independent teams could not provide consistent rules, equipment, or facilities, all of which are essential if the NFL is to be able to produce an entertaining product. If the teams were independent, the result would be a loosely fashioned and inconsistently regulated handful of games, rather than the formulaic and regulated seasons to which NFL fans had become accustomed. "The NFL, in short, made a market in which individual [teams] are unable to compete fully effectively."[9]

Justice Rehnquist acknowledged that the teams do compete to a certain degree. However, he carefully noted that the competition between teams is generally athletic competition rather than economic competition. He recognized only one limited instance in which there is intraleague economic competition between teams: when two teams are located in the same city, such as New York or Los Angeles, and therefore compete to some extent for local broadcast revenues and local ticket sales. These examples notwithstanding,

Justice Rehnquist argued that "in all other respects, the league competes as a unit against other forms of entertainment."[10] Justice Rehnquist thus articulated the single-entity concept as applied to a sports league, and although the full Supreme Court refused to revisit the Second Circuit's decision, his dissenting opinion laid a firm foundation for leagues' subsequent arguments in favor of single-entity treatment.

Copperweld Corp. v. Independence Tube Corp.

Two years later, the Supreme Court's decision in *Copperweld Corp. v. Independence Tube Corp.* advanced the single-entity defense outside the sports context. The *Copperweld* Court held that a parent corporation and its wholly owned subsidiary are incapable of conspiring with each other for purposes of Section 1 of the Sherman Act. The Court explained that, as Justice Rehnquist had argued in his dissent, business entities may lawfully join together in various arrangements such as joint ventures, mergers, and other vertical arrangements that increase their efficiency and profitability and allow them to compete more effectively in the market. Certain forms of concerted activity are permissible, but all concerted activity must be carefully scrutinized. Justice Warren Burger, writing for the majority, explained the reason for such scrutiny:

> Concerted activity is inherently fraught with anticompetitive risk. It deprives the marketplace of the independent centers of decisionmaking that competition assumes and demands. In any conspiracy, two or more entities that previously pursued their own interests separately are combining to act as one for their common interest. This not only reduces the diverse directions in which economic power is aimed but suddenly increases the economic power moving in one particular direction. Of course, such mergings of resources may well lead to efficiencies that benefit consumers, but their anticompetitive potential is sufficient to warrant scrutiny[.][11]

Thus, *Copperweld* held that the actions of a single, unitary firm do not pose the type of antitrust dangers that Section 1 was designed to prevent. As noted earlier, by definition, a single person or entity is incapable of conspiracy because a conspiracy requires a minimum of two actors acting in concert. *Copperweld* applied the same reasoning to the corporate form and held that a firm (and arrangements of officers, employees or other entities within the firm) is a single economic unit for antitrust purposes. The Court explained,

> The officers of a single firm are not separate economic actors pursuing separate economic interests, so agreements among them do not bring together

economic power that was previously pursuing divergent goals.... [O]fficers or employees of the same firm do not provide the plurality of actors imperative for a § 1 conspiracy.[12]

The Court extended this reasoning to subsidiaries of parent corporations. A parent and a subsidiary have unified interests—where the parent owns 100 percent of the subsidiary, the two ultimately have a common and aligned economic purpose. Accordingly, if a parent and a subsidiary agree on a particular course of action, there is no joining of economic resources as described above, because the parent and subsidiary are ultimately pursuing common interests. The Supreme Court directed lower courts to evaluate such organizations based on the reality of the parent's control over the subsidiary, regardless of the formal nature the business may choose to form the parent-subsidiary relationship.[13] In broad words that could be read to extend far beyond the parent/wholly owned subsidiary context, the Supreme Court opined: "Especially in view of the increasing complexity of corporate operations, a business enterprise should be free to structure itself in ways that serve efficiency of control, economy of operations, and other factors dictated by business judgment without increasing its exposure to antitrust liability." Thus, *Copperweld* indicated the Court's willingness to recognize a wider array of business arrangements as single entities for Section 1 purposes.

Post-*Copperweld* Decisions

Nonetheless, lower courts did not immediately accept the single-entity defense in subsequent challenges to leagues' actions. The NFL faced two separate Section 1 challenges in 1992 and 1994, and argued the single-entity defense unsuccessfully each time.

McNeil v. NFL

In *McNeil v. NFL*, several NFL players whose contracts had expired alleged that the NFL's proposed wage scale constituted an illegal horizontal price-fixing arrangement between separate teams. Under one provision of its proposed "Plan B," the NFL proposed to eliminate individual contract negotiations between NFL players and NFL teams. Instead, the league would establish a unified wage scale that would set all NFL players' salaries, or, viewed another way, "set the price for all NFL players' services."[14] The players filed suit to enjoin the NFL from adopting the proposed wage scale because it violated Section 1: they argued, in the alternative, that the wage scale was either a horizontal price-fixing arrangement and therefore *per se* illegal, or that it failed to satisfy the Rule of

Reason test because there were no plausible pro-competitive or business justifications for its implementation.

The NFL responded in part that because its teams functioned as a single economic unit, the agreement among teams to fix player salaries should not be subjected to Section 1 scrutiny. NFL Commissioner Paul Tagliabue submitted a declaration in support of the NFL's single-entity defense in which he stated that the business relationship among the NFL teams is not a relationship of independent economic competitors, but rather co-owners of a single entity engaged in a common business enterprise—"the production and marketing of professional football entertainment."[15]

The District Court was not receptive to the commissioner's plea. The court noted a variety of cases, including *NFL v. NASL*, in which the NFL's single-entity defense had previously been rejected. The court then explained that since the NFL had failed to make clear how its current structure differed from the league structure alleged in earlier cases where the NFL's single-entity defense was rejected, the NFL's latest articulation of the single-entity defense in *McNeil* similarly failed.

The NFL argued that *Copperweld* effectively overruled *NFL v. NASL* and other similar cases and that, in light of *Copperweld*, the NFL's single-entity defense should prevail notwithstanding previous instances where the argument had been rejected. The District Court examined the pre-*Copperweld* decisions that rejected sports leagues' single-entity defenses and held that *Copperweld* did not overrule that line of cases. It explained that the NFL's interpretation of *Copperweld* could not be reconciled with the Supreme Court's *NCAA v. Board of Regents* (decided earlier in 1984 than *Copperweld*), which held that while some horizontal restraints are necessary to govern sports leagues, such restraints are nevertheless subject to abbreviated Rule of Reason scrutiny. Therefore, the actions of the NFL teams were within the scope of Section 1 scrutiny.[16]

Sullivan v. NFL

In 1994 the NFL faced another Section 1 challenge to its internal rules. In *Sullivan v. NFL,* the owner of the New England Patriots sued the NFL under Section 1, challenging the NFL's policy against public ownership. In 1960 Billy Sullivan, then the owner of the AFL's New England Patriots, sold nonvoting shares in the Patriots to the public. When the NFL and AFL merged in 1966, the combined league adopted the NFL's ban on public ownership of teams (although the Patriots were allowed to retain their premerger level of public ownership as a grandfathered exception). In 1976 Billy Sullivan reacquired all of the publicly owned shares.

However, in the mid-1980s, Sullivan's family experienced financial difficulties and sought to raise capital to alleviate its rising debt burdens. The Sullivans proposed that they be allowed to offer 49 percent of the Patriots to the public as part of a public offering, as an exception to the NFL's prohibition on public ownership. Sullivan's proposal did not garner much support among other NFL owners and the league. Eventually, the proposal was tabled and Sullivan never sought a formal vote from the NFL owners. Instead, he sold the Patriots to a limited partnership led by Victor Kiam for $83.7 million. Four years later, Kiam sold his interest in the Patriots to James Orthwein for approximately $110 million.

Sullivan filed suit against the NFL under Section 1, seeking damages and arguing that but for the NFL's prohibition on public ownership, he would have been able to retain a majority interest in the Patriots and capture the appreciating value of the franchise. Instead, he argued, he had been forced to sell the team at an extremely low price to private buyers in order to meet his existing debt obligations. Therefore, the NFL's public ownership ban operated in restraint of trade in violation of Section 1. Following a trial, the jury returned a verdict for $38 million in favor of Sullivan, which the judge reduced to $17 million on remittur.

On appeal, the NFL again argued that it was a single entity for antitrust purposes. The league cited *Copperweld* for the proposition that it functioned as a single economic unit in relation to its public ownership policy. The First Circuit rejected this argument. Under *Copperweld,* it opined, the deciding factor for whether a business was a single entity was whether the divisions had a "complete unity of interest." In its view, the NFL teams did not have complete unity of interest when it came to sale of ownership interests. The panel ruled that the NFL teams compete with one another in several ways, not only on the field but also off the field in certain areas, specifically in the market for sale of ownership interests. Thus, it held that NFL owners act as competitors when they market their teams to the same group of prospective owners interested in joining the NFL.

The court cited several NFL owners' comments suggesting the existence of competition between teams. For example, Arthur Rooney II of the Pittsburgh Steelers and Ralph Wilson of the Buffalo Bills both expressed concern that consolidated ownership interests or large corporations who owned NFL teams would possess an unfair competitive advantage over individually or family-owned teams. NFL Commissioner Pete Rozelle acknowledged that other NFL owners had expressed similar sentiments.[17]

The court concluded that these statements were sufficient evidence to show that the potential for economic competition between teams existed. Based on this evidence of NFL teams pursuing diverse interests both on and off the field, the court rejected the NFL's single-entity defense.

Chicago Prof. Sports & WGN v. NBA

Despite these decisions, the other leagues and their lawyers were not deterred. The issue arose once again when the Chicago Bulls and their telecast partner, WGN, challenged the NBA and its rules restricting the number of games that individual teams could license for certain telecasts. For many years, pursuant to the NBA's television rules, the league entered into agreements with national carriers—both over-the-air broadcast networks (such as NBC or ABC) and national cable networks (such as TNT), while it permitted each member team to enter into local arrangements with over-the-air and cable outlets in their territory. Starting in 1976 and growing through the 1980s, a form of hybrid entity—"superstations"—emerged. Under the NBA's rules adopted by its board of governors, the NBA defined a superstation as "any commercial over-the-air television station whose broadcast signal is received outside of the local designated market area . . . by more than 5% of the total number of cable subscribers in the U.S."[18] Under this definition, there were three superstations in the United States: WWOR in New York, WGN in Chicago, and WTBS in Atlanta. All three carried NBA games. Each of these carriers had long been local carriers within their own home markets; however, as a superstation, each arranged for its signal to be retransmitted to cable systems throughout the United States and evolved into national cable networks.

In 1990 the NBA board of governors amended its rule and reduced the number of games that individual teams could license to superstations from twenty-five to twenty games. The Bulls and WGN sued the NBA seeking an injunction against enforcement of the new twenty-game rule. The District Court held that the NBA, like the NFL, was a joint venture of separate legal entities and thus subject to Section 1 Rule of Reason scrutiny. It then concluded that an agreement among teams through its board of governors is analogous to a cartel and held that its superstation rule was unlawful under Section 1. The Seventh Circuit affirmed the District Court's decision, but set forth certain guideposts suggesting how the NBA might alter its rules to withstand antitrust scrutiny.

Following the Seventh Circuit's lead, the NBA, among other things, entered into exclusive agreements with its national carriers with limited carve-out for licenses to other national cable networks (including superstations), ensured that the league held the copyright in all games telecast, and imposed a fee (for the benefit of all teams) for any games licensed by a club to a national cable network. Again, the Bulls and WGN challenged the modified rule. Following an extended trial, the District Court held that the NBA's arrangements still violated the antitrust laws. As part of that ruling, the court rejected the NBA's single-entity defense and again ruled that the teams that comprise the NBA were joint venturers with diverse interests, who were actually competitors, both on the field in athletic competition and off the field in competition for players, coaches, attendance, television viewers, and advertising. The court noted that some cooperation exists and that mutual agreement is necessary to create the product of the games themselves, but held that in general "the profit seeking interests of one team are often contrary to those of other teams," and therefore the joint-venture characterization is appropriate.[19]

The case was once again appealed to the Seventh Circuit. This time the NBA fared much better. The NBA argued that despite the fact that its twenty-nine teams and central organization comprised thirty separately owned legal entities, and the twenty-nine teams were obviously not subsidiaries of the central organization, the NBA is nevertheless a single entity because it functions as a single entity and creates a single product—NBA basketball—that competes with other major sports and other forms of entertainment. Separate ownership of the teams, the NBA argued, did not imply that their concerted action was like a cartel, no more than various chain restaurant franchises pursuing a common goal or members of a cooperative would be considered a cartel. The NBA noted that antitrust law encourages cooperation between divisions of a single business and argued that cooperation among its teams to create internal policy fostered the creation and distribution of its products.

In its ruling, the Seventh Circuit expanded upon *Copperweld* in explaining what degree of "unity of interest" was necessary among cooperating actors in order for them to be considered a single economic unit. The court noted that *Copperweld*'s reference to "complete unity of interest" was too stringent to be the definitive consideration in single-entity analysis because any single firm may include diverse interests that can occasionally be in tension. In considering the NBA, the court observed that it has characteristics of both a single entity and a joint venture. It is a single entity insofar as the NBA has no existence independent of sports, and only the NBA can make NBA basketball games. Moreover, the court opined that in connection with the licensing of television content in particular, the NBA looks and acts very much like a single firm. On the other hand, the court noted the existence of various elements of competition that preempted it from concluding that the NBA was a single entity as a matter of law.

The court ultimately held that applying the *Copperweld* analysis to sports leagues cannot be a blanket designation of all sports leagues as either joint ventures or single entities as a matter of law; rather, it requires investigating each league separately, paying special attention to different facets of each league's operations and how the analysis might differ between them. The court explained:

> Sports are sufficiently diverse that it is essential to investigate their organization and ask *Copperweld*'s functional question one league at a time—and perhaps one facet of a league at a time, for we do not rule out the possibility that an organization such as the NBA is best understood as one firm when selling broadcast rights to a network in competition with a thousand other producers of entertainment, but is best understood as a joint venture when curtailing competition for players who have few other market opportunities.[20]

Thus, the court concluded that a league might be considered a single entity when it licenses television rights, yet be closer to a joint venture and subject to Section 1 when it signs and negotiates with players, where teams are arguably competing against one another for players' services.[21] Accordingly, the Seventh Circuit reversed the District Court decision and remanded the case for full consideration of this analysis in light of its opinion. However, before the court could undertake this analysis, the parties settled the case. Nonetheless, the Bulls cases provide the most exhaustive explorations of the single entity defense in sports leagues after *Copperweld*.

If Form Matters, Change the Form: *MLS v. Fraser*

In response to courts' refusal to recognize joint ventures and unincorporated associations of separate teams as single entities for antitrust purposes, entrepreneurs starting new leagues began to adopt new forms aimed at addressing the courts' concerns. In the early 1990s Major League Soccer L.L.C. (MLS), the Women's National Basketball Association (WNBA), the Women's United Soccer Association (WUSA), the American Basketball League (ABL), the World Wrestling Federation's XFL, and others were created with single and centralized corporate structures.

The strategic decision to structure MLS as a single corporate entity was undertaken in part in response to the courts' repeated rejection of sports leagues' single-entity arguments. MLS intended to take proactive steps at its formation to structure the league in a form that would be more likely to fall within the ambit of the Supreme Court's definition of a single entity for antitrust purposes.

Accordingly, MLS was organized as a single corporate entity (a Delaware limited-liability company) that would own and operate all of the MLS teams around the country. Investors would hold equity interests in MLS and some would sit on its management committee, which would oversee MLS policies. However, unlike traditional sports leagues, the league would retain extensive control over the operations of individual teams and the signing and trading of players among teams. Players signed contracts with MLS as employees of MLS itself, not the individual teams. League revenues were used to pay player salaries, stadium costs, coaching staff salaries, and other expenses incurred running the league. Profits, if any, would then be paid as dividends to MLS's investors.

Prior to the launch of the league, MLS made certain modifications to its structure to attract investors. MLS was still organized as a Delaware limited-liability company, and continued to own the intellectual property, player contracts, and other assets that comprised the teams themselves. But in eight markets, MLS relinquished certain control of various teams to individual investors, each of whom was granted the right to operate a team. These so-called operator/investors purchased a special class of membership unit and served as managers of the league, which entitled them to make separate decisions about team staffing, local broadcast rights, local ticket sales, and marketing. In return, MLS paid the operator/investors management fees that reflected their team's financial performance. However, MLS retained 100 percent of national broadcasting and merchandising revenues and planned to use these funds to pay player salaries and league expenses.

Thus, MLS retained—and to this day continues to retain—a degree of control over players that is unique among major sports leagues. This centralized control was a core component of its founders' original design for the league. MLS negotiates, signs, and pays players directly. The league—like a law firm—decides how much to pay its employees without the involvement of its constituent partners (subject to a limited exception). Each player negotiates his own deal with MLS, which, like the law firm, may impose a salary scale or cap the aggregate amount it pays its employees.

The players, however, saw the league's unique single-entity structure as an alleged sham designed to circumvent the antitrust laws. In 1998 several MLS players challenged the structure under Section 1. They alleged that MLS and its operator/investors had unlawfully combined to restrain trade by contracting for players' services centrally through MLS, which eliminated the competition for players that could exist among the teams in the absence of a centralized contracting arrangement.

The District Court applied *Copperweld* and held that MLS and its operator/investors functioned as an integrated single entity. Because a limited liability company was the equivalent of a corporation for corporate law purposes, the court treated MLS and its operator/investors in the same manner as the *Copperweld* Court treated a subsidiary and its parent: as a single economic unit. The plaintiffs argued that MLS and its operator/investors could not be a single entity because MLS's members had divergent interests, arising primarily from the management fees paid to each operator/investor based on the performance of that operator/investor's team. The court rejected this argument, explaining that operator/investors' successful operation of their teams did not simply benefit the operator/investors; rather, their success benefited the entire league by increasing the revenues that were retained by MLS and shared by all of its members.

The District Court further held that the contracting arrangement between MLS players and MLS, rather than the individual teams, did not violate Section 1. The court framed the issue as an internal decision made by the members of the company as a united group. It stated that the MLS members calculated that the surrender of autonomy in player contracting will benefit MLS as a whole, by lowering and controlling player salaries and increasing parity in talent among teams. The court noted: "this is a calculation made on behalf of the entity, and it does not serve the ulterior interests of the individual investors standing on their own."[22]

The District Court also dismissed the plaintiffs' argument that the MLS structure was simply a "sham to allow what is actually an illegal combination of plural actors to masquerade as the business conduct of a single entity."[23] The plaintiffs had urged the court to disregard the fact that MLS was a lawfully incorporated limited-liability company—a single corporate form—for antitrust purposes and treat the league as a conspiracy of plural actors. The court declined, explaining that to do so would contravene antitrust policy of encouraging trade because it would eliminate any security that corporations had in making their internal decisions without being vulnerable to Section 1 examination.

Thus, the court emphasized the importance of the investor's selection of the limited-liability company form and their right to form an entity to pursue a common goal. As the court stated, "In sum, plaintiffs' deconstruction efforts are unavailing. *MLS is what it is*. As a single entity, it cannot conspire or combine with its investors in violation of § 1 and its investors do not combine or conspire with each other in pursuing the economic interests of the entity."[24]

On appeal, however, the First Circuit cast some doubt on the District Court's ruling. Nevertheless, it refused to reverse the District Court's decision. The panel explored the ramifications of applying the *Copperweld* analysis to MLS or any other corporate entity that has a structure more complex than a parent and a wholly owned subsidiary, noting that there were functional differences between the complex structure employed by MLS and the parent-subsidiary relationship in *Copperweld* that it viewed as relevant to the antitrust analysis. The court ultimately concluded that MLS presented a "hybrid" arrangement, "somewhere between a single company (with or without wholly owned subsidiaries) and a cooperative arrangement between existing competitors" and that the single-entity issue with respect to such hybrid arrangements could not be definitively answered on motion in that case.[25] The court did not decide the single-entity issue definitively, noting its view that "the case for expanding *Copperweld* is debatable," but also concluding that even if Section 1 did apply to MLS, the challenged rule was not a *per se* violation and was a debatable case under the Rule of Reason. The court did not remand for any potential further findings to determine the applicability of the single-entity defense because it affirmed the jury verdict for MLS dismissing the case.[26]

Back to First Principles: *Texaco v. Dagher*

As we have seen, for the past twenty-five years, judicial decisions in antitrust cases involving sports leagues have employed a hodgepodge of balancing tests and exhaustive factual analysis. Courts have considered both form and substance, often disagreeing on the appropriate standards and even the outcome. Despite the Supreme Court's recognition that joint ventures are not inherently unlawful,[27] sports leagues—even those that in response to years of adverse judicial decisions organized themselves as limited liability companies instead of associations or joint ventures—have long been viewed from varying perspectives. While the single-entity defense remained available, few leagues were able to successfully avail themselves of *Copperweld* and its principles.

Then, in February 2006, the Supreme Court announced a decision in *Texaco v. Dagher* that, while unanimously reiterating existing law, may nonetheless represent a dramatic shift in the antitrust law framework applicable to sports leagues. *Texaco* confirmed what leagues have argued for years—that is, a legitimate joint venture consisting of separate companies that would otherwise be competitors may lawfully establish uniform terms for the venture's products without running afoul of the antitrust laws. Having formed a "lawful, economically integrated joint venture," these separate companies were no longer competitors with one another. Rather, like the lawyers who join together to form a law firm, they participated in the market jointly through what the court referred to as "an important and increasingly popular form of business organization."[28]

The facts of *Texaco* were simple and will be familiar to anyone who has ever formed a partnership with one or more other people or companies. In 1998 Texaco and Shell Oil began to collaborate in a joint venture called Equilon Enterprises, under which they agreed to refine and sell gasoline in the western United States under the original Texaco and Shell brand names.

Under their joint-venture agreement, they agreed to pool their resources and share the risks of and profits from Equilon's activities. The court emphasized that their venture was both "legitimate" and "lawful," not a sham designed to evade antitrust scrutiny. Indeed, it noted that Equilon's formation had been approved by an Federal Trade Commission (FTC) consent decree as well as by the state attorneys general of California, Hawaii, Oregon, and Washington.

Equilon decided to set a single price for both Texaco and Shell brand gasoline. Soon after, several Texaco and Shell service-station owners brought suit, arguing that by unifying prices for both brands, Texaco and Shell had violated Section 1's *per se* rule against price fixing. The District Court awarded summary judgment to Texaco and Shell, but the Ninth Circuit overturned its decision, characterizing the joint venturers' position as a request for "an exception to the *per se* prohibition on price fixing."

The Supreme Court reversed the Ninth Circuit, holding that while Equilon's pricing policy "may be price fixing in the literal sense, it is not price fixing in the antitrust sense."[29] The Court concluded that this was not the sort of horizontal price-fixing agreement between competitors that had long been condemned as *per se* illegal. Texaco and Shell were not competitors, each pursuing its own economic interests; instead, they were participating in the market jointly by pooling their investments and sharing profits and losses. Accordingly, Equilon's pricing policy amounted to "little more than price setting by a single entity."[30] The fact that it sold two different brands for the same price was outside the purview of the courts. Justice Clarence Thomas explained: "As a single entity, a joint venture, like any other firm, must have the *discretion* to determine the prices of the products that it sells, including the discretion to sell a product under two different brands at a single, unified price."[31]

Throughout its brief opinion, the Court emphasized two factors in justifying its ruling. First, it characterized Equilon's pricing policy an "internal" determination because it directly involved the operation of Equilon itself. Of course, representatives of Texaco and Shell were undoubtedly involved in the decision. Yet, by characterizing Equilon as "a single firm competing with other sellers in the marketplace," the Court essentially immunized its partners' joint decision-making process on account of their respective investments and profit-sharing arrangements. As the Court had recognized twenty-seven years earlier in *Broadcast Music, Inc. v. Columbia Broadcasting System, Inc.*, "[w]hen two partners set the price of their goods or services they are literally 'price fixing,' but they are not *per se* in violation of the Sherman Act."[32]

Second, the Court noted that the business practice being challenged in this instance was a "core activity of the venture itself." It rejected the Ninth

Circuit's application of the ancillary restraints doctrine, explaining that Equilon's pricing policy was integral to its business. Again, Justice Thomas cited *Broadcast Music* for the proposition that price-fixing by joint ventures is not unlawful "where the agreement on price is necessary to market the product at all."[33] In effect, the Court was saying that if Equilon could not determine the price of its own product, there would be no purpose or reason for having a joint venture.

At a minimum, *Texaco* stands for the proposition that the "internal" decisions of a "lawful, economically integrated joint venture" with respect to its "core activities" do not fall within the category of activities that are *per se* illegal under Section 1. Of course, this does not necessarily mean that the protection is absolute: for example, if Equilon's actions had affected the conduct of Texaco or Shell outside of the operation of the venture, that conduct would likely be fully subject to a Rule of Reason analysis under Section 1. In *Texaco*, the issue was made simpler because, as the Court recognized, Texaco and Shell were not competing with one another in the western United States. In the end, the Court found that Equilon was a legitimate, separate economic unit that, like Copperweld and its subsidiary or the partners in a law firm, was incapable of combining or conspiring with itself. Thus, whether evaluated under *per se* analysis or the Rule of Reason, legitimate restraints imposed by joint ventures on their core business activities should be presumptively permissible in light of the Court's decision in *Texaco*.

APPLYING *TEXACO* TO SINGLE-ENTITY DEFENSES OF SPORTS LEAGUES

The *Texaco* decision has been greeted favorably by sports leagues. As the cases discussed above illustrate, courts have typically rejected sports leagues' single-entity arguments, instead characterizing leagues as combinations or cartels among independent economic actors that have the potential to unreasonably restrain trade. Under *Texaco*, however, a joint venture formed for legitimate business purposes should be regarded as a single entity when it produces a joint product and makes internal decisions regarding its core activities, such as setting prices and determining output.

Like the agreement that formed Equilon, an agreement among dozens of teams or events to form a league and abide by its rules and decisions constitutes joint participation in a single, economically integrated joint venture. When teams pool, for example, their television rights and share the proceeds (whether pro rata or otherwise), they are not acting as competitors, but as investors in a single product—the professional sport—that competes against other forms of sports and entertainment for viewers, broadcasters and advertisers in the global marketplace. Just as Equilon or the law firm, a sports league should be recognized as a "lawful, economically integrated joint venture" and thus a separate, single entity for antitrust purposes. As such, to the extent its internal decisions involve "the core activity of the joint venture," they should be outside the purview of Section 1.

Therefore, the outcome of various earlier antitrust cases involving sports leagues should be reconsidered in light of the decision in *Texaco*. To be sure, many of the challenged actions can be justified under *Texaco*, as they represent properly characterized as internal decisions regarding core activities of a legitimate joint venture.

For example, when, as in *McNeil*, a league adopts a salary cap limiting the amount any team can pay its players (whether on an individual or aggregate basis) to promote competitive balance, or like MLS, allocates its players among the various teams, the league is clearly making an internal decision regarding a core function. In any sport, the players are an integral and indispensable part of creating the league's product. Thus, there can be little doubt that rules and restrictions regarding the allocation of players are "necessary to market the product at all." Few matters are more integral to the operation of a league than its rules regarding the composition, number, nature, and location of its teams. Under *Texaco*, the league should be treated as a single entity when it makes such internal decisions, even if the decisions impact the salary—or price—any member of the league can pay a particular player. If, as the Court held in *Texaco*, a joint venture can set a uniform price when it acts as the seller of a product, surely it can establish a uniform or maximum rate it is willing to pay when it acts as the buyer of a product, regardless of whether that product is gasoline or athletic talent.

Likewise, when a league determines how to exploit its telecasting rights, its choices should be regarded as internal decisions regarding a core activity. National and local telecasting is today the primary means by which sports leagues convey their product to the consumer market. Indeed, television coverage is integral to the product itself—many of the decisions a league makes regarding the rules of play that govern the sport are designed to enhance the product's television appeal. A league's decision to telecast—or to allow its constituent partners to telecast—a limited number of games is no less "integral to the running of a business" than any other company's determination to set output at a particular level. Thus, a plaintiff should have no better luck attacking the number of games telecast—or, for that matter, played— by a particular league than it would challenging the number of cars that General Motors produces in any given year.

Logically, the holding in *Texaco* should not be limited to decisions directly regarding price and output. Rather, any "internal decisions" on "core activities" should be outside the scope of Section 1 so long as the league is operating as a legitimate, economically integrated joint venture. Any league's decisions on where to place its franchises—expansion, relocation, and even contraction—should be immune from antitrust attack, just as a law firm may decide to open or close an office in any city, or to relocate its office from one part of town to another.[34] The nature of league sports requires that the number of teams be limited and that they play in a diverse group of markets in order to foster fan loyalty and promote geographic rivalries.[35] Thus, geographic allocation of franchises is as much a "core activity" as its decisions regarding price and output.

Finally, *Texaco* suggests that newly created sports leagues may be able to employ traditional structures—such as joint ventures and unincorporated associations—without jeopardizing their antitrust position. This would largely assuage the concerns that prompted the founders of MLS to employ a unique and complex limited-liability company structure in an effort to gain recognition as a single entity under *Copperweld*. While a single structure should still be highly significant, *Texaco* allows leagues also to argue, consistent with an expansive view of the "economic reality" test set forth in *Copperweld*, that their substance mandates treatment as a single entity for antitrust purposes. As discussed above, *Copperweld* looked past the fact that a parent and subsidiary were separate legal entities and instead focused on the unity of interests between the two. Likewise, the *Texaco* Court focused the economic integration of the joint venture, the partners' investment in the joint venture and the fact that they shared Equilon's profits. Based on Justice Thomas's opinion, future leagues should be free to choose their structures—whether they be joint ventures, associations, limited-liability companies, not-for-profit corporations, or other entities—based on valid business reasons rather than fear of antitrust challenges.

It remains to be seen exactly what effect *Texaco* will have on sports leagues and the players, broadcasters, facilities, licensees, and others with whom they conduct business. At the very least, however, the opinion suggests a trend toward recognizing the possibility that a sports league can be treated as a single economic unit for many purposes under Section 1. Indeed, in November 2006 Judge Loretta Preska of the U.S. District Court for the Southern District of New York cited *Texaco* in refusing to grant a preliminary junction in an antitrust action brought by a Russian hockey club against the NHL after its Pittsburgh Penguins signed Russian superstar Evgeni Malkin. There, the plaintiff asserted, *inter alia*, claims under the antitrust laws challenging the NHL's rules that required the Russian club to negotiate only with the league, and not with any individual NHL club, regarding the transfer of foreign players. While Judge Preska gave several other reasons for her decision, in concluding that the plaintiff had failed to show any likelihood of success on its antitrust claims, she stated that the NHL's activities "seem to be included within the meaning of the Supreme Court's recent *Texaco* case as the core activities of a joint venture, and thus would not constitute a combination in restraint of trade."

More recently, the NFL relied on *Texaco* to establish that it constitutes a single entity when it licenses team trademarks to clothing manufacturers. In *American Needle, Inc. v. New Orleans Louisiana Saints, et al.,* the plaintiff alleged that that the NFL teams violated Section 1 by pooling their respective intellectual property rights and delegating licensing authority to a jointly-owned affiliate, NFL Properties.[36] American Needle, a manufacturer of hats and other headwear, filed suit against the teams after losing its license to use their trademarks when NFL Properties entered into an exclusive relationship with Reebok. The District Court quickly recognized the value of exclusive licensing agreements and turned to the question of whether the teams could designate a common actor to exploit their various intellectual property rights. The court concluded "yes," explaining that "they have so integrated their operations that they should be deemed to be a single entity."[37] It cited that "obvious" reasons why the NFL teams would choose to delegate this authority to a jointly owned entity: "To require the 32 teams to each take total responsibility for the protection and marketing of its own logos and trademarks in a nationwide market would cause each to be at a competitive disadvantage with other leagues with integrated marketing."[38] The Court also acknowledged that, in this case, one of the purposes of the challenged cooperation was to promote the attractiveness or the league's product, as it emphasized that the joint licensing arrangement facilitated league-wide revenue sharing that was designed in part to prevent large market teams from gaining an unfair advantage.[39] Finally, while American Needle argued that the teams' separate ownership of the intellectual property rights rendered their delegation to NFL Properties unlawful, the court noted that "[o]wnership (and, thus, ultimate control) does not necessarily defeat the single entity argument" and "[t]he economic reality is that the separate ownerships had no economic significance in and of itself."[40] The court ultimately granted summary judgment in favor of the NFL and its teams, concluding that they acted as a single entity in licensing their intellectual property.

CONCLUSION

For many years, courts struggled with the question of how to characterize a professional sports league under the antitrust laws. Although they recognized that these joint ventures generate a product—the games themselves—that competes with other sports and entertainment offerings, they fixated on the divergence of interests among the teams that comprise each league and the fact that those teams compete against one another on the playing field, if not in the economic marketplace. Often, judges employed an exhaustive, fact-based analysis that led to prolonged discovery and lengthy proceedings that, in many cases, lasted for years. In the end, many disputes settled before the courts could issue a decision on the merits, thus further delaying the judicial guidance sought not only by the leagues, but by potential plaintiffs as well.

With the question still unresolved, new leagues attempted to develop structures based on limited-liability companies—with team operators as investors rather than joint venturers—in the hope that courts would be more amenable to a structure that more closely resembled the facts of *Copperweld*. While Major League Soccer ultimately won a victory, the First Circuit's decision failed to definitively resolve the issue. Although the appellate court recognized that the league's corporate form was not dispositive, it refused to ignore MLS's unique economic and corporate integration. In the end, it acknowledged that despite dozens of decisions and decades of case law, the law in this area still required further development.[41]

The Supreme Court's most recent decision on the subject suggests that the question may not be so difficult to answer after all. Under *Texaco*, a legitimate joint venture must, at least to some substantial extent, be treated as a single economic unit for antitrust purposes, and therefore its internal decisions regarding its core activities should be beyond Section 1 scrutiny. While the ultimate impact of the Court's opinion will no doubt be shaped by future cases, the opinion has rekindled the "single entity" debate. Ironically, only months after Chief Justice Rehnquist's death, lawyers will again be reading his prescient dissent in *NFL v. NASL* and advancing his arguments. This time, if *Texaco* is any indication, his former colleagues on the Supreme Court will apparently be more receptive to his characterization of a sports league as a "unit" competing against other forms of entertainment. Simply put, it's a whole new ballgame.

NOTES

1. The principal exception is Major League Baseball, which was granted an exemption by the Supreme Court in the 1922 *Federal Baseball Club* case. Although the rationale for the initial decision is no longer applicable, the Court extended the exemption in the case of *Flood v. Kuhn*, 407 U.S. 258 (1972), holding that Congress was long aware of its prior holding and had not taken any steps to reverse it. Certain leagues also have received a statutory exemption to pool television rights and license such rights to "sponsored telecasters."

2. 15 U.S.C. § 1.

3. *Chicago Bd. v. U.S.,* 246 U.S. 231, 238 (1918).

4. See *Copperweld Corp. v. Independence Tube Corp.,* 467 U.S. 752, 769 (1983).

5. *Id.*

6. 15 U.S.C. § 2.

7. *NCAA v. Board of Regents,* 468 U.S. 85, 101 (1984).

8. *NFL v. NASL,* 670 F.2d 1249, 1253–1257.

9. *NFL v. NASL,* 459 U.S. 1074, 1077.

10. *Id.* at 1078.

11. *Copperweld* at 768–769.

12. *Id.* at 769.

13. For example, the Court explained that whether or not the subsidiary was wholly owned or unincorporated would not affect the single entity analysis.

14. *McNeil v. NFL,* 790 F. Supp. 871, 875–876 (1992).

15. *Id.* at 878.

16. *Id.* at 880.

17. *Sullivan v. NFL,* 34 F.3d 1091, 1100 (1st Cir. 1994).

18. *Chicago Prof. Sports Ltd P'ship v. National Basketball Ass'n*, 754 F. Supp. 1336, 1345 (N.D. Ill. 1991).

19. 874 F. Supp. at 848–850.

20. *Chicago Prof. Sports Ltd. P'ship v. Nat'l Basketball Ass'n*, 95 F.3d 593, 600 (7th Cir. 1996).

21. *Id.*

22. *Fraser v. MLS,* 97 F. Supp. 2d 130, 137 (D. Mass. 2000).

23. *Id.* at 137–138.

24. *Id.* at 139.

25. *Fraser v. MLS,* No. 01-1296, 1st Cir. March 20, 2002.

26. *Id.*

27. See *Arizona v. Maricopa Cty. Med. Society,* 457 U.S. 332, 356 (1982) (When "persons who would otherwise be competitors pool their capital and share the risks of loss as well as the opportunities for profit … such joint ventures [are] treated as a single firm competing with other sellers in the market"); *Broadcast Music, Inc. v. Columbia Broad. Sys., Inc.,* 441 U.S. 1, 23 (1979) ("Joint ventures and other cooperative arrangements are also not usually unlawful, at least not as price-fixing schemes, where the agreement on price is necessary to market the product at all").

28. *Texaco v. Dagher,* 126 S. Ct. 1276, 1279 (2006).

29. *Id.* at 1280.

30. *Id.*

31. *Id.*

32. *Broadcast Music,* 441 U.S. 1, 9 (1979).

33. *Id.* at 23.

34. See *Los Angeles Memorial Coliseum Comm'n v. NFL,* 726 F.2d 1381 (9th Cir. 1984) ("[T]he nature of NFL football requires some territorial restrictions in order both to encourage participation in the venture and to secure each venturer the legitimate fruits of that participation"); see also *NBA v. San Diego Clippers Basketball Club,* 815 F.2d 562 (9th Cir. 1987); *St. Louis Convention & Visitors Comm'n v. NFL,* 154 F.3d 851 (8th Cir. 1998).

35. See *Major League Baseball v. Crist*, 331 F.3d 1177, 1183 (11th Cir. 2003) ("It is difficult to conceive of a decision more integral to the business of major league baseball than the number of clubs that will be allowed to compete," quoting *Major League Baseball v. Butterworth*, 181 F. Supp. 2d 1316, 1332 [N.D. Fla. 2001]).

36. See *American Needle, Inc. v. New Orleans Louisiana Saints, et al.*, 496 F.Supp.2d 941, 941–942 (N.D. Ill. 2007).

37. *Id.* at 943.

38. *Id.*

39. *Id.* at 943–944.

40. *Id.* at 944.

41. See *MLS*, 284 F.3d, at 58 ("The law at this point could develop along either or both of two different lines. One would expand upon *Copperweld* to develop functional tests or criteria for shielding [or refusing to shield] such hybrids from section 1 scrutiny for intra-enterprise arrangements. This would be a complex task and add a new layer of analysis. . . . The other course is to reshape section 1's rule of reason toward a body of more flexible rules for interdependent multi-party enterprises").

Three

Competitive Balance and Attendance in the Sports Industry

Brian P. Soebbing

Competitive balance is currently a hot topic in sports. Fans, media, and sports leagues all stress the importance of "competitive balance," but what is it? Andrew Zimbalist compares competitive balance to wealth by saying competitive balance is a good thing to have, but nobody is able to discover how much competitive balance a person or league needs.[1] David Forrest and Robert Simmons define competitive balance as "a league structure which has relatively equal playing strength between league members."[2] This definition will become important later on in this essay. Competitive balance is important mainly for fan welfare. Fan interest and welfare are critical to both teams' and leagues' success because gate revenues and broadcasting revenues impact these entities' financial stability.

This chapter will give an introduction to sports leagues motives and discuss how competitive imbalance occurs among teams in professional sports leagues. Next will be a quick introduction to some of the competitive balance measurements that analyze competitive balance in professional sports leagues. The third section will examine some of the research and implications within competitive balance and attendance in professional sports.

COMPETITIVE BALANCE

To understand the concept of competitive balance, it is important to consider the work of Simon Rottenberg on how professional sports teams operate.[3] In sports economics, two types of team motives emerge: profit maximizing and wins maximizing. These two motives inspect the tradeoff between wins and profits differently. Put simply, the profit-maximizing teams will not acquire additional talent beyond the point where marginal revenue equals marginal cost. In contrast, win maximizers maximize wins and sacrifice profit. They generally acquire talent past the point where marginal revenue equals marginal cost. The general thought is teams in North American sports (Major League Baseball, National Football League, National Basketball Association, and National Hockey League) are profit maximizers, whereas teams in European and some other international sports leagues are win maximizers.

Rottenberg studies how playing talent accumulates among baseball teams. Put simply, players go to teams who value them the most. This forms his invariance principle. However, under profit maximization, teams will not acquire talent that exceeds the profit-maximizing marginal revenue. Therefore, this limits the accumulation of talent to any one particular team. What, then, is the profit-maximizing point for teams?[4]

Rodney Fort and James Quirk developed an economic model to explain the disparity among teams in professional sports, particularly in Major League Baseball (MLB). Their goal was to investigate the effect of free agency, reverse order drafts, and salary caps on competitive balance. However, the model of professional sports leagues they develop provides an excellent introduction to how a professional sports league operates and introduces readers to the disparity in win percent that teams in professional sports leagues have. This disparity produces competitive imbalance within professional sports leagues.[5]

Three underlying assumptions are present in Fort and Quirk's model. The first is that teams are profit maximizing. The second is players in leagues attempt to maximize their income. The third is the market generates equilibrium outcomes.[6]

An illustration of their one-team model shows that revenues increase until a certain winning percentage (see Figure 3.1). After that, revenues decline as winning percentage increases. This reflects the law of diminishing marginal returns, which states that as people keep consuming one additional good, the return from that good decreases. In fact, Walter Neale infers the law of diminishing marginal returns with his example of the New York Yankees. In the late 1950s, the Yankees were in one of their multiple World Series title streaks. When they did not win the championship one year, bigger crowds started to attend the games. This reflects both the law of diminishing marginal return and the uncertainty of outcome. An in-depth discussion on uncertainty of outcome occurs later in this chapter. Neale notes that the Yankees prayer is, "Oh Lord, make us good, but not that good."[7]

FIGURE 3.1
A Team's Profit-Maximizing Level of Success

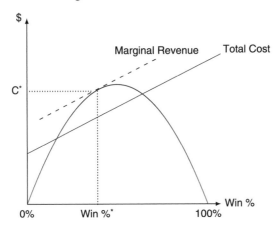

Source: Adapted from Rodney Fort and James Quirk, "Cross-Subsidization, Incentives, and Outcomes in Professional Team Sports Leagues," *Journal of Economic Literature* 33, no. 3 (1995): 1265–1299.

The cost function is the straight line on the figure. The intercept reflects the fixed costs of operating a team. The slope of the line reflects a constant marginal cost of acquiring talent and thus increasing winning percentage. The more wins a team choose, the higher the cost. Finally, marginal revenue is the slope of a line that is tangent to the revenue curve at any point. The slope of the marginal revenue line is equal to the slope of the cost line at the point of profit maximization. These two lines are parallel at this point. Thus, a profit-maximizing team will choose a winning percentage at that point where marginal revenue equals marginal cost.[8]

This model is an abstraction. The revenue curve captures all differences between teams. The slope of the revenue curve affects a team's marginal revenue, which in turn determines the profit maximizing win percent. This interaction of market potential in a simple two-team league is shown in Figure 3.2. The three assumptions made before still hold. Also, the combined win percents of the two teams has to equal 1. For example, if one team has a 0.700 winning percentage, the other team's winning percentage has to be 0.300. Figure 3.2 shows that a team with a lower revenue curve (hence a smaller marginal revenue) chooses a lower winning percentage than the team with a higher revenue curve (larger marginal revenue). This disparity in the marginal revenue line reflects the disparity in win percents and thus competitive balance.[9]

FIGURE 3.2
Equilibrium in a Two-Team League

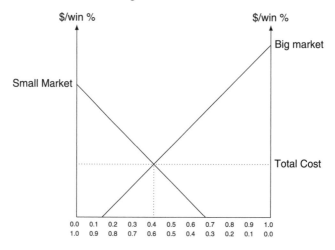

Source: Adapted from Rodney Fort and James Quirk, "Cross-Subsidization, Incentives, and Outcomes in Professional Team Sports Leagues," *Journal of Economic Literature* 33, no. 3 (1995): 1265–1299.

The key to the model by Fort and Quirk is the issue of market size. The disparity in win percentage does not come from what happens on the field. Two teams with the same market size each choose a 0.500 winning percentage in the long run. However, when two teams have different market sizes, the win percentages each team chooses are not equal. So in a two-team model, a 0.600/0.400 split could be possible as well as a 0.700/0.300 split. The disparity in market size creates competitive imbalance in the long run.[10] This prediction supports Rottenberg's conclusion.[11]

Now with an understanding of how competitive imbalance occurs within sports leagues, we can examine the measurements of competitive balance. Rodney Fort and Joel Maxcy partition competitive balance research into two distinct analytical areas. The first area is the analysis of competitive balance, which focuses on measures of competitive balance and analyzes its changes over time. This area mainly focuses on how policy changes in professional sports leagues affect competitive balance. Some examples of policies include free agency, revenue sharing, reverse order draft, and salary caps. The second area of research, according to Fort and Maxcy, is the uncertainty of outcome hypothesis, which applies to competitive balance and its affects on consumer behavior (fan attendance).[12] Both areas of research are equally important in the study of competitive balance in professional sports leagues. Since the purpose of this essay is to examine competitive balance and attendance, the focus is almost exclusively on the uncertainty of outcome hypothesis area of competitive balance research.

COMPETITIVE BALANCE MEASUREMENTS

Since competitive balance is a difficult concept to define, many different measures of competitive balance exist. Competitive balance measures partition in two areas: intraseason and interseason. This next section will examine some of the main ways to measure competitive balance and will also discuss some of the strengths and limitations of each of these measures.

The standard deviation of winning percentage (SDWP) is the most common measure of competitive balance. It reflects the dispersion of wins in a sports league. A standard deviation of zero indicates perfect competitive balance within a league. This will occur when each team in the league wins 50 percent of its games in a season. The higher the SDWP, the worse the competitive balance is for a league.

In order to compare competitive balance across leagues, sports economists use the idealized standard deviation of winning percentage (ISDWP) ratio. The calculation for the ISDWP ratio is dividing the SDWP by the ISDWP. The ISDWP in any league is simply the actual standard deviation divided by the square root of the number of games played in a season. The closer the ratio is to 1, the better the competitive balance for a league.

This one-dimensional number does not have much explanatory power. Its power lies in the ability to compare one period's level of competitive balance to another period's level. The ISDWP ratio's main function is to compare competitive balance across professional sports leagues by correcting for differences in the number of regular-season games ($\sqrt{G}$) for each professional sports league. This is important because professional sports leagues play different regular-season schedules. For example, MLB plays 162 games, the National Football League (NFL) plays 16 games, and the English Premier League plays 38 games.

The primary advantage of SDWP is simplicity. This measure gives a quick snapshot of the competitive balance in a league during a period of time. Disadvantages do exist, though. One of the limitations of the SDWP is that this measure does not vary across teams within a particular season. For example, if the SDWP for a particular season is 0.005, each team's measure in that season is 0.005 so that measure does not vary across teams in that particular season. Brad Humphreys notes this limitation of the SDWP.[13]

Another limitation of this measure is that the SDWP does not reflect changes in league standings. For example, consider a league that has two teams, A and B. These two teams play each other ten times. Team A finishes with six wins and four losses and, of course, Team B finishes with the exact opposite record. In year two, the two teams' records are reversed: Team A finishes with a four-win and six-loss record, whereas Team B finishes with a six-win and four-loss record. In calculating the SDWP, the result is the same for both seasons. However, the standings were different from one year to the next. This illustrates another limitation of the SDWP measure.[14]

Two alternative measures extend from the SDWP. E. Woodrow Eckard examines cartel behavior and competitive balance in NCAA Division I football. In his paper, Eckard recognizes one of the limitations of the SDWP measure. He tries to correct this limitation by decomposing the observed variation in winning percentage into two parts: the average of the variance in win percentage across schools and the variance of win percentage across teams. In Eckard's paper, the calculation of total variance is across each member of a particular conference. This approach captures some of the interdependence between teams in a sports league and/or conference. When a decrease in the time variance couples with an increase in the cumulative variance, competitive balance declines within the subject area. If the exact opposite occurs (an increase in time and a decrease in cumulative) competitive balance in the sports league declines. Eckard notes both terms (time and cumulative) rarely move in unison.[15]

Humphreys adds to this section of the literature with his competitive balance ratio (CBR). The CBR is useful "because it also reflects the average amount of team-specific variation in won-loss percentage that will not be reflected in σ_L."[16] The CBR is just the ratio of team-specific win percentage variation during a season, and the winning percentage in each season from all the teams in the league. The CBR bounds are between 0 and 1. A value of 0 shows no competitive balance whereas 1 shows perfect competitive balance. The biggest benefit of this measure is "unlike standard deviation of winning percentage, this ratio is easier to compare during different time periods because it does not have to be compared to an idealized value that depends on the number of games played in each season."[17]

Two main limitations of the CBR exist. One limitation of this measurement is "because of the manner in which it is defined, however, it is incapable of separating the impact of intra-seasonal from inter-seasonal balance on attendance." Another limitation of the CBR is its time constraint. It "can only be calculated during a period of seasons."[18]

The Herfindahl-Hirschman Index (commonly known as HHI) is a concentration measure. The most common use of the HHI is in measuring the concentration of championships over a certain period in a sports league. However, the HHI can measure concentration of first-place finishes within a division as well as the concentration of wins/points within a sports league.[19] The measure is simple to calculate: take the market share of each team (whether market share is first-place finishes, World Series titles, or wins), square that number, and then sum the values for all teams to get the HHI score. The higher the HHI, the higher the concentration of the wins/points, championships, or first-place finishes in the sample. Increasing concentration shows increasing competitive imbalance. For example, in the 1990s the HHI is high in MLB because of the multiple World Series titles by the New York Yankees and Toronto Blue Jays. However, in the 2000s, the concentration is low because no team is a multiple World Series winner so far in this decade.

A positive aspect of the HHI is its emphasis on the distribution of championships and first-place finishes. In general, championships and first-place finishes mean that a given team reaches postseason play. Postseason play, or playoffs, can benefit teams in two ways. First, the fans retain their energy through the whole season as their team battles for a spot in the playoffs. The second benefit is playoffs can generate an unexpected league champion. This uncertainty benefits the fans of weaker teams throughout the league because once the playoffs begin, every team began again from scratch.[20]

The HHI captures to some extent the reordering of standings that the SDWP does not measure. However, one of the negative aspects is the HHI did not vary across the teams with that season. This is the same problem with the SDWP. In addition, a championship model in its pure form (measuring the distribution of championships) is a bad predictor when comparing it to a win-percent predicting model.[21] Another problem with analyzing playoffs and competitive balance is variation in the number of teams who make the playoffs for a professional sports league. An example of this situation would be MLB. The definition of the Blue Ribbon Panel for competitive balance is that every team has a chance of making the playoffs.[22] However, one change that took place in MLB a few years before is the expansion of the playoffs. Instead of two teams making the playoffs in each league, now four teams make the playoffs in each league. Certainly, this "improves" competitive balance according to the definition from MLB. However, the question is did this really improve competitive balance or just artificially deflate the HHI?

Gini coefficients are another measure of win dispersion in a professional sports league. Gini coefficients are a "conventional economic measure of inequality." Gini Coefficients "are used to measure to measure inequality in league playoff outcomes."[23] Its bounds are 0 and 1, where 0 signals perfect equality. In the framework of competitive balance, a 0 happens when each team wins 50 percent of its games.

The main drawback is the Gini coefficient "ignores that one team cannot possibly win all of the leagues games."[24] Other constraints when calculating Gini Coefficients for within-season competitive balance are unbalanced schedules, interleague play, and expansion of the number of teams in professional sports leagues.

Neale hypothesizes that "the closer the standings, and within any range of standings the more frequently the standings change, the larger the gate receipts."[25] This is the basis behind the Spearman rank correlation coefficient (SRCC). The SRCC measures changes in leagues' standings from one season to the next. The range of this measurement is from −1 and 1. The value −1 is a perfect reordering of the standings whereas 1 means no reordering in the standings.[26]

The main benefit with using the SRCC is its ability to describe the reordering of the standings. The SRCC captures the place in the standings that the previous competitive balance measures cannot capture. The reordering of standings not only is a competitive balance benefit because of its potential lack at unpredictable outcomes, but it is also a benefit in examining the distribution of talent and the effect of free agency among a league. Another benefit is the simplicity of the measurement, which is similar to the properties of the SDWP.

The main drawback to the SRCC in measuring competitive balance is its inability to capture closeness of the finishes. For example, the 2006 MLB season, National League Central Division came down to the final day of the season. The Houston Astros finished in second place to the Saint Louis Cardinals. In the National League East Division, the Philadelphia Phillies finished in second place to the New York Mets. However, unlike the Astros, the Phillies finished twelve games behind in the standings. The SRCC did not account for the difference in second-place finishes, which is a limitation. When examining the reordering or standings and its effect on competitive balance, one needs to scrutinize both the reordering of standings from one year to the next but also the number of games back each team is from one season to the next. The question is even if perfect reordering in the standings occur, if the games behind do not change from one year to the next, then does good competitive balance really exist in the context of the league?

The main measures, SDWP, HHI, SRCC, and Gini coefficients, vary across seasons but not across teams in a season. Markov transitional probabilities capture variation by teams within seasons. Markov Transitional Probabilities assume that what happens in the past helps determine what will happen in the future. This unique measure of competitive balance has some benefits. The first one is that transitional probabilities track teams' performance from one season to the next season, which other competitive balance measures fail to do. It also captures the cyclical aspect of performance by professional sports teams. Under the assumption that teams were profit maximizers, the probabilities show how difficult it can be for a bad team to "jump the curve," and win or how reluctant teams are to choose extra wins because of the effects on profits.

A negative aspect to transitional probabilities is they do not take into account how many games a team would need to make the playoffs. This is similar to the problem with the SRCC. This might help more accurately predict a team's chances from one season to the next since not all losers were equal. A team that finishes two games away from making the playoffs is certainly more likely to make the playoffs next season than a team that finishes thirty games out of the playoffs.

All competitive balance measures have their own unique way of capturing competitive balance, including win dispersion, concentration of championships, first-place finishes, or reordering of the standings. However, the measures each have their own limitations, which is important for researchers to recognize within the context of analyzing competitive balance within professional sports.

UNCERTAINTY OF OUTCOME HYPOTHESIS

The uncertainty of outcome hypothesis (UOH) is the second proposition of Rottenberg's paper. (Recall that the invariance principle is the first proposition of Rottenberg's paper.) Rottenberg remarks that the profits of a sports league decline as competitive balance declines. This is the uncertainty of outcome hypothesis.[27] Neale talks about the UOH in his League Standing Effect, noting that in order for fans to attend sporting events, listen to events on radio, or watch teams on television, some uncertainty of outcome must be present.[28] The earlier example of the New York Yankees is an example of the UOH and the importance of fan welfare for a professional sports league.

Similar to competitive balance, it is important to define what exactly uncertainty of outcome is. One definition is "a situation where a given contest within a league structure has a degree of unpredictability about the result and, by extension, that the competition as a whole does not have a predetermined winner at the outset of competition."[29] This definition describes two of the three types of uncertainty that sports economists investigate in their research. The first type is game uncertainty, which examines the closeness of a match between two clubs. The second is playoff or championship uncertainty, which examines how likely it is to predict a winner of a professional sports league. No mention of the third type of uncertainty, consecutive-season uncertainty, occurs in the above definition. Consecutive-season uncertainty examines the absence of dynasties, these perennial winners in leagues.

MEASUREMENTS AND STUDIES

The metrics present in the uncertainty of outcome literature are, for the most part, different from those that appear in competitive balance literature. This exposes a slight disconnect across these two areas of study. Many UOH studies specify a demand function for attendance in a particular professional league. Uncertainty of outcome is an individual factor within those demand functions. MLB and European football (soccer) are the two sports that undergo the most analysis when examining uncertainty of outcome and its effects on attendance. However, some uncertainty of outcome research focuses on other major professional sports leagues. An article by Jeffery Borland and Robert McDonald, an essay by Rodney Fort, and an article by Stephen Syzmanski contain thorough reference lists of research done on uncertainty of outcome.[30] I recommend consulting all three articles for additional reading. The focus here will not be to critique and analyze each individual study, but rather, to use some of the previous research to provide thorough examples of the uncertainty of outcome measures and to discuss some issues when testing uncertainty of outcome and the UOH.

One uncertainty of outcome measure is games/points behind the leader. Using this measure, or some transformation of this measure (for example, combined games behind, average games behind, or difference of games behind) captures uncertainty of outcome in both game and season levels. This measure gives a snapshot of the relative quality of each individual team and is easy to calculate.

Two main limitations exist when using the games/points behind the leader to measure uncertainty of outcome. The first limitation when examining this measure in the context of game uncertainty is it does not consider the impact of home-field advantage present within a particular sports league. Home-field advantage is a big factor in game uncertainty because it potentially raises the quality of the match when the weaker team plays a home game against the stronger team. This makes the game outcome more uncertain than if that same game occurs at a neutral site or at the home of the higher-quality team. This measure does not factor in the effect of home-field advantage, and certainly when testing the effect of uncertainty of outcome on attendance, this is an important consideration.

The second limitation with using this measure is using the measure in leagues that engage in postseason playoffs. This measure, in its pure form, works well in leagues such as the English Premier League that does not engage in a postseason championship. For leagues such as MLB, National Hockey League (NHL), and NFL that engage in some sort of playoff system, the games behind the leader measure needs modification. Major League Baseball provides a good illustration of this phenomenon. From the 1969 baseball season to the end of the 1994 season, MLB partitioned each league (American and National) into two divisions (East and West). The winners of each division played each other to see who would represent the league in the World Series. In that time period, using games behind the leader to measure uncertainty of outcome is appropriate. At the beginning of the 1995 season, MLB realigned both leagues so these days three divisions (East, Central, and West) exist within each league. With the three divisions in each league, this creates an odd number for a playoff format. In order to correct for the odd number of teams, MLB institutes a wild-card team in each league. This team is the nondivisional winning team that comprises the best regular season record in the league. The institution of the wild-card team institutes two simultaneous races in MLB: the race for the division winner and the race for the wild-ard winner. The games behind the leader measure would now be an inappropriate measure at both the game and seasonal uncertainly level. A simple adjustment would be to calculate the games behind from making the playoffs. Recall the example earlier with the Philadelphia Phillies. In 2006 the Phillies finished twelve games behind the division-winning New York Mets. In that same year, however, the Phillies only finished three games behind the Los Angeles Dodgers in the wild-card race. Using the games behind the leader measure would not accurately measure the degree of uncertainty in games involving the Philadelphia Phillies.

Roger Noll conducted one of the earliest studies of uncertainty of outcome. Noll examined total season attendance demand for the 1970 and 1971 MLB seasons and used games behind the leader as an argument in the demand function. His results show that the games behind variable is not significant, but Noll comments this is probably the case because of strong correlation with other variables within his demand function.[31]

James Richard Hill, Jeff Madura, and Richard A. Zuber tested uncertainty of outcome in a different way. Instead of examining long-run seasonal uncertainty of outcome similar to Noll, Hill and colleagues studied short-run, game-by-game uncertainty of outcome. In their model, they included many game-specific variables, including the time of game, pitching records for the opposing pitchers, and if a promotion occurred for that game. The uncertainty of outcome measure in their function is both the home and visitor games behind the leader. They hypothesize both of these numbers would have an inverse relationship to attendance for that particular game. The results confirm their hypothesis (the UOH) with the home team having the bigger effect on attendance than the visiting team that intuitively makes sense.[32]

Using games behind the leader measure is not exclusive to MLB. Jeff Borland used a deviation of this measure in describing the seasonal demand for Australian Rules Football. In his research, Borland contemplated four different types of uncertainty of outcome measures. He settled on using the average games behind the leader measure to test the effect of uncertainty of outcome in the league. For his average, Borland generated the games behind the leader at four different points during the season. Even though the relationship between uncertainty of outcome and attendance is the correct relationship (inverse), it is not statistically significant in the demand equation.[33]

A second common uncertainty of outcome measure includes a group of measures. These "probability-based measures" encompass betting odds, the probability of a home team winning a game, and the probability of a team winning a championship. These measures, when used to examine game uncertainty, capture the home-field advantage. By capturing the home-field advantage of teams, researchers can more accurately calculate the effect outcome uncertainty has on game or seasonal attendance. What these probability measures can also do is begin to examine a big underlying question: Do fans of particular sports leagues prefer short-term uncertainty (game uncertainty) or do they prefer more balance in league structures (competitive balance)?

A limitation with these measures involves the betting market in which betting odds are set. An accepted theory in the financial market literature is the efficient market hypothesis. Put simply, the market in setting its prices (point, spreads, betting odds, and so on) reflects all the relevant information available. Therefore, the betting odds give fans and researchers more information regarding the result for a particular match. Past research uncovers some biases regarding the setting of these betting odds and therefore slight inefficiencies of the sports betting market. One example is the long-shot bias where odds setters overinflate the odds of a favorite to win a particular match. Previous research uncovers biases in the betting markets of European football (soccer), MLB, and NHL.[34] Knowing and correcting for these biases will allow a better articulation on the effect of uncertainty of outcome on attendance.

Glen Knowles, Keith Sherony, and Mike Haupert improved on the research previously done by Hill and colleagues by adding the probability of the home team winning the game. They examined National League home games for the 1988 season. Knowles and colleagues hypothesized that the uncertainty of outcome generates a positive effect on attendance. In the model, Knowles and colleagues used the probability of the home team winning the game. They also sum the total number of games behind the two opposing teams are from the leader. The results confirm the UOH for both the games behind the leader and the probability of the home team winning. In fact, attendance is at its maximum point when the probability is 0.6 of the home team winning the contest.[35]

David Peel and Dennis Thomas conducted a series of studies examining betting odds and their determination of the effect of the uncertainty of outcome. For the first study, they used the 1986–1987 season of the English Football League matches. They used betting odds to test the probability of the home team winning and found a negative and significant effect with attendance that confirms the UOH. More specifically, they concluded match attendance follows a U-shape curve in relation to the probability of the home team winning.[36]

The next study by Peel in Thomas examines matches in the 1991–1992 Scottish Football League season. The study uses the betting odds similar to their previous study. This study, though, gives mixed results. It does confirm the U-shape relationship. However, they conclude that this is for core fans. For noncore fans, Peel and Thomas concluded these fans just want to see the home team win.[37]

Finally, Peel and Thomas examined British Rugby League matches in the 1994–1995 seasons. They again used betting odds for the league and found "potential effects of a leveling of standards amongst competing teams."[38] In summary, mixed results exist regarding the effect on uncertainty of outcome at both the game and seasonal uncertainty levels using all types of measurements. This shows certainly the difficulty of locating an adequate measure to capture uncertainty of outcome in sports leagues. It also shows the complexities of sports teams and leagues as business entities.

Referring back to Fort and Maxcy's research, one omission in their study of UOH is the lack of a competitive balance measure. Earlier in this chapter, the main measures of competitive balance were discussed. However only two studies, both in North American sports, actually test for the UOH using a competitive balance measure.

Martin Schmidt and Dave Berri used Gini coefficients on team winning percentage to test the UOH in MLB. They tested the relationship between competitive balance and attendance in two ways. The first way is by testing the effect of competitive balance on attendance throughout the entire sample, which is from 1901 to 1998. Their results confirmed the UOH. However, they note that the change in attendance is somewhat small. The second way is including price data for a subset of the data sample. Their analysis showed mixed results. For short-term attendance (the authors define short term as one year or less) fans actually respond negatively to competitive balance. However as time progresses and competitive balance improves, fans respond in a positive manner. The exact opposite holds true for competitive imbalance. This suggests that the phenomenon of competitive balance and attendance might act in more than just one-year time frames and it is important to examine the impact of competitive balance on attendance in three- or five-year spans.[39]

Brad Humphreys used his CBR to test competitive balance and attendance in MLB as well. Humphreys compares three separate measures of competitive balance in his model to help explain league attendance from 1901 through 1999. The sample time period divides into five-year sections for his CBR. Humphreys's two other competitive balance measures are the SDWP and the HHI. Only the CBR is statistically significant of the three measures. It confirms the UOH as well as Walter Neale's League Standing Effect.[40]

CONCLUDING THOUGHTS

It is important to refer back to Rottenberg's 1956 hypothesis when utilizing the concepts and definitions occurring during this chapter. He hypothesized that profits decline as competitive balance declines. His hypothesis would suggest testing uncertainty of outcome on more on a league-wide, seasonal basis. More seasonal uncertainty, absence of dynasties, and playoff uncertainty are what comprises the UOH. This then feeds into the competitive balance research which, as the discussion in the previous section explains, is lacking on studies using a competitive balance measure to examine the effects on attendance in professional sports leagues. Therefore, this leads to a particular distinction between uncertainty of outcome and the UOH.

All this leads to a simple question in theory, but something I argue has been overlooked in the literature: Should sports leagues maximize team profits or league profits? If it is better to maximize team profits, then certainly research would want to emphasize game uncertainty and intraseasonal competitive balance. However, if leagues want to maximize league profits, then research should focus on both playoff uncertainty and interseasonal competitive balance. This would also address Rottenberg's second hypothesis. The answer to this question is certainly different for each professional sports league. However, the answer clearly has implications to fans, managers, commissioners, and owners of sports teams in professional leagues.

I second the comment made by Fort, when he mentions the lack of research examining the effect of broadcast games.[41] Certainly, with the explosion and increasing amount of sporting events on television, demand for sporting events is changing. It also creates an interesting extension of the UOH. A couple of recent studies in European sports leagues began investigating this phenomenon. However, no studies test this phenomenon in North American sports.

The competitive balance and uncertainty of outcome literature is crucial to professional sports leagues. It possesses many implications in policy, marketing, and human resources for both teams and leagues. More work needs to be done in both these areas to get a better grasp on not only these two concepts, but on pinpointing the actual importance for all the different professional sports leagues.

NOTES

1. Andrew S. Zimbalist, "Competitive Balance in Sports Leagues: An Introduction," *Journal of Sports Economics* 3, no. 2 (2002): 111–121.

2. Dave Forrest and Robert Simmons, "Outcome Uncertainty and Attendance Demand in Sport: The Case of English Soccer," *The Statistician* 51, no. 2 (2002): 229.

3. Simon Rottenberg, "The Baseball Players Labor Market," *Journal of Political Economy* 64 (1956): 242–258.

4. Ibid.

5. Rodney Fort and James Quirk, "Cross-Subsidization, Incentives, and Outcomes in Professional Team Sports Leagues," *Journal of Economic Literature* 33, no. 3 (1995): 1265–1299.

6. Ibid.

7. Walter C. Neale, "The Peculiar Economics of Professional Sports," *Quarterly Journal of Economics* 78, no. 1 (1964): 2.

8. Fort and Quirk, "Cross-Subsidization," 1265–1299.

9. Ibid.

10. Ibid.

11. Rottenberg, "Baseball Players Labor Market," 242–258.

12. Rodney Fort and Joel Maxcy, "Comment: 'Competitive Balance in Sports Leagues: An Introduction,'" *Journal of Sports Economics* 4, no. 2 (2003): 154–160.

13. Brad R. Humphreys, "Alternative Measures of Competitive Balance in Sports Leagues," *Journal of Sports Economics* 3, no. 2 (2002): 133–148.

14. E. Woodrow Eckard, "Free Agency, Competitive Balance, and Diminishing Returns to Pennant Contention," *Economic Inquiry* 39, no. 3 (2001): 430–443; Humphreys, "Alternative Measures," 133–148.

15. E. Woodrow Eckard, "The NCAA Cartel and Competitive Balance in College Football," *Review of Industrial Organization* 13, no. 3 (1998): 347–369.

16. Humphreys, "Alternative Measures," 138.

17. Ibid., 137.

18. Anthony C. Krautmann and Lawrence Hadley, "Dynasties Versus Pennant Races: Competitive Balance in Major League Baseball," *Managerial and Decision Economics* 27 (2006): 288; Humphreys, "Alternative Measures," 146.

19. Zimbalist, "Competitive Balance in Sports Leagues," 111–121.

20. Fort and Quirk, "Cross-Subsidization," 1265–1299.

21. Ibid.

22. Richard C. Levin, George J. Mitchell, Paul A. Volcker, and George F. Will, "The Report of the Independent Members of the Commissioner's Blue Ribbon Panel on Baseball Economics" (2000), in http://www.mlb.com/mlb/downloads/blue_ribbon.pdf. (accessed October 8, 2006).

23. Martin B. Schmidt and Dave J. Berri, "Competitive Balance and Attendance: The Case of Major League Baseball," *Journal of Sports Economics* 2, no. 2 (2001): 147; Joshua Utt and Rodney Fort, "Pitfalls to Measuring Competitive Balance with Gini Coefficient," *Journal of Sports Economics* 3, no. 4 (2002): 367.

24. Utt and Fort, "Pitfalls to Measuring Competitive Balance," 360.

25. Neale, "Peculiar Economics of Professional Sports," 3.

26. Joel Maxcy, "Rethinking Restrictions on Player Mobility in Major League Baseball," *Contemporary Economic Policy* 20, no. 2 (2002): 145–159.

27. Rottenberg, "Baseball Players Labor Market," 242–258.

28. Neale, "Peculiar Economics of Professional Sports," 1–14.

29. Forrest and Simmons, "Outcome Uncertainty and Attendance Demand," 229.

30. Jeffery Borland and Robert MacDonald, "Demand for Sport," *Oxford Review of Economic Policy* 19, no. 4 (2003): 478–502; Rodney Fort, "Competitive Balance in North American Professional Sports," in *Handbook of Sports Economics Research*, ed. J. Fizel (Armonk, N.Y.: M. E. Sharpe, 2006), 190–206; Stefan Szymanski, "The Economic Design of Sporting Contests," *Journal of Economic Literature* 41, no. 4 (2003): 1137–1187.

31. Roger G. Noll, "Attendance and Price Setting," in *Government and the Sports Business*, ed. R. G. Noll (Washington, D.C.: Brookings Institution, 1974), 115–157.

32. James Richard Hill, Jeff Madura, and Richard A. Zuber, "The Short Run Demand for Major League Baseball," *Atlantic Economic Journal* 10, no. 2 (1982): 31–35.

33. Jeff Borland, "The Demand for Australian Rules Football," *Economic Record* 63, no. 182 (1987): 220–230.

34. Forrest and Simmons, "Outcome Uncertainty and Attendance Demand," 229–241.

35. Glen Knowles, Keith Sherony, and Mike Haupert, "The Demand for Major League Baseball: A Test of the Uncertainty of Outcome Hypothesis," *American Economist* 36 (1992): 72–80.

36. David Peel and Dennis Thomas, "The Demand for Football: Some Evidence on Outcome Uncertainty," *Empirical Economics* 17, no. 2 (1992): 323–331.

37. David Peel and Dennis Thomas, "Attendance Demand: An Investigation of Repeat Fixtures," *Applied Economics Letters* 3, no. 6 (1996): 391–394.

38. David Peel and Dennis Thomas, "Handicaps, Outcome Uncertainty and Attendance Demand," *Applied Economics Letters* 4, no. 9 (1997): 569.

39. Schmidt and Berri, "Competitive Balance and Attendance," 145–167.

40. Humphreys, "Alternative Measures," 133–148.

41. Fort, "Competitive Balance," 190–206.

Four

Franchise Relocations, Expansions, and Mergers in Professional Sports Leagues

Daniel A. Rascher

Sports league executives constantly face important questions: How many teams should be in the league? Where should expansion teams be located? What expansion fee should be charged? What are the economic effects if a particular team moves from its current city to another city? What is the competitive nature of rival leagues, and what is to be done about them? While the economics of expansion and relocation have many similar aspects, such as the financial return to a particular location, there are also many differences in practice. For instance, relocations are often very controversial and pit cities, teams, and leagues against each other. Expansions, on the other hand, while making the loser of the bid or beauty contest unhappy, do not create the same controversy because there is no incumbent city and its fans losing a team.

Rival leagues and their dissolution, often by partial absorption or merger with the dominant league or via financial failure, are a disruption to the equilibrium in North American professional sports. This equilibrium is characterized by one dominant league at the highest level. All league rivalries in major professional sports in North America have always reverted back to a single league. Whether or not this single league is a "monopoly" in the antitrust sense is left for discussion in other chapters.

This chapter discusses the economics of expansion, relocation, and mergers in professional sports by (1) examining the underlying economic forces, (2) surveying recent real-world expansions, relocations, and mergers in the National Football League (NFL), Major League Baseball (MLB), the National Basketball Association (NBA), and the National Hockey League (NHL), and (3) examining optimal locations for expansion or relocation using the NBA as an example.

EXPANSION

Unlike other businesses and industries, sports teams desire competition. Although sports franchises are often considered separate entities, in many ways they are interrelated and interdependent because the league product (games) requires the interreliance of teams. Without access to a regular-season format of structured competition via scheduled games, the team itself would not have a forum for its product. So while teams compete for inputs in the form of coaches and players, they are interdependent in terms of their output, which are games played within the league. The very nature of the teams is to compete with one another in sport but, in the context of a league, they have no interest in running one another out of business.

Sports franchises themselves are in fact governed by leagues, which control such matters as player selection (through a draft), player compensation (through a salary cap, in some leagues), revenue sharing, and expansion. Leagues have had less success in controlling franchise relocation, although recent legal cases have given leagues a bit more power in this regard.

The competitive balance generated by league control allows the league to operate effectively, and to produce a consistent output in the form of game attendance and television ratings. Unlike organizations with joint governance mechanisms in which an independent governing board attempts to align the interests of the executives and shareholders, in the NFL many of the board members and executives with controlling interest are majority owners, making it likely that decisions will be self-motivated. However, individual self-motivation is not always in the interests of the league as a whole, as in when a team relocates to a market that serves the team better but not the league (to be discussed in the next section).

A league restricts the number of franchises to maintain the overall playing quality of the league by maintaining the competitive balance between teams and by keeping playing quality sufficiently high. However, Lee and Fort show that expansion actually did not harm competitive balance in MLB since at least as far back as 1954.[1] Moreover, leagues restrict the number of teams to markets the league feels can both support a team and provide enough excess income to the rest of the teams in the league to justify the expansion in the first place. Additionally, adding expansion teams may result in a reduction in the fan base for existing clubs and the possibility that the expansion team will detract from, and not add to, the pool of revenues that are shared among teams. The expansion fee helps cover the gap, if there is one, but also adds income for the incumbent teams.

Kahn shows that, under many different conditions, too much expansion lowers the overall quality of the product.[2] This lowers welfare for fans of incumbent teams (as their teams' quality decreases because talent is spread across more teams), even though it raises welfare for fans in the new expansion markets that did not have a team at all.[3] The net effect is that overall fan welfare is higher when leagues do not have as many teams as would be the case under pure competition.

The economics of expansion are fairly straightforward, as described by Fort.[4] The league sets the expansion fee based on its expectations of the value potential bidders place on owning an expansion franchise and whether this fee will more than offset the future reduction in shared revenues. These revenues typically consist of media, sponsorship, and licensing. Also, the impact on gate receipts (whether shared, as with the NFL, or not, as with the NHL) for the existing teams by having the expansion team come to town or by visiting the expansion team at its home is also an issue of consideration. Given the relative bargaining power of the league, it will try to extract as much of the expansion teams' future profit and value as possible via the expansion fee.[5]

On the other side of the market, the potential expansion team owners determine the value (based on future income flows, capital gain upon sale of the team, and consumption value) of buying an expansion franchise in a particular location. Consumption value is based on the notion that some owners are "sportsmen owners" who gain nonfinancial value from owning a team because they might enjoy the process of owning and running the team, and are therefore willing to pay more for a team, as compared to owning a coal-extraction company. For instance, the major reason the NHL did not accept the Game Plan/Bain offer to purchase the entire league was because a number of owners did not want to sell at any price. They liked owning a hockey franchise. Economist Rod Fort stated that "the portion of ownership value not associated with annual operations appears to be significant."[6] In other words, "sportsmen owners" are willing to pay for the privilege of owning a team above and beyond its cash-flow potential.

If the total value to the potential owner is higher than the expansion fee set by the league, then the owner might place a bid for an expansion team. Often there is more than one bidder. The term "bidder" does not imply that each potential owner tries to financially outbid each other. It is interesting that an auction model has not been used by the leagues to determine expansion fees and locations.[7]

Similar to the discussion by Fort, the expansion fee chosen by the profit-maximizing league is equal to the discounted value of the revenue sources available to the expansion team owner (gate receipts, television, concessions, merchandise, parking, licensing, sponsorship), *minus* the team owner's expected costs (player payroll, operations, capital costs for facility, and the owner's opportunity cost), *minus* the loss to the league if the expansion team generates lower than average revenues that are shared with the league, *plus* the consumption value (which is hard to measure).[8]

Bruggink and Eaton show that expansion teams in MLB that are lower quality in terms of wins have a negative impact on attendance while on the road, but their novelty effect has a positive impact on attendance while on the road.[9] The net effect is actually positive for the league overall because the substantial losses for the expansion team are wins for the rest of the teams in the league. This, combined with the novelty effect, causes a net positive effect on MLB in terms of attendance, and therefore revenue, from expansion teams. Whether the league or the potential bidders for an expansion team will take this into account is unknown. Similarly, expansion teams have higher attendance, all else being equal, at home because of the novelty effect but this honeymoon lasts about four years in MLB, after which the team needs to play well as all teams' fans demand.[10]

In some instances, such as that of an NFL expansion team in Los Angeles, the expansion team may add revenues directly to the other league members via a larger national television contract. Interestingly, even though the NFL not having a team in Los Angeles is a disequilibrium outcome because it is the second-largest market in the United States, the league only gets one chance to expand into that market (unless it adds two teams). Securing an expansion team is so valuable that the league wants to optimize it perfectly and, perhaps, may be forgoing all of these years of being there and generating revenues. Looking back, though, it is hardly feasible that forgoing over a decade of net value by being in Los Angeles has been worth it to try to obtain the perfect expansion situation.

Without outside forces, a league does the calculations described above to determine whether to expand and at what price based on how much a bidder is willing to pay and if that amount exceeds any losses to the existing teams in the league. Historically, though, expansion was not motivated by financial gain but was undertaken in order to thwart a rival (see the section on mergers below). However, recent expansions appear to have been purely financial and not strategic. Strategic expansions may occur at prices and in locations that would be less than optimal but for the start-up or rival league's threats. For instance, the NFL expanded into Cleveland in 1937 in the face of competition from the second incarnation of the American Football League (AFL II) by transferring the AFL II Cleveland franchise to the NFL (today's St. Louis Rams).

The exact opposite economic force also exists, namely that a city may be left unoccupied by a league in order to have a bargaining chip with existing teams vis-à-vis their city and stadium leases and subsidies. The team can always threaten to relocate to this new city if it doesn't get the subsidies it is looking for in its current city. A more credible and instant threat is when a city without a team actually builds a stadium with the hopes of luring a team to town. Currently, Kansas City is building an arena; a number of NBA franchises have used this arena in bargaining with their incumbent locations. Moreover, if a team eventually moves into the arena, it often requires millions of dollars in upgrades and changes to the facility to fit with the owner's vision of the arena. An owner is able to negotiate these changes (often to be paid for by local government) because of its relative leverage compared with the facility owner.[11] For example, in 1990 the Suncoast Dome was opened in St. Petersburg at a cost of $138 million with the hopes of luring an MLB team. When the Tampa Bay Devil Rays finally began play in the facility in 1998, the team required upgrades of $70 million—50 percent of the original construction cost.

A further complication is that expansion into markets with existing teams is complicated even though it may be preferred from the league's perspective. A third MLB team in New York City might possibly be more profitable for other MLB teams than expansion into Portland, for instance. However, expansion into Portland is easier because no one team is harmed (although the Seattle Mariners would protest) and all should benefit from the expansion fees. A team moving into New York City would harm the Yankees and Mets, so side payments from the league would need to be made to compensate those teams. These negotiations are complicated by determining the value of those side payments. For instance, the merger of the All American Football Conference (AAFC) and the NFL in 1950 (see below) required the Colts to pay $150,000 to the Redskins owner, George Marshall, for invasion of his territory. Similarly, the American Football League (AFL) paid the NFL $20 million to merge, with much of that money going to the owners of the Giants and 49ers, who were going to share territories with the Jets and Raiders, respectively.

The opposite of expansion is contraction. Recently, however, there is not much to say on this issue in major professional sports. As Rodney Fort points out, the criteria used to decide whether to expand needs to exceed the threshold by a large margin because once a league expands, it is very hard to contract.[12] The players' union and local, state, and national public officials will fight contraction because of the "public good" aspect of professional sports. Whether or not warranted, politicians can gain political capital by preventing a team from moving or contracting.

MLB mentioned contraction as a possibility prior to the 2002 season on the basis of financially struggling franchises in Oakland, Minnesota, Montreal, and Florida. According to MLB, contraction was not proposed for the purpose of bargaining with the players association, yet, since contraction would reduce the number of players in the league, it could still be used as leverage in negotiating other collective-bargaining issues. It is unclear whether MLB would have contracted any teams or that it was simply using the threat as leverage with players and with cities to get new stadia. In Minnesota the contraction of the Twins was thwarted due to its lease with the Minneapolis Sports Facilities Commission, which required the team to play that season.

Staudohar states that MLB has not contracted since 1899, when the National League lost four teams.[13] The NFL lost thirty-eight franchises from 1920 to 1959, the NHL contracted six franchises from 1917 through 1979, and the NBA had fourteen franchises dissolved between 1946 and 1959. The last contraction in major professional league sports was in 1979 when the Cleveland Barons (formerly the California Seals) contracted or, depending on how it is viewed, merged with the Minnesota North Stars.

To summarize, prospective owners calculate the overall value of owning a franchise, including revenues, expenses, opportunity costs, and consumption value. The league does the same calculation, but also accounts for impacts on the teams in the rest of the league due to the expansion team's operations and interdependency with the league. Based on this, the league chooses an expansion price and opens it up for potential owners to formally bid based on different locations. Additionally, a league may expand for strategic reasons such as thwarting the entry of a rival league, or may not expand, even when it profitably could, in order to keep viable relocation alternatives open for its existing members. What follows are examples of how expansion is handled in the four major leagues.

Expansion in the NFL

As the value of franchises have increased, so to have expansion fees. In the NFL, the steep increase in expansion fees served to limit the number of entrants initially (and to increase the quality of owners of those who can afford entry into the league). When the league was chartered in 1920, entrance fees were set at $100, which many teams neglected to pay. When the league expanded in 1930, the expansion fee was $500, along with a $2,500 deposit with the league office. In 1932, when the Boston Braves (now the Washington Redskins) joined the league, the fee rose to $1,500 with an additional $1,500 deposit to guarantee that the team would finish the season. Over the next five years, fees more than doubled, growing to $10,000 when the Cleveland Rams (now the St. Louis Rams) joined the league in 1937. Expansion fees increased nearly sixfold from 1937 to the 1960s when

TABLE 4.1
NFL Franchise Expansions Since 1960

Franchise	Year	Expansion Fee (millions of US$)	Location and Notes
Cowboys	1960	0.60	Irving, TX (awaiting new facility in Arlington, TX)
Vikings	1961	0.60	Minneapolis
Falcons	1965	8.50	Atlanta
Dolphins (AFL)	1965	7.50	In 1970, team joined NFL in merger
Saints	1966	8.00	New Orleans
Bengals (AFL)	1967	7.50	In 1970, team joined NFL in merger
Seahawks	1976	16.00	Seattle
Buccaneers	1976	16.00	Tampa Bay
Panthers	1995	140.00	Charlotte
Jaguars	1995	140.00	Jacksonville
Browns	1998	530.00	Cleveland; original Cleveland Browns moved to Baltimore as the Ravens
Texans	1999	700.00	Houston

the NFL added four teams to compete with the rival American Football League (AFL IV), awarding franchises to Dallas and Minnesota (1961), for $600,000 apiece—much higher than the $25,000 the AFL required to join its league. See Table 4.1 for information related to NFL expansions after the 1950s.

Fees increased another 42 percent to $8.5 million when the Atlanta and New Orleans franchises joined the league in 1965 and 1966, respectively. When the AFL merged with the NFL in 1970, AFL teams had to pay $7.5 million to become part of the league. When the league expanded to 28 teams in 1976, expansion fees had risen an additional 88 percent to $16 million for the entry of the Tampa Bay Buccaneers and the Seattle Seahawks.

The league did not expand again until the 1990s, when it added Carolina and Jacksonville for $140 million apiece in 1995.[14] Since then, expansion fees have risen dramatically over the previous four entrants, growing at an annual rate for the last five years of greater than 50 percent. The Cleveland Browns re-entered the NFL as the thirty-first franchise in 1998 for a $530-million expansion fee, fulfilling the NFL's commitment to return the Browns to the field because of the relocation of the former Browns to Baltimore.

The NFL decided to further expand in an effort to have a symmetrical thirty-two-team league with expanded playoffs and tabbed Los Angeles as the next possible expansion location, with Houston as a fallback in the event Los Angeles could not get its stadium situation straightened out. The NFL gave potential owner Ed Roski and the LA Coliseum five months between March and September of 1999 to put together a financial package that would bring the Coliseum up to NFL standards. Los Angeles stumbled, and Houston owner Robert McNair was awarded the NFL's thirty-second franchise, which began play in 2002 as the Houston Texans. Comparing the Houston franchise with its Texas counterpart, the Dallas Cowboys, expansion fees have increased at a compounded annual growth rate of over 15 percent from the $6 million paid for the Cowboy's expansion fees in 1966, to the $700 million paid for the Houston franchise expansion in 1999.

Expansion in MLB

In response to pressure from the Continental League (see below), MLB expanded in 1961–62 for the first time in fifty years with four teams (Mets, Senators, Colt 45s, and Angels). The Senators moved to Texas to become the Rangers in 1971 and the Colt 45s changed their name to the Astros a few years after inception (as shown in Table 4.2). In 1969 MLB expanded into San Diego, Montreal, Kansas City, and Seattle. The Seattle Pilots went bankrupt

TABLE 4.2
MLB Franchise Expansions Since 1960

Franchise	Year	Expansion Fee (millions of US$)	Location and Notes
Senators/Rangers	1961	2.10	In 1971, moved from Washington, D.C. to Texas and became the Texas Rangers
Angels	1961	2.10	In 1965, team moved to Anaheim from Los Angeles
Mets	1962	1.80	New York City
Colt 45s/Astros	1962	1.80	In 1964, team renamed Houston Astros
Padres	1969	12.50	San Diego
Expos/Nationals	1969	12.50	In 2005, team moved from Montreal to Washington, D.C. to become the Nationals
Royals	1969	5.55	Kansas City
Pilots/Brewers	1969	5.30	In 1970, team moved from Seattle to Milwaukee to become the Brewers
Mariners	1977	6.25	Seattle
Blue Jays	1977	7.00	Toronto
Rockies	1993	95.00	Denver
Marlins	1993	95.00	Miami
Diamondbacks	1998	130.00	Phoenix
Devil Rays	1998	130.00	Tampa Bay area

in 1970 and the American League turned down an offer by a local ownership group (reportedly due to financing concerns), so the team was sold to Bud Selig, who moved it to Milwaukee as the Brewers. In 1977 MLB expanded again into Seattle, on the heels of lawsuits related to the original Pilots relocation, and Toronto. In 1993 MLB expanded into Denver and Miami and a few years later into Phoenix and Tampa Bay. The league didn't expand at all for fifty years, and then added fourteen teams in a little over thirty years.

Expansion in the NBA

As was often the case in professional sports, there were many versions of professional basketball leagues, each with a constantly changing number of teams, team locations, and team names. The NBA was created from National Basketball League (NBL) teams, which had been around for a decade (mostly in the Midwest), merging with the newly formed Basketball Association of America. The BAA was formed in 1946 by arena owners who wanted to fill nights alongside the major tenant, either NHL or minor-league hockey teams. Most BAA teams were located in the east. During 1948, the Minneapolis Lakers, Fort Wayne Pistons, Indianapolis Olympics, and Rochester Royals left the NBL and joined the BAA.

The following year, the NBL dissolved and six more of its teams moved into the BAA. After the merger (of sorts), the league settled into eight teams, with the relatively smaller market Rochester Royals, Fort Wayne Pistons, Milwaukee Hawks, and Minneapolis Lakers moving to larger cities (Cincinnati, Detroit, St. Louis, and Los Angeles, respectively) over the next decade. Five expansion teams were added in 1966–1968, bringing the total NBA franchises to thirteen, as shown in Table 4.3. The second wave of expansion in the NBA, not related to mergers with or acquisitions of rival leagues, was in the late 1980s and early 1990s. The NBA added four teams in 1988–1989 and two Canadian franchises in 1995.

Finally, as we saw with the NFL replacing franchises that had left for other cities in Cleveland and Houston, the NBA replaced the Charlotte Hornets (moved to New Orleans) with the Charlotte Bobcats in 2004.

Expansion in the NHL

The NHL has struggled financially recently, mostly due to high player salaries in proportion to total revenues. In other words, relative to its professional brethren, the NHL overpaid its players. The recent collective-bargaining process resulted in a salary cap that appears to have allowed the league to remain stable. The prior financial struggles were exacerbated by

TABLE 4.3
NBA Franchise Expansions Since 1960

Franchise	Year	Expansion Fee (millions of US$)	Location and Notes
Wizards	1961	Unknown	Began as Chicago Packers (see Table 4.6 for details)
Bulls	1966	1.25	Chicago
Rockets	1967	1.75	Began in San Diego and moved to Houston in 1971
Supersonics	1967	1.75	Seattle
Bucks	1968	2.00	Milwaukee
Suns	1968	2.00	Phoenix
Clippers	1970	3.70	Began as Buffalo Braves, moved to San Diego in 1978 and Los Angeles in 1984
Cavaliers	1970	3.70	Cleveland
Trailblazers	1970	3.70	Portland
Jazz	1974	6.15	Began as New Orleans Jazz and moved to Salt Lake City in 1979
Mavericks	1980	12.00	Dallas
Hornets	1988	32.50	Began as Charlotte Hornets and moved to New Orleans in 2002
Heat	1988	32.50	Miami
Timberwolves	1989	32.50	Minneapolis
Magic	1989	32.50	Orlando
Raptors	1995	125.00	Toronto
Grizzlies	1995	125.00	Began as the Vancouver Grizzlies and moved to Memphis in 2001
Bobcats	2004	300.00	Charlotte

Note: Does not include the four teams acquired from the ABA in 1976 (Nets, Nuggets, Pacers, Spurs).

the substantial expansion beginning in 1991, much of it into the southern United States, a region not known for its hockey fanaticism (however, with larger populations). As shown in Table 4.4, the addition of the Tampa Bay Lightning (1992), Florida Panthers (1993), Nashville Predators (1998), and Atlanta Thrashers (1999) through expansion and the relocation of the Quebec Nordiques to Denver (1995), the Winnipeg Jets to Phoenix (1996), and the Hartford Whalers to Raleigh (1997) cemented the NHL broadly across the United States. With relatively low television ratings (at least partially due to the difficulty of showing the sport on television because of the fast action and very small puck), it is unclear if the southern strategy will work.

In general, expansion from the "Original Six" has been successful despite often occurring in large waves.[15] From 1967 through 1974, the NHL added

TABLE 4.4
NHL Franchise Expansions Since 1960

Franchise	Year	Expansion Fee (millions of US$)	Location and Notes
Stars	1967	2.00	Began as Minnesota North Stars and moved to Dallas (as Stars) in 1993
Kings	1967	2.00	Los Angeles
Flyers	1967	2.00	Philadelphia
Penguins	1967	2.00	Pittsburgh
Blues	1967	2.00	St. Louis
Sabres	1970	6.00	Buffalo
Canucks	1970	6.00	Vancouver
Flames	1972	6.00	Began as Atlanta Flames and moved to Calgary in 1980
Islanders	1972	6.00	New York City
Devils	1974	6.00	Began as Kansas City Scouts and moved to Denver in 1976 and to New Jersey in 1982
Washington Capitals	1974	6.00	Washington, D.C.
Sharks	1991	45.00	San Jose
Senators	1992	45.00	Ottawa
Lightning	1992	45.00	Tampa Bay
Ducks	1993	50.00	Anaheim; changed name from Mighty Ducks of Anaheim to Anaheim Ducks in 2006
Panthers	1993	50.00	Miami
Predators	1998	80.00	Nashville
Thrashers	1999	80.00	Atlanta
Blue Jackets	2000	80.00	Columbus
Wild	2000	80.00	St. Paul, MN

twelve expansion teams (with the aforementioned California Seals contracting in 1979). Additionally, in 1979 four teams from the rival World Hockey Association were integrated into the NHL (see mergers below). This was followed by a dozen years of league stability (including two relocations) before the next wave of expansion with the 1991 San Jose Sharks took place.

RELOCATION

Mildner and Strathman analyze the causes of team relocation in MLB and the NBA.[16] The probability of a franchise moving is based on population growth, attendance growth, winning percentage, league-wide expansion, and stadium ownership. Their hypothesis is that a having stadium owned by a team owner is likely to prevent a team from moving because the stadium itself would be devalued. The consequence is that publicly owned stadiums actually increase the likelihood that a team will move. The empirical results are consistent with this notion for MLB, but mixed for the NBA.

Another reason for relocation is to increase stadium-related revenues. Owners often posit that the increased revenues from a new sports facility will put a franchise in a better position to bid for quality players, resulting in a better team, drawing more fans, resulting in more revenues, and so on. Not only are the market economics important, but the structure of the lease allows the owner to capitalize on those economics.

For instance, in the NFL, a few teams have relocated to smaller markets in order to play in new stadiums with "sweetheart" lease agreements. These leases allow the owner to keep a higher proportion of revenue, create more revenue from a newer stadium, host more events raising the revenue even more, and reduce expenses. The Rams moved from Los Angeles to St. Louis and the Raiders moved from Los Angeles (the second-largest market in the country) back to Oakland in 1995. In 1996 the Browns moved to Baltimore to become the Ravens, while the Oilers moved to Tennessee from Houston (becoming the Titans) the following year. The new market was smaller (in terms of population) than the former market in each of these situations. Moreover, the NBA's Hornets' move from Charlotte to New Orleans was primarily due to a more appealing agreement with New Orleans for a state-of-the-art facility; however, the relocation placed the team in a smaller media market and a less affluent city.[17] Market size is less important in football because the small number of games make sellouts much more likely than in baseball, basketball, or hockey, where market size is more important.

Team relocations and the threat thereof have commensurately increased the value of major-league clubs. Franchises are constantly considering new locations (e.g., Oakland A's, Sacramento Kings, LA Clippers, San Diego Chargers, Minnesota Vikings). As discussed above, the leagues control the number of teams and the rate of expansion. In fact, since the NFL and AFL merged in 1966, the NFL has added only seven other teams, even though many other markets desire franchises.[18]

Which cities should teams choose when considering their ideal locale? The choice of a city depends on at least three major factors, as described by Daniel Rascher and Heather Rascher: the owner's personal preference, the political climate, and the economics of the location.[19] While many team owners are profit-maximizers and make decisions accordingly, some owners may be more personally motivated, perhaps choosing to move a team to a city because it is where they live or prefer to live. For instance, Georgia Frontiere, owner of the St. Louis Rams, moved the team from Los Angeles to her hometown of St. Louis, Missouri. Similarly, the Minnesota Vikings were considering a move to San Antonio, Texas, because owner Billy Joe "Red" McCombs is from there.[20] Personal preference, as in these cases, is idiosyncratic and will therefore not be investigated in this analysis.

Political support for a major-league team within a city is very important because arenas and stadiums are often financed in part or in full by local and state governments.[21] The locational decision is usually the result of a bidding competition between the governments of various cities, each offering various amenities to the teams in order to attract the team to their locale.

Finally, the economics of the market matters. Regions with larger, richer populations containing a sufficient number of large businesses or numerous corporate headquarters are assumed to be more able and willing to support a team than a smaller city that lacks these desirable demographic features. However, the three overarching decision criteria can be interrelated. For instance, the degree of public funding is likely to correspond to the size and economic demographics of the market. In fact, there is a correlation of 0.33 (significant at the 1 percent level) between the percentage of public funding and the population for six cities with NBA teams that are in relatively smaller population centers. Also, an owner's preferences are likely to be in favor of locating in a large metropolitan area because of the potential favorable economics.

In practice, franchise relocation is rare in the modern era. In the 1950s, with the growth of airplane travel and disproportionate growth of population in the western United States, many MLB teams moved. For instance, the Athletics, Browns, Braves, Giants, and Dodgers all relocated during that time. Mildner and Strathman show that in MLB, 3.1 percent of the number of franchises per year relocated in the 1950s.[22] This decreased to 1.5 percent in the 1960s, 0.8 percent in the 1970s, to 0 percent in the 1980s and 1990s. Since then, the Montreal Expos relocated to Washington, D.C., to become the Nationals. The NBA saw a similar trend with 5.5 percent in 1960s, 2.6 percent in 1970s, 0.8 percent in 1980s, and 0 percent of teams relocating in 1990s. As with MLB, it has picked up slightly in the 2000s with the Grizzlies moving to Memphis from Vancouver in 2001 and the Hornets moving to New Orleans from Charlotte in 2002.

The early NBA relocations were part of the maturation of the league from a regional to national sport with its beginnings in smaller towns like Waterloo, Iowa, or Fort Wayne, Indiana. Relocations in the early formative years of a league were rarely viewed negatively by leagues because they were attempts to stay in business and find sustainable markets. Many of the more recent moves have been at odds with league desires (e.g., Raiders, Rams) as franchises may be benefiting at the expense of the league and not just trying to survive.

Carlton et al. show that relocated teams experience about 5 percent lower attendance, all else equal, when that team travels to other NHL cities during the following seasons.[23] In other words, the natural rivalries that had developed seem to disappear once the team relocates. This is an example of where the relocation positively affects the franchise but has a negative externality on the rest of the league, a big part of the drama associated with franchise relocation.

Relocation restrictions by leagues have been tightened lately, but are still not under complete control of the leagues. However, MLB has complete control based on its antitrust exemption.[24] Prior to last year's move by the Montreal Expos to Washington, D.C., no MLB team had moved since the Seattle Pilots became the Milwaukee Brewers in 1970. In MLB the franchise has to negotiate with the league as well as with the prospective cities in order to move. The league wants to ensure that the other members of the league are not harmed by the move or, if so, that appropriate compensation is forthcoming. The other leagues do not have an antitrust exemption, making it harder for them to control franchise movement.

Sometimes relocation is followed by expansion into the "lost" market. This is often the case because the league did not necessarily want the team to relocate but could not stop it. Or the league understands that the city is a good location, but that there is an irreconcilable disconnect between the current owner and city, and the league cannot make the owner sell the franchise. The NBA's Hornets moved to New Orleans because Charlotte was not interested in working with the current owners (who had allegedly spoiled the relationship with the community) and the league followed up with an expansion into Charlotte almost immediately. In the NFL Baltimore lost the Colts in the middle of the night to Indianapolis. Los Angeles, Cleveland, Houston, and St. Louis all lost teams to relocation to smaller markets. Cleveland and Houston have received expansion franchises and St. Louis got the Los Angeles Rams to come calling. Los Angeles is likely to receive an expansion team, although the stadium process has been a big problem.

Standard techniques to prevent relocation are lease provisions containing a long lease term or one that costs a lot to break. The application of eminent domain is also an option, but it has failed in the past. Some cities have considered purchasing a team, but most leagues prevent that type of ownership. Larger cities have more bargaining power because threats to move are idle. Would the Yankees leave New York City? The Cowboys, with everyone knowing that they wouldn't leave the Dallas area, chose to cause competition among local cities and counties (specifically, Irving, Arlington, Dallas, and Dallas County). The result is that they are getting a whopping $325 million in subsidies from Arlington, yet they are paying $325 million themselves. What follows are examples of how relocation is handled in each of the four major leagues.

Relocation in the NFL

Perhaps surprisingly, the NFL and NHL have much in common when it comes to relocation. Both leagues saw more franchises relocate—four—during the 1990s than in any previous decade since 1950. However, NFL teams were so valuable that they were able to shop themselves around to different cities, while NHL franchises needed to relocate in order to survive.

The Chicago Cardinals, the oldest professional football team in the United States, was the lesser loved of the two Chicago football teams. That, combined with poor performances during the 1950s, caused the team to get the league's permission to move to St. Louis in 1960. It wasn't until twenty-two years later that another NFL team moved, this time without league permission. See Table 4.5 for a summary of NFL relocations since the 1950s.

In one of the most contentious moves in league history, Al Davis sought permission to move the Raiders from Oakland to Los Angeles in 1980 in an effort to obtain better revenue opportunities in a bigger market. Davis needed a three-quarters vote of the owners to be able to move, and was nearly unanimously blocked 22–0 (with five abstentions, and the Raiders not tendering a vote because Davis felt that he did not need league approval to relocate). Davis subsequently filed suit against the NFL claiming that the rules in the NFL Constitution dealing with relocation decisions violated the antitrust laws preventing him from operating his business where he so chose. In 1982 the court found for Davis, as did the subsequent appeals court. The opinion against the NFL hinged on two factors: (1) that the league was not a single entity, and (2) preventing the Raiders from relocating did in fact unreasonably restrain competition. Although the NFL was able to delay the move for two seasons, the Raiders eventually were awarded nearly $11.55 million in damages (trebled to nearly $36 million) for lost revenues due to the NFL first preventing and then delaying the team relocation. On appeal, the Supreme Court refused to hear the case in 1984. The case opened the floodgates for teams to move without permission from the NFL.

The city of Oakland later filed an eminent domain suit, claiming that the Raiders are a civic asset and that the city should be able to purchase the Raiders at a fair price in order to retain the team. The courts found for

TABLE 4.5
NFL Franchise Relocations Since 1960

Franchise	Year	From	To	Location and Notes
Cardinals	1960	Chicago	St. Louis	After a poor-performing 1950s on the field and at the gate, the team moved to St. Louis.
Raiders	1983	Oakland	Los Angeles	A fierce legal battle won by the Raiders allowing it to stay in LA, despite the NFL's resistance.
Colts	1984	Baltimore	Indianapolis	The team infamously cleared out of the facility in the middle of the night to avoid eminent domain attempts by the State.
Cardinals	1988	St. Louis	Phoenix	Moved to Phoenix as Phoenix Cardinals and was renamed the Arizona Cardinals in 1994.
Raiders	1995	Los Angeles	Oakland	Against the backdrop of a number of lawsuits, team relocates back to Oakland.
Rams	1995	Los Angeles	St. Louis	The Rams moved into an already existing domed stadium with a very good lease.
Ravens	1996	Cleveland	Baltimore	Moved from Cleveland to Baltimore to become the Ravens. NFL retained team histories, etc., for use by the new Cleveland Browns.
Oilers	1997	Houston	Nashville	The team, renamed the Tennessee Titans, moved to Memphis until its stadium was ready in Nashville.

the Raiders, although it did find that the notion of a football team potentially being a civic asset was upheld.

The results of the Raiders litigation facilitated the Colts' move, which was done without NFL consent, when Robert Irsay quickly abandoned Baltimore for Indianapolis in 1984. Irsay first considered relocating the Colts in the 1970s, considering the cities of Jacksonville, Memphis, Phoenix, and even Los Angeles, which was vacated after the Rams relocated to Anaheim after the 1979 season. Irsay's desire to relocate was due in part to the lack of support for Irsay; the city wanted the team, but not him. The team infamously cleared out of the facility in the middle of the night on March 29, 1984. As soon as the vans left Maryland, Indianapolis mayor William Hudnut announced the move, and the Maryland legislature quickly drafted a bill that would permit the Colts to be seized by eminent domain, which failed.

Following failed attempts at getting a stadium funded primarily by the public and given the results of the Raiders litigation, Bill Bidwill moved the St. Louis Cardinals to Phoenix in 1988. The city of St. Louis was unable to stop the team based on other failed eminent-domain cases. The Phoenix Cardinals changed its name to the Arizona Cardinals in 1994.

In the mid-1990s there was a lot of franchise relocation in the NFL. The Rams moved from Los Angeles into a new domed facility in St. Louis, owner Georgia Frontiere's hometown, in 1995. The St. Louis Convention and Visitors Commission (CVC) sued the NFL, who argued that the relocation of the Los Angeles Rams to St. Louis resulted in an adverse affect on league rivalries and television revenue. To offset these losses, the league imposed a $29-million relocation fee on the Rams (which used CVC money to pay for this, hence the lawsuit). Also, the Raiders moved back to Oakland in 1995. This was followed by lawsuits against the NFL for interfering with the franchise's choice of location and with the city of Oakland for allegedly failing to uphold its promise to sell out the stadium.

In another contentious relocation, the Cleveland Browns moved to Baltimore to become the Ravens in 1996 essentially because the stadium lease was much better, in a new facility in Baltimore, than local Cleveland officials could muster. In a rare move, the NFL retained the name "Cleveland Browns" and all of the team's history (including multiple NFL championships) and other intellectual property for an expansion team that began play in 1999 under the same name.

In 1997 the Houston Oilers moved to Memphis, Tennessee, and kept the "Oilers" moniker, but the geographic name was Tennessee, not Memphis. Once its new stadium was completed in Nashville in 1999, the team relocated and once again changed its name, to the Tennessee Titans. As with the Browns, the NFL expanded back into Houston in 1999, granting a franchise to what is now known as the Houston Texans.

Relocation in the NBA

The NBA has seen the most franchise relocations since 1960, fourteen, of the four major professional sports leagues. The dispersion of relocations was fairly consistent through 1985 (twelve relocations). It wasn't until sixteen years later with the Grizzlies' move to Memphis that the two most recent relocations took place. See Table 4.6 for a summary of NBA relocations since the 1950s.

In 1960, after George Mikan retired, the Lakers' attendance dropped dramatically and the team relocated to Los Angeles. New owner Bob Short (who would later purchase and move the Washington Senators baseball

TABLE 4.6
NBA Franchise Relocations Since 1960

Franchise	Year	From	To	Location and Notes
Lakers	1960	Minneapolis	Los Angeles	After Mikan retired, attendance dropped dramatically and new owner Bob Short followed the successful Dodgers to Los Angeles.
Warriors	1962	Philadelphia	San Francisco	After Chamberlain's record-setting game and season, the team was sold and packed up and left.
Wizards	1963	Chicago	Baltimore	The Zephyrs became the Bullets.
76ers	1963	Syracuse	Philadelphia	The Nationals became the 76ers, after the franchise moved from a mid-sized market under new owner Irv Kosloff.
Hawks	1968	St. Louis	Atlanta	Under new ownership, the team moved to Atlanta and in a few years received a new arena to play in.
Rockets	1971	San Diego	Houston	Under new ownership, the team moved to Houston.
Kings	1972	Cincinnati	Kansas City	The Royals became the Kings.
Wizards	1973	Baltimore	Washington, D.C.	Became the Capital Bullets, then Washington Bullets (1974), and Washington Wizards in 1997.
Clippers	1978	Buffalo	San Diego	Celtics owner Irv Levin wanted to own a team in California, so he switched franchises with Buffalo's owner, knowing that the Braves were allowed to break their lease and move.
Jazz	1979	New Orleans	Salt Lake City	Why did this franchise not change its name?
Clippers	1984	San Diego	Los Angeles	Under new ownership and poor play and attendance, the team moved to Los Angeles.
Kings	1985	Kansas City	Sacramento	Kansas City continues to be a temporary stopping point for teams moving west.
Grizzlies	2001	Vancouver	Memphis	Under new ownership, the team shopped around and settled in Memphis.
Hornets	2002	Charlotte	New Orleans	After discussions with the city failed to produce a new arena, the team moved.

club) saw how successful the Dodgers had quickly become moving west so he continued in their footsteps. Amazingly, the season after Wilt Chamberlain set the NBA single-game scoring record at 100 points in a game versus the Knickerbockers, the team was sold to Franklin Mieuli, a California native who moved the team to San Francisco. The next year, 1963, saw the Chicago Zephyrs leave for Baltimore, which left Chicago without an NBA team for a few years. The Zephyrs were renamed the Bullets. And, finally, the Syracuse Nationals moved to Philadelphia in 1963, filling the void left by the Warriors' departure. This was the last of the NBA teams moving from mid-sized markets to large markets.

Five years later, in 1968, another round of relocations took place beginning with the St. Louis Hawks moving to Atlanta. The team was purchased by an Atlanta-based ownership group who planned, and succeeded, in building a state-of-the-art facility, the Omni Coliseum. In 1971 the San Diego Rockets moved to Houston under new ownership. The next year, the Cincinnati Royals moved to Kansas City and became the Kings (to avoid confusion with MLB's local Royals franchise). Finally, in 1973 the Baltimore Bullets moved to Washington, D.C., and became the Capital Bullets, then the Washington Bullets the next year, and the Washington Wizards in 1997.

In 1978 a strange event took place allowing the Buffalo Braves to relocate to San Diego to become the Clippers. Boston Celtics owner Irv Levin wanted to own a team in his native California, so he switched franchises with Buffalo's owner, knowing that the Braves' lease was breakable, allowing the team to move. A similar transaction took place, although without the immediate relocation of the teams involved, when Carroll Rosenbloom swapped his Baltimore Colts in 1972 with Robert Irsay's Los Angeles Rams. The next year, the New Orleans Jazz left for Salt Lake City after only five unsuccessful years in New Orleans.

The San Diego Clippers moved to Los Angeles in 1984 after the aforementioned Irv Levin sold the team to Donald Sterling. The team drew poorly in San Diego. The Los Angeles Lakers sued for invading their territory and won $6 million. In the lawsuit *NBA v. San Diego Clippers Basketball Club*, the court reaffirmed the right for the NBA to require league approval before a team relocates. The following season, the Kings left Kansas City and relocated to Sacramento.

Before the 2001–2002 season, the Vancouver Grizzlies decided to move out of Canada and created a short list of possible locations that they believed could successfully support the franchise. The list contained the cities of San Diego, Las Vegas, New Orleans, Memphis, and Louisville. San Diego showed no interest in obtaining the Grizzlies because at the time the city was embroiled in a half-built, publicly financed baseball stadium issue. The NBA ruled out Las Vegas because of its ties to gambling. St. Louis had been a contender the year prior to the sale, with the failed purchase of the team by St. Louis Blues (NHL) owner, Bill Laurie, who would not open the Savvis Center to an NBA team unless he owned the team. The three final locations were quickly narrowed to two, as New Orleans was unable to generate an offer that was suitable to the Grizzlies. The decision between Memphis and Louisville was tipped in favor of Memphis when Federal Express (FedEx), whose headquarters are in Memphis, made a naming rights offer and equity purchase of the team.[25]

The most recent NBA relocation is the Hornets' move from Charlotte to New Orleans. The Hornets considered Louisville, Norfolk, Virginia, and New Orleans for their relocation out of Charlotte before agreeing to terms with New Orleans. The move is from a relatively larger more affluent market into a smaller one. New Orleans's median household income is $38,800 a year, below the national average and below Charlotte's median income of $51,000. New Orleans's TV market, ranked forty-third nationally, is the smallest in the NBA; Charlotte's TV market ranks twenty-seventh. As discussed in the next section, it is not surprising that the franchise has struggled financially. There are objective criteria that can be used to help the decision process of where to relocate (or which city to expand into).

A Model for Choosing a Franchise Location

Once an expansion or relocation is approved, how do franchises determine the optimal market in which to operate? A recent study was undertaken to determine the economics of potential markets for NBA expansion or relocation.[26] Rather than using the current methodology, which involves separate comparisons of cities by population and a few other measures, this analysis utilized an integrated approach that captures the relationships between the factors and relative importance of each factor.

A hierarchical two-equation system is employed. In the first equation, the twenty-five U.S. markets that had NBA franchises (as of 1999) are examined to determine the relationship between the underlying factors which allow the city to support a franchise.[27] The model is then used to forecast the relative likelihood of other cities without an NBA franchise to be able to support a team (again based on economic factors, not personal preference or political factors). This model is similar to the analysis for baseball teams by Bruggink and Zamparelli, except that the NBA model has additional variables, two stages, and uses a substantially different econometric approach.[28] The second equation is a revenue equation, the forecasts from which are used as inputs into the first equation. The logic is that the potential revenues that each location could generate are certainly important factors in an owner's location decision.

One objective of the overall analysis is to be able to aid in the financial decision regarding league expansion or team relocation. A set of models such as described here can be used to rank cities for further, more in-depth analysis, across many sports in many countries.

The cross-sectional data consist of forty-eight observations, with twenty-five being cities with NBA teams and twenty-three being cities without NBA teams in 1999 that potentially are the most eligible cities for league expansion or team relocation.[29] There are twelve potential explanatory variables, some of which are correlated (e.g., 1995 MSA population and 2000 MSA population).[30] Each observation represents information for the year 1999 (except where specified).

Utilizing a number of estimation techniques to test for sensitivity and robustness, the results provide a prediction of which cities would be likely to succeed in hosting an NBA franchise, as shown in Table 4.7. The results lend credence to the Grizzlies' decision to include Memphis and Louisville in the final relocation list. Also, the model predicts that a New Orleans franchise would struggle. As shown, Charlotte is a much stronger market, as is Louisville, yet the owners chose New Orleans. It is not surprising that the team struggled financially from the beginning in New Orleans prior to the impact of Hurricane Katrina. After just one season into the honeymoon phase following relocation, the New Orleans Hornets attendance was 15 percent below the league average and overall ticket sales continued to struggle.

MLB

Every few years from 1955 through 1972, an MLB team relocated, as shown in Table 4.8. Most of the eight relocations were teams moving west as the population grew more quickly in the west. In 1955 the Philadelphia Athletics were purchased by Chicago businessman Arnold Johnson, who moved out of a two-team market into Kansas City. Perhaps the most famous and controversial relocation is that of the Brooklyn Dodgers in 1958 to Los Angeles. Despite tremendous success in Brooklyn, the owner could not get a satisfactory stadium deal. That coupled with the growth potential in the west caused the team to move. Similarly, the New York Giants moved to San Francisco, providing visiting teams a two-team road trip in California.

In 1961, after nearly six decades in Washington, D.C., the Washington Senators moved to Minneapolis and became the Minnesota Twins. The team had not fared well on the field in Washington, drew poorly, and

TABLE 4.7

Cities Likely to Succeed in Hosting an NBA Franchise

City/Team (Sorted by Attendance)	Forecasted Probability (Attendance)	Forecasted Probability (Gate Receipts)	Forecasted Probability (Total Revenue)
Boston Celtics	1.000	1.000	1.000
Chicago Bulls	1.000	1.000	1.000
Dallas Mavericks	1.000	1.000	1.000
Houston Rockets	1.000	1.000	1.000
Los Angeles Lakers	1.000	1.000	1.000
Los Angeles Clippers	1.000	1.000	1.000
Minnesota Timberwolves	1.000	1.000	1.000
New York Knicks	1.000	1.000	1.000
New Jersey Nets	1.000	1.000	1.000
Golden State Warriors	1.000	1.000	1.000
Philadelphia 76ers	1.000	1.000	1.000
Washington Wizards	1.000	1.000	1.000
Atlanta Hawks	1.000	1.000	1.000
Detroit Pistons	1.000	1.000	1.000
Portland Trail Blazers	1.000	1.000	1.000
Seattle SuperSonics	0.997	0.998	0.990
Utah Jazz	0.963	0.962	0.912
Phoenix Suns	0.937	0.989	0.947
Charlotte Hornets	0.919	0.954	0.896
Indiana Pacers	0.873	0.953	0.901
Orlando Magic	0.816	0.862	0.817
Louisville	0.740	0.743	0.751
San Diego	0.696	0.677	0.658
Denver Nuggets	0.675	0.707	0.715
Miami Heat	0.675	0.585	0.615
Milwaukee Bucks	0.501	0.709	0.520
Memphis	0.486	0.241	0.331
Las Vegas	0.416	0.345	0.442
San Antonio Spurs	0.404	0.703	0.549
Cleveland Cavaliers	0.351	0.262	0.323
Pittsburgh	0.333	0.163	0.328
St Louis	0.271	0.279	0.299
Baltimore	0.252	0.288	0.256
Norfolk, Virginia Beach, Newport News	0.220	0.255	0.352
Hartford	0.209	0.155	0.164
Sacramento Kings	0.130	0.107	0.087
Nashville	0.125	0.115	0.152
Austin, San Marcos	0.073	0.055	0.118
Kansas City	0.017	0.015	0.036
Cincinnati	0.003	0.001	0.004
New Orleans	0.002	0.000	0.004
Columbus	0.002	0.000	0.004
Jacksonville	0.000	0.000	0.000
Albuquerque	0.000	0.000	0.000
Buffalo, Niagara Falls	0.000	0.000	0.000

Note: Bolded cities are those without an NBA team in 1999.

TABLE 4.8
MLB Franchise Relocations Since 1955

Franchise	Year	From	To	Location and Notes
Athletics	1955	Philadelphia	Kansas City	Chicago businessman Arnold Johnson purchased the team and moved it out of a two-team market.
Dodgers	1958	Brooklyn	Los Angeles	One of the most storied franchises couldn't secure a favorable stadium situation so moved out west.
Giants	1958	New York	San Francisco	Suffering from similar stadium-building issues, the team relocated with the Dodgers to the West Coast.
Twins	1961	Washington, D.C.	Minneapolis	The Senators became the Minnesota Twins. MLB then granted an expansion franchise to the nation's capital, also called the Senators.
Braves	1966	Milwaukee	Atlanta	Under a new ownership group, the team moved to a brand-new stadium in a larger media market.
Athletics	1968	Kansas City	Oakland	The franchise's final step towards moving to the west coast.
Brewers	1970	Seattle	Milwaukee	The Seattle Pilots were purchased by Bud Selig and moved to Milwaukee and became the Brewers.
Rangers	1972	Washington, D.C.	Dallas	Under new ownership, the Senators were approved to relocate to Dallas and become the Texas Rangers.
Nationals	2005	Montreal	Washington, D.C.	The nation's capital gets another chance at hosting MLB.

played in an aging stadium. The team did not relocate until MLB promised an expansion franchise for the next season. In 1966 the Milwaukee Braves, under new ownership, moved the team to Atlanta to play in a new stadium and in front of a larger media market.

After barely more than a decade, the Athletics left Kansas City for the West Coast and set up in Oakland. Charlie Finley, the team's owner, tried to move the team many times (to many different locations, including Louisville and Dallas). After six years of trying, he was allowed to move the team in 1968. Missouri senator Stuart Symington tried unsuccessfully to prevent the relocation, but was able to secure an expansion franchise to begin in 1969.

The Seattle Pilots played one season in the American League (1969), only to be purchased by Bud Selig and moved to Milwaukee the following season to play as the Brewers. The Pilots immediately struggled financially and Selig offered to bail them out of near-bankruptcy. The second incarnation of the Washington Senators was purchased by Bob Short in 1968. Less than a decade earlier, Short had moved the Lakers from Minneapolis to Los Angeles. This time, he moved the Senators, in 1972, to Dallas to become the Texas Rangers.

While many teams relocated in the other leagues, MLB witnessed a long period of locational stability. Over three decades passed before the Montreal Expos (who had been purchased by MLB itself) were moved to Washington, D.C., in 2005 and eventually sold to Ted Lerner (who owns shares of the local NHL and NBA teams). This relocation is one of the few where a franchise in the same league allegedly moves into another team's territory. It has been debated whether the Baltimore Orioles have territorial rights, or would be economically harmed, by the relocation of the Expos to Washington, D.C. However, as compensation for the move, the Orioles have become the majority shareholder in a new television network that will broadcast Nationals and Orioles games. Additionally, MLB guarantees that the Orioles and their share of the TV network will sell for at least $365 million whenever Angelos sells the team. Interestingly, Bruggink et al. show that Washington, D.C., would be the best location for a new or relocated MLB team, based on their analysis of 1994 data.[31]

NHL

Recent relocation in the NHL, coupled with recent expansions, have changed the league from a northern/Canadian-based league to a North American league. A number of studies coauthored by J. C. H. Jones show that the Canadian/U.S. exchange rate and general differences in the economies can cause incentives to move the teams to U.S. markets that aren't necessarily hockey havens (e.g., player salaries are in U.S. dollars while most revenues for Canadian teams are in Canadian dollars).[32]

The California Golden Seals, after poor performances on the ice and at the gate and under new ownership, relocated. The franchise moved from Oakland to Cleveland (as the Barons) in 1976. The team was later absorbed into the Minnesota North Stars (1978), and then undone to create the San Jose Sharks in 1991. Along with the Golden Seals' relocation, the Kansas City Scouts became the first NHL team to relocate since 1934. Poor attendance and financial performance caused the team to move to Denver to become the Colorado Rockies in 1976. This was followed by multiple

TABLE 4.9
NHL Franchise Relocations Since 1976

Franchise	Year	From	To	Location and Notes
Sharks	1976	Oakland	Cleveland	The Seals became the Cleveland Barons, which were later absorbed into the North Stars (1978). That merger was undone in 1991 to create the Sharks.
Devils	1976	Kansas City	Denver	The Scouts, after weak attendance, became the Colorado Rockies in the first HL relocation since 1934.
Flames	1980	Atlanta	Calgary	Local ownership group could not make it work financially and sold the team for a then record $16 million to a Canadian group who moved it to Calgary.
Devils	1982	Denver	East Rutherford, NJ	With multiple ownership changes during the short history in Denver, the Rockies were sold and relocated to New Jersey as the Devils.
Stars	1993	Minneapolis	Dallas	Despite the North Stars playing well in the early 1990s, the community and new owner could not settle stadium issues, so the team moved to Dallas as the Stars.
Avalanche	1995	Quebec City	Denver	Financial troubles were exacerbated by the NHL lockout and local government's bailout fell through, causing a sale and relocation of the Nordiques to Denver.
Coyotes	1996	Winnipeg	Phoenix	Financial troubles caused the Jets to move to Phoenix as the Coyotes.
Hurricanes	1997	Hartford	Raleigh	Amid financial difficulties and a failed agreement on a publicly funded arena, the Whalers moved to Raleigh and became the Hurricanes.

ownership changes, which resulted in a move, in 1982, to East Rutherford, N.J., as the New Jersey Devils. See Table 4.9 for more information on NHL franchise relocations.

A few years earlier in 1980, the Atlanta Flames' ownership group could not succeed financially and sold the team for a then-record $16 million to a Canadian group who moved the team to Calgary. It wasn't until nearly two decades later that the Atlanta Thrashers expansion team, for $80 million in franchise fees, brought top-level hockey back to Atlanta. The mid-1990s saw four NHL franchises relocate to warmer climates with the expectation of tapping into larger population centers. As discussed earlier, the financial results have been mixed. The North Stars played well in the early 1990s, but new owners wanted a better stadium situation so the team moved, in 1993, to Dallas to eventually play in the new, highly regarded American Airlines Center.

The NHL lockout of 1994–95 caused existing financial troubles for the Quebec Nordiques to worsen. The local government bailout fell through and the team relocated to Denver and became the Colorado Avalanche, where it has seen much success. For similar reasons, the Winnipeg Jets moved to Phoenix to become the Phoenix Coyotes in 1996. The most recent relocation in the NHL was the Hartford Whalers' move to Raleigh, North Carolina. The team has struggled financially, but did win the Stanley Cup in 2006.

RIVAL LEAGUES AND MERGERS

An Ounce of Prevention

An ounce of prevention is worth a pound of cure, so the saying goes. This appears to be the case with respect to rival leagues. It is economically beneficial to reduce the incentives for rival leagues to form rather than to try to fight them once formed. When leagues expand, they are able to collect an expansion fee commensurate with the value of the new franchise. If a rival league is formed and causes some of its franchises to be picked up by the existing league as expansion franchises or as part of a merger, the fees paid by these expansion teams is often lower than what a regular expansion team would pay. This is because the rival league has some leverage in that it can threaten not to dissolve if entry into the incumbent league is not granted. This is also true because the harm caused by the rival, in terms of reduced profit, will end. Thus the expansion fee is really the cash fee plus the increase in profits associated with a rival disappearing, so the dominant league is often willing to accept the lower expansion fee.

In general, incumbent leagues try to create barriers to entry to prevent rival leagues from forming. In professional team sports, these barriers have included long-term player contracts, boycotting players who switched to a rival league, long-term exclusive television and stadium contracts, an anti-trust exemption for MLB, and high switching costs caused by a strong his-torical brand and positive consumption network externalities. As a result of the rivalry with the U.S. Football League (USFL), the NFL began signing players to multiyear contracts and staggered the last years of the contracts so there wouldn't be a sufficient number of players whose contracts were ending during the same year (enabling a rival to steal a big chunk of quality, well-known players). Similarly, MLB allegedly boycotted players who switched to the Mexican League during the 1940s.

When there were just three television networks (ABC, CBS, and NBC), an incumbent sports league could contract with all three to show its games, thereby preventing a rival league from getting into enough households. A sufficiently modern stadium is practically necessary to be able to host sporting events for a rival. If all or most of the suitable stadiums in the country have exclusive contracts with teams from the incumbent league, it is not feasible for a rival to be able to find satisfactory locations for playing its games. These last two barriers to entry have faded somewhat recently with the growth of cable television and the many quality college stadiums that have become available (at least for basketball and football).

As described below, on its face it is amazing that the United States has had a single dominant league for each of its major sports for most of those leagues' existence. Is it because the incumbent leagues have been better managed? Maybe, but likely an important factor is that history, tradition, and statistics are critical elements of the product that sports leagues sell. Each year the incumbent league adds to its history. The common experience that bonds fans of the same team may mean that, for another league to start up and be successful, it would have to compensate fans (presumably through higher enjoyment) for the "cost" of learning the new teams and players and tossing out the history of the existing league. This branding factor makes the "switching costs" for fans very high. A fan would have to learn all of the new teams, players, coaches, rules, and then not mind that there are no natural rivalries. Therefore, incumbent leagues have a natural advantage over potential entrants that grows each year.

Similarly, part of what sports sells is the camaraderie with other fans of the sports league. The more fans there are of a particular sports league, the stronger is the camaraderie (e.g., imagine if Raider Nation had only one member, how unsatisfying that would be for that member). If there aren't other fans to play Monday morning quarterback with, a rival will find it difficult to compete, so it needs a large fan base immediately (not typically the way any business is able to start off). Each additional person that becomes a fan of a particular sports league increases the value of being a fan of that league for all of the existing fans. Thus, it can be argued that leagues such as the NFL exhibit positive consumption network externalities.[33] As the size of the fan base increases, there are more opportunities for sports-based conversations, and increased attendance typically adds to the excitement of a given game. For a rival to be successful, it may have to make an all-or-nothing move for primacy. Given that the major North American sports leagues have millions of fans, it will always be hard for any rival to break down this natural barrier to entry.

Structure of Rivalry

If a rival league is not prevented, it often forms what Quirk and Fort call a classic rival league where it places a few teams in large markets in direct competition with the incumbent league.[34] This is because the population of some large markets can support more than one team, and in order to get a good media deal a league needs to be in some of the large markets. Additionally, it puts the remaining teams in the comparable cities left open by the incumbent (typically measured in terms of population).

When a rival enters, the market goes from a single provider of the sport to two providers, that is, the market goes from monopoly to a duopoly that may manifest itself in more competition. This is not necessarily true in the antitrust sense. For instance, the NFL can be viewed as a single provider of top-level professional football or as one of many sports entertainment offerings, depending on how one attempts to define the relevant market. From an antitrust perspective, these definitions are continuously debated. However, history has shown that when a rival league enters, the incumbent league sees increased player salaries (costs) due to higher labor demand, and often lower attendances. The incumbent may respond to decreased demand by lowering ticket prices (or not raising them as much).

Some rival leagues are not necessarily rivals in terms of the quality of product. The Pacific Coast League (PCL) began evolving into a rival league so MLB went to the West Coast to thwart the rivalry (see below for more details). Many of the minor-league hockey leagues in the United States and Canada have been successful precisely because they are not trying to be rivals to the NHL. If a rival begins to raid the existing top league for players, then it is claiming to be a rival league and history has shown that it will likely fail or perhaps send a few of its teams into the existing league, while the remaining teams will have lost substantial money in the process of competing.

A current rivalry exists between the Indy Racing League (or IndyCar Series) and Champ Car. These racing leagues were once a single league, but Indy Racing League formed in 1994. Each league suffers from the rivalry and Champ Car had recently filed bankruptcy. If the future is anything like the past, these leagues will merge or one of them will die off. The long-run equilibrium is a single dominant major league for each sport.

This begs the question, are sports leagues natural monopolies?[35] Sports fans may prefer to have the very best athletes concentrated in a single league rather than spread across numerous competing leagues. If this is true, then sufficient support may not exist for multiple top-level leagues. Additionally, high "switching costs" and the impact of the positive consumption network externality (both described above) further move sports leagues toward natural monopoly.

Sports leagues also produce a very high fixed cost, low marginal cost product, similar to actors, singers, and software creators. This may enhance the tendency toward natural monopoly. Once a league is created and a season of competitive play is in progress, the cost of selling an extra seat or of having one more fan tune in is quite inexpensive. Moreover, consumption by one television-viewing fan does not inhibit another fan from consuming the product on TV, which when combined with low marginal costs, enables a sports league to sell its product simultaneously to millions of fans around the world.[36] Unlike a carpenter who can only sell his or her services to one construction project at a time, a sports league can remain the only firm in an industry and still satisfy 100 percent of the market. Additionally, the low marginal cost allows an incumbent league to engage in limit pricing to prevent the entry of a competitor, leading to a version of a winner-take-all market. In short, if fans only want to see the best, and the best can be purchased for about the same price as the second best, the market may not support the second best at all.[37]

The extent to which the NFL and other sports leagues are natural monopolies is extremely important for policy decisions. It may be that consumers demand only one league, so efforts by the courts to encourage competition will be in vain or contrary to consumers' interests.

The two previous sections on expansion and relocation show two measures for preventing a rival league from springing up: either expand into open territories or relocate teams into important territories for rivals (e.g., PCL). However, relocation is not always under the control of the league. A team owner may move on its own to a less strategic city. This can have the opposite effect by opening up a valuable market for a rival league to fill, as Quirk and Fort point out.[38] It is for these reasons that many rival leagues that have managed not to fold are eventually consolidated in whole or in part into the incumbent league.

Consolidation in Baseball

Prior to 1900 the American Association (AA) competed with the National League (NL). In 1882 both leagues competed directly with each other for talent, but played in different cities. Within a few years the AA had moved into a couple of larger NL cities, but the leagues had signed an agreement not to compete with each other for players.[39] The AA disbanded in 1891 when renewed competition for players resulted in the NL acquired the four strongest AA teams. Additionally, four AA teams had moved over into the NL over the previous decade. Thus, the twelve-team NL consisted of eight former AA teams.

In 1903, after a few years of direct competition for players and fans, the National League (NL) and American League (AL) reached an agreement not to compete (effectively merging). Prior to this, in 1900, the AL wanted access to players alongside the NL, so it ignored the reserve clause and competition for players ensued. Also, the AL moved some teams in NL markets. Attendance for the leagues was similar in 1901 and 1902 and in competing markets the AL outdrew the NL. As Quirk and Fort state, "The AL rates as the most successful rival league in the history of team sports in the United States."[40]

For different reasons, an equally important rival league was the Federal League (FL) because of the ensuing antitrust lawsuit that resulted in professional baseball's antitrust exemption. The league began as a minor league in 1913, but started courting MLB players and signing them to long-term contracts. Perhaps as many as 221 MLB players made the switch, significantly increasing their salaries. MLB fought back by blacklisting MLB players and trying to prevent them from making the switch. The Federal League sued and did get a settlement from MLB, but the FL's Baltimore Terrapins filed its own suit, leading to the famous decision that baseball is not interstate commerce, but purely state affairs.

MLB has not been severely challenged by a rival league since 1914–1915. However, the Pacific Coast League (PCL) was in the process of gaining major league status in the 1950s. Then, as described above, the Giants and Dodgers moved west, displacing a number of PCL teams and moving PCL fans' attention to the National League. Some of the remaining PCL teams were purchased by MLB teams as minor-league teams, firmly cementing the differences in the majors and minors.

Additionally, in 1959–1960, the Continental League (CL) was able to get four of its owners to receive MLB expansion franchises, without ever playing a single game, because Senator Estes Kefauver held hearings to limit MLB's ability to keep its players (and its minor leaguers) out of the CL.[41] MLB pledged to cooperate with the fledgling league in exchange for Kefauver's bill not being passed (but sitting in committee). The cooperation led to the expansion of the Twins, Angels, Astros, and Mets. Twelve of the thirty teams that constitute MLB today are from rival leagues.

Consolidation in Basketball

The American Basketball League (ABL) lasted for seven years during the Roaring Twenties, but were beset with competitive imbalance problems that may have been cured, but for the Depression limiting the league's growth. The ABL re-formed in 1934 in New York and Philly and, despite a large number of teams folding and new ones entering, lasted through World War II and until 1947 (when it reverted to a minor league). At about the same time (1937), in the Midwest, the National Basketball League formed with some teams owned by Firestone, Goodyear, and General Electric. In 1946 the Basketball Association of America was formed by arena owners who needed to fill nights not being used by the NHL or minor-league hockey teams. They saw the success of college basketball and wanted to capture some of that. The BAA was located in seven of the top ten markets while the NBL was only in two of them, and the BAA controlled the big arenas in those markets. In 1948 the Minneapolis Lakers, Rochester Royals, Fort Wayne Pistons, and Indianapolis Olympics moved to the BAA. The next season six more teams switched from the NBL to the BAA, breaking the NBL. The 1949–1950 season consisted of seventeen BAA teams, but by 1954 had shrunk to eight stable teams. In 1961 another ABL formed with George Steinbrenner and Abe Saperstein (Harlem Globe Trotters) as owners. The league lost money and folded two years later.

In 1967 the ABA was formed by Gary Davidson (who would later form the World Football League [WFL] and World Hockey Association [WHA]). The league played nine seasons before merging with the NBA in 1976. According to Quirk and Fort, the ABA followed the prescription for a classic rival league to succeed by setting up in the major markets of New York and Los Angeles (because of the relative lack of basketball teams there) and filling in the mid-sized cities that the NBA neglected. The merger took only New York, Indiana, Denver, and San Antonio into the NBA. Each team paid an expansion fee of $3.2 million, with the Nets paying the Knicks $4 million for invading its territory (New York). The four teams also paid the Utah and Kentucky franchises to close down. Overall, it is estimated that the ABA teams lost about $40 million in its nine-year history and the original owners were gone by the time it merged with the NBA, so the league, according to Quirk and Fort, was not a successful rival even though it moved four teams into the NBA.[42] Today, the thirty teams in the NBA consist of nine from rival leagues.

Consolidation in Hockey

The NHL began as a four-team league in 1917. The Pacific Coast Hockey League (Calgary, Edmonton, Saskatoon, and Regina) played the

NHL for the Stanley Cup beginning in the 1917–1918 season. Another league, the Western Canada Hockey League, began play in 1921, and all three leagues played for the Stanley Cup until 1924 when the PCHL folded. The NHL bought the league for $258,000, distributing the player contracts across the newly expanded NHL (expanding into the United States). The Depression hit the NHL hard and knocked it down to six teams (the "Original Six") that constituted the league for twenty-six years. In 1967 the league added six expansion teams for a $2-million expansion fee, in 1970 two more (at $6 million per expansion franchise), and in 1972 another team at $6 million. At the same time, in 1972, the WHA began its run of seven years ending in 1979 with four teams (Hartford Whalers, Quebec Nordiques, Edmonton Oilers, and Winnipeg Jets) joining the NHL and two (Birmingham and Cincinnati) compensated for not joining the NHL, but being forced to disband. The four teams had to pay $6 million in "expansion" fees to join the NHL and also pay Birmingham and Cincinnati $6 million each.

The WHA was able to sign many NHL players, and players from the NHL minor-league system, causing NHL salaries to rise in response to the competition. Attempted mergers by the WHA into the NHL were voted down by the NHL until boycotts of Molson beer (owner of the NHL's Toronto Maple Leafs) reportedly caused enough votes to shift to allow the four-team merger. Most owners in the WHA lost money, except those who were able to merge with the NHL. Additionally, the New York Islanders were formed by the NHL in 1972 to prevent the WHA expansion into Long Island, so five of the current thirty NHL teams were a result of the WHA.

Consolidation in Football

In June 1922 the American Professional Football Association changed its name to the National Football League and began restructuring to provide for territorial rights. The early NFL was simply a loose confederation of local club teams who typically played many nonleague teams along with their NFL schedule. The league membership fee increased to $1,000, but most teams did not pay the fee. Any team that had eleven players to field was likely to be granted an expansion team. It was later required that expansion teams not be located in small towns, and all small-town teams were eliminated after the 1926 season, with the exception of Green Bay. As the league found its footing, there was much instability. In the 1920s, there were ten franchise sales, twenty-seven expansion teams, four franchise relocations, and twenty-nine abandoned franchises.

The American Football League (AFL I) was formed in response to a rejection for a franchise in New York to capitalize upon the drawing power of the Galloping Ghost, Red Grange. A sensation at the box office in his collegiate and professional career, Red Grange was signed by George Halas's Chicago Bears the day after Grange's collegiate eligibility at the University of Illinois ended in 1925. At a time when the typical NFL game drew around 5,000 fans, one of the Bears games, against the New York Giants at the Polo Grounds in New York, drew over 64,000 fans, a record that held for two decades.

Red Grange and his manager, C. C. "Cash and Carry" Pyle, continued leading the Bears around the country playing exhibition games and earning over $250,000 for the pair during and after the 1925 season. When Halas rejected Grange and Pyle's bid to buy a piece of the Bears, the two petitioned for an NFL franchise, to play in New York's Yankee stadium. Every NFL owner was in favor of bringing Grange's drawing power into the NFL, with the exception of Tim Mara, owner of the New York Giants and would-be local competitor to Grange's team. At the time, expansion decisions needed 100 percent approval from the owners and Mara voted against Grange's entry into the league. Grange and Pyle responded by forming the first rival professional football league, the original American Football League, in 1926.

After one season of turmoil, the AFL disbanded, but the NFL made a side payment to Tim Mara and the Giants in order to entice his vote to allow Grange's Yankees to enter the NFL for the 1927 season. Part of the agreement was that the Yankees had to play thirteen of their sixteen games on the road. Grange was injured during that campaign, and the Yankees went 7-8-1, and folded at the end of the season. Grange returned to the Chicago Bears to play out his career, which ended with his retirement in 1934.

Ten years after the formation of the first American Football League, the second incarnation of the AFL (AFL II) was formed in 1936. At that point, the NFL had contracted to nine franchises, all located in large population centers. This time, AFL II directly competed with the NFL in many of these same cities, rather than staking out other locales. However, rather than raiding NFL teams for talent, the AFL primarily filled its rosters with recent college graduates, which kept salary costs down for both leagues. AFL II success at the gate was limited, with the exception of the New York Yankees and the Boston Shamrocks, which faired well in comparison to their NFL counterparts. Average per-game attendance in AFL II for the 1936 season was 8,384, dropping to 8,075 in its second and last season. The limited financial information available for the AFL showed that each franchise lost money.[43]

The AFL II Boston Shamrocks drew crowds rivaling that of the NFL's Boston Redskins. The Redskins' owner, George Marshall, was so disappointed by the lack of fan support for his team that he relocated the Redskins to Washington, D.C., for the 1937 season and beyond. In the face of competition, the NFL granted an expansion franchise to the AFL's Cleveland Rams for a franchise fee of $10,000. To replace the Cleveland team, AFL II added the Los Angeles Bulldogs, who proceeded to finish the 1937 season with a 9-0 record, becoming the only AFL team to have a winning record that year. In fact, the lack of competitive balance within the league was likely one of the causes for its failure following that season.

The next rival league to the NFL, initiated by Arch Ward (sports editor of the *Chicago Tribune*), opted for a different name other than AFL, the All American Football Conference (AAFC), and actually posed a credible threat to the NFL. The league was formed in 1944, but opted to wait until the end of World War II before beginning operations. It offered higher salaries than the NFL and located in both big cities with NFL competition and in smaller cities (e.g., San Francisco, Cleveland, and Miami). It competed effectively with the NFL, drawing higher crowds in its second season (approximately 32,800 compared with 30,600 for the NFL).

Reportedly, the AAFC and NFL lost $5 million and $3 million, respectively, during the 1946–1949 seasons, with only the Cleveland Browns (AAFC's dominant team), Chicago Bears, and Washington Redskins turning a profit. Despite setting a team attendance record in 1949, the Los Angeles Rams (NFL) were unprofitable from 1946 to 1949. The on-field domination of the Browns hurt attendances for other AAFC franchises. The fierce rivalry ended after four years in 1949 with a partial merger of the AAFC and NFL. Under the agreement, the San Francisco, Cleveland, and Baltimore teams moved from the AAFC into the NFL. The NFL's New York Bulldogs closed down, with owner Ted Collins purchasing the New York Yankees of the AAFC and moving them into the NFL. As reciprocation for having their territory invaded, the NFL's New York Giants were allowed to choose six players from the New York Yankees' lineup (the Yankees folded in 1952 and their assets were transferred to the Dallas franchise). Similarly, Redskins owner George Marshall received $150,000 for the invasion of his team's local territory by the Baltimore Colts. The Colts franchise went under a year after the merger, and, after re-forming in 1951, the team became financially successful in the NFL.

In the aftermath of the merger, the NFL was relatively stable, with no rival leagues being introduced from 1952 to 1960, when the fifth and most successful rival league, American Football League (AFL IV), was introduced. The AFL played until 1966 when the NFL voted to merge the leagues. However, congressional approval was needed because the merger would possibly have violated antitrust laws by creating an alleged monopoly from a duopoly. Commissioner Pete Rozelle convinced Louisiana's Rep. Hale Boggs and Sen. Russell Long to pass the merger bill in exchange for the NFL expanding into New Orleans. The Browns, Colts, and Steelers were each paid $3 million to switch to the AFC in order to create two balanced conferences (NFC and AFC).

In August 1973 Gary Davidson, the founder of the American Basketball Association and the World Hockey Association, started talks with investors about potentially starting a world-wide football league. By January 1974 the first meeting of what would become the World Football League was held, with representatives from Anaheim, Birmingham, Boston, Chicago, Detroit, Honolulu, Memphis, New York, Orlando, Philadelphia, Toronto, and Washington attending. Soon after, the twelve-team WFL commenced, beginning its twenty-game season in July 1974 in order to get a head start on the NFL. The season would conclude in November, ending in a "World Bowl" championship, which also occurred before the NFL championship game.

The league was divided into six large market teams competing directly with NFL franchises and six smaller market teams (with populations less than 1 million). The investors in the league were underfinanced from the beginning. Each of the initial twelve franchises cost $100,000, with subsequent franchises fees ranging from $250,000 to $1.6 million. Although the league did not get a major network contract, the WFL did get a television contract with Eddie Einhorn's TVS network.[44] The large market teams helped to secure a national television contract that paid each team $130,000 per year, compared with $2.2 million per team for the NFL television contracts that year.

Another rivalry was resolved in July 1986, when, following an eleven-week trial and just five days of deliberation, a jury in U.S. District Court in New York awarded the United States Football League (USFL) one dollar in its $1.7 billion antitrust suit against the NFL, trebled to $3 in damages. The jury rejected all of the USFL's television-related claims, which were the lifeblood of the USFL's case. In 1988, in a unanimous 3-0 decision, the 2nd Circuit Court of Appeals in New York upheld the verdict of the jury. The USFL needed the large damage award to survive, and subsequently folded in 1986 after effectively losing the case. Overall, thirteen of the thirty-two teams that exist in the NFL today come from rival leagues.

CONCLUSION

All three sections in this chapter are interrelated. Expansions and relocations, especially in the early years of a league, are often the response to upstart rival leagues. More recently, relocations have occurred because another city offers a better facility lease regardless of whether the league as a whole is better off or not. Relocations, more so than expansions, often end up in court whether as an antitrust case accusing the league of monopolistically restricting business or as an eminent domain suit attempting to prevent a team from relocating. Recent rulings have allowed a league to enforce a relocation fee that is commensurate with the harm caused to the rest of the league because of the move.

Rivalries often begin with a few teams in major cities competing head-to-head with the existing dominant league. Inevitably, the sport ends up with one major league providing top level play, begging the question of whether sports leagues are natural monopolies. This occurs either with a merger, a partial merger, an acquisition or, most commonly, a failed rival league. Often the incumbent league emerges from the rivalry a stronger, more stable business, having been forced to address a weakness exploited by the rival (e.g., MLB failing to recognize the western markets). Additionally, the new locations of franchises have often been vetted by the upstart rival to determine which few are most profitable and sustainable.

NOTES

1. Young Hoon Lee and Rodney Fort, "Structural Change in Baseball's Competitive Balance: The Great Depression, Team Location, and Racial Integration," *Economic Inquiry* 43, no. 1 (2005): 168.

2. Lawrence M. Kahn, "Sports League Expansion and Economic Efficiency: Monopoly Can Enhance Consumer Welfare," CESifo Working Paper 1101, 22.

3. In economic parlance, "welfare" can be thought of as a measure of the well-being of a group of people. Fans in new markets are happier with a new team, but fans in existing markets are less happy than before expansion because their teams are of lower quality.

4. Rodney Fort, *Sports Economics* (Upper Saddle River, N.J.: Prentice-Hall, 2003), 135–145.

5. Occasionally, the expansion fee may be a combination of actual payments to the league and foregone future shared revenues from the league. For instance, the Carolina Panthers did not receive annual shares of the national television revenues from the NFL for a number of years.

6. Rodney Fort, "The Value of Major League Baseball Ownership," *International Journal of Sport Finance* 1, no. 1 (2006): 9.

7. Some reasons for this are that a league wants to have control over who becomes an owner (because factors beyond price matter), and it may be able to determine the approximate auction price based on recent transactions of existing franchises. However, the free agent market for athletes in most sports leagues is similar to an auction in that multiple franchises often bid for a player's services. At times the resulting "price" is higher than most pundits thought would be the case (see Alex Rodriguez's contract in MLB).

Additionally, the Federal Communications Commission has auctioned off wireless spectrum to bidders at prices that have gone for much more than when sold at predetermined prices.

8. Fort, *Sports Economics,* 135–145. Opportunity cost is the value of the next best alternative. For instance, if a franchise owner broke even in terms of revenues and expenses, one might think that the owner did not lose anything. However, if the owner could have used the money invested in the franchise to invest in something else that would have made money, then, in this sense, the owner did lose money. The lost money compared with the opportunity foregone. Additionally, the owner's time has value and if the owner did not pay him- or herself a salary (as part of this example), then they forewent the opportunity to earn a salary elsewhere. Thus, opportunity cost should be included in the overall calculation.

9. Thomas H. Bruggink and James W. Eaton, "Rebuilding Attendance in Major League Baseball: The Demand for Individual Games," in *Baseball Economics: Current Research*, ed. J. Fizel, E. Gustafson, and L. Hadley (Westport, Conn.: Praeger, 1996), 26–28.

10. Donald A. Coffin, "If You Build It Will They Come? Attendance and New Stadium Construction," in *Baseball Economics: Current Research*, ed. J. Fizel, E. Gustafson, and L. Hadley (Westport, Conn.: Praeger, 1996), 42–46.

11. Coates and Humphreys analyze the ability for franchise owners to pay for the bulk of stadium upgrades and new construction from the incremental gain in revenues that the owner will receive in the new stadium. The extent to which public financing is needed is different than the amount that a franchise owner can get via his or her leverage. See Dennis Coates and Brad R. Humphreys, "Novelty Effects of New Facilities on Attendance at Professional Sporting Events." *Contemporary Economic Policy*, 23, no. 3 (2005): 436–455.

12. Fort, *Sports Economics,* 135–45.

13. Paul D. Staudohar, "Baseball's Contraction Pains," *NINE: A Journal of Baseball History and Culture* 11, no. 2 (2003): 73–84.

14. The NFL's twenty-ninth franchise was unanimously awarded to the Carolina Panthers on October 26, 1993. The thirtieth franchise was awarded to the Jacksonville Jaguars on November 30, 1993. However, the expansion teams did not play until after their stadiums were constructed in 1995. Of this additional $280 million in new revenue for the NFL, each team within the league received approximately $9.9 million annually through 1998.

15. The "Original Six" consist of the Boston Bruins, Chicago Blackhawks, Detroit Red Wings, Montreal Canadiens, New York Rangers, and Toronto Maple Leafs, who were the only NHL teams from 1942 to 1967.

16. Gerard S. Mildner and James G. Strathman, "Baseball and Basketball Stadium Ownership and Franchise Incentives to Relocate," in *Sports Economics: Current Research*, ed. J. Fizel, E. Gustafson, and L. Hadley (Westport, Conn.: Praeger, 1999), 75–94.

17. The agreement is for a ten-year lease. The team will pay $2 million annually in rent and receive all of the revenue from premium seating, advertising, naming rights, concessions, novelty and parking—a guarantee of at least $18 million in annual arena revenue. If attendance falls below 11,000 per game, the rent can be adjusted, but will be at least $1 million. The city of New Orleans covered all relocation expenses, too. The

team moved into New Orleans Arena, which the city spent $15 million to upgrade to NBA-quality.

New Orleans's median household income is $38,800 a year, below the national average and below Charlotte's median income of $51,000. New Orleans's TV market, ranked forty-third nationally, is the smallest in the NBA; Charlotte's TV market ranks twenty-seventh.

18. Those teams are the New Orleans Saints (1966), Seattle Seahawks (1974), Tampa Bay Buccaneers (1974), Carolina Panthers (1994), Jacksonville Jaguars (1994), Cleveland Browns (1999), and Houston Texans (2002).

19. Daniel A. Rascher and Heather Rascher, "NBA Expansion and Relocation: A Viability Study of Various Cities," *Journal of Sport Management* 18, no. 3 (2004): 274–295.

20. Minnesota Vikings owner Red McCombs said the Vikings cannot remain competitive unless they get a new stadium to replace the Metrodome. Getting a new stadium built for the Vikings was Red McCombs's top priority, but measures to finance a stadium in Minnesota have twice failed. McCombs's suggestion that the team relocate to San Antonio is unlikely, due to the fact that San Antonio is another small market in a state with two teams, the Dallas Cowboys and the Houston Texans.

21. For an in-depth discussion of the politics of stadium financing see Dean V. Baim and Larry Sitsky, *The Sports Stadium as a Municipal Investment* (Westport, Conn.: Greenwood, 1994), and Wilbur C. Rich, *The Economics and Politics of Sports Facilities* (Westport, Conn.: Quorum Books, 2000).

22. Gerard S. Mildner and James G. Strathman, "Baseball and Basketball Stadium Ownership and Franchise Incentives to Relocate," in *Sports Economics*, ed. Fizel, Gustafson, and Hadley, 79.

23. Dennis W. Carlton, Alan S. Frankel, and Elizabeth M. Landes, "The Control of Externalities in Sports Leagues: An Analysis of Restrictions in the National Hockey League," *Journal of Political Economy* 112, no. 1 (2004): 268–288.

24. The Curt Flood Act of 1998 only changed the exemption with regards to labor relations. Although *Brown v. Pro Football*, as Andrew Zimbalist (*May the Best Team Win: Baseball Economics and Public Policy* [Washington, D.C.: Brookings Institution, 2003]) notes, prevents the players from receiving protection under both labor law and antitrust law.

25. Memphis had attracted enough investors to buy a 49 percent interest in the team, while Louisville investors were only able to offer a 20 percent stake in the team. FedEx helped to seal the deal for Memphis by agreeing to pay $100 million for naming rights for a new stadium in Memphis, matching the offer of Tricon Global Restaurants (parent company of Kentucky Fried Chicken, Pizza Hut, and Taco Bell), which reportedly offered $100 million for the naming rights of the new arena.

26. Rascher and Rascher, "NBA Expansion and Relocation," 274–295.

27. In 1999 there were twenty-nine teams in the NBA, with two located in Canada (the Vancouver team has recently moved to Memphis, Tennessee), and two each in the Los Angeles and New York areas.

28. T. H. Bruggink and J. M. Zamparelli, "Emerging Markets in Baseball: An Econometric Model for Predicting the Expansion Teams' New Cities," in *Sports Economics*, ed. Fizel, Gustafson, and Hadley, 49–60.

29. The choice of the twenty-three non-NBA cities is simply based on MSA population.

30. These variables were chosen based on a review of the literature, on the availability of data, and on knowledge regarding the theory of demand. Ultimately, the data will determine their applicability.

31. Bruggink and Zamparelli, "Emerging Markets in Baseball," 49–60.

32. J. C. H. Jones and D. G. Ferguson, "Location and Survival in the National Hockey League," *Journal of Industrial Economics* 36 (1988): 443–457; Glen Seredynski, J. C. H. Jones and D. G. Gerguson, "On Team, Relocation, League Expansion, and Public Policy: Or, Where Do We Put This Hockey Franchise and Why Would You Care?," *Seton Hall Journal of Sport Law* 4 (1994): 663–700; Angelo Cocco and J. C. H. Jones, "On Going South: The Economics of Survival and Relocation of Small Market NHL Franchises in Canada," *Applied Economics* 29 (1997): 1537–1552.

33. A positive consumption network externality is often associated with network technology products, such as an operating system where each addition to the installed base of users of the incumbent product adds value for each of the existing and potential users. Another classic example is the telephone—it is valueless to a user if he or she is the only one with a phone, but as more users purchase telephones, the value of a phone to each user increases.

34. Quirk and Fort offer concise economic histories of rival leagues. Some of the information in the remainder of this chapter draws on their descriptions. James Quirk and Rodney D. Fort, *Pay Dirt: The Business of Professional Team Sports* (Princeton, N.J.: Princeton University Press, 1992).

35. A natural monopoly is an industry whose profitability is positive only if one firm is in the industry, whereas if two or more firms were present, each firm's profits would be negative. Similarly, an industry is a natural monopoly if the cost of producing a particular good is minimized if only one firm produces it. The policy issue balances how society can benefit from low-cost production by one producer, but not be subject to the potential abuse of a monopolist.

36. This is an example of what economists call nonrival production, where consumption by one does not reduce the amount available to others.

37. In limit pricing an incumbent sets the price just below the minimum long-run average cost of the most formidable potential entrant, thus dissuading the entrant from entering at all.

38. Quirk and Fort, *Pay Dirt*.

39. Ibid., 304.

40. Ibid., 312.

41. Zimbalist, *May the Best Team Win*.

42. Quirk and Fort, *Pay Dirt*, 325–327.

43. Ibid., 340–341.

44. Evan Weiner and Heather Rascher, "A Business History of Professional Football," unpublished manuscript (2005).

Five

The Financial Valuation of Sports Franchises

Mitchell Ziets and David Haber

As the sports industry has grown into big business over the past twenty years, the need to drill down on the value of sports assets has grown. From estate tax planning to limited partnership sales, from change in control events to features incorporated into partnership agreements, franchise valuations have become a part of the sports business landscape.

A number of texts have focused on sports franchise valuation methodology. Rather than repeat what has already been written, this chapter takes a different approach: It raises the question as to the appropriate methodology of sports franchise valuation and provides the reader with the tools to develop an informed opinion.

According to *Forbes* and *Financial World* magazines, values in the four major U.S. sports leagues—Major League Baseball (MLB), National Basketball Association (NBA), National Football League (NFL), and National Hockey League (NHL)—have grown at an average annual rate of 11.7 percent from 1991 to 2006. While the value of sports franchises has grown dramatically in recent years, valuation techniques differ from those in other businesses, both in methodology and rigor. While many well-established industries are valued based on operating profits or cash flow, the sports industry derives value based on revenue multiples. This methodology frequently discounts the expense side of the ledger and pays short shrift to the unique features inherent in a sports franchise.

After providing background on trends in sports franchise values, this chapter focuses on the differentiating factors, or drivers, of franchise value. It then discusses key considerations regarding the current preferred sports franchise methodology, revenue multiple analysis. Finally, it makes a case for valuing franchises based on the discounted cash flow. It is important to note that this chapter does not conclude that revenue-multiples valuation methodology should be scrapped in favor of discounted cash flow. It simply raises the question and provides sufficient ammunition for the reader.

HISTORICAL FRANCHISE VALUES

In order to analyze trends in sports franchise values, it is useful to examine franchise valuations from a historical context. In that regard, Figure 5.1 shows the average franchise valuations for each of the four leagues since 1991, as reported by *Financial World* magazine and *Forbes* magazine.

Clearly, franchise values have steadily increased across all four leagues since 1991. This can be attributed to a number of factors, but perhaps the most relevant is the evolution of the overarching attitude toward sports franchise ownership. In recent years, an increasing emphasis has been placed on the business operations of franchises, as opposed to the traditional focus on the competitive, game-related aspects. Historically, sports franchises were generally considered to be expensive toys or hobbies for wealthy individuals. However, as the dollars associated with franchise operations increased

FIGURE 5.1
Franchise Valuations

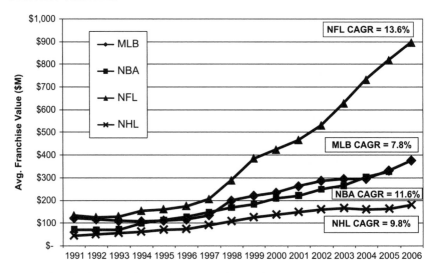

Source: Adapted and compiled from Rodney Fort, "Rodney *Fort's Sports Economics*," Sports Business Data page, 2005, http://www.rodneyfort.com/SportsData/BizFrame.htm (accessed January 2007).

exponentially in recent years, owners began to recognize and take advantage of opportunities to turn their franchises into real moneymaking ventures, rather than mere outlets for their competitive instincts. Accordingly, demand and sales prices for franchises have increased across all four leagues, as seen in Figure 5.1.

It should be noted that these valuations, while providing public benchmarks, are a source of debate within the sports finance community. *Forbes* began attempting to value franchises in the four primary leagues in 1998, picking up where *Financial World* magazine left off in 1997. *Forbes*'s valuation methodology is kept confidential, but does ultimately result in valuations for each franchise based on four primary components: (1) value attributable to revenues shared by all franchises within a given league; (2) value attributable to a franchise's city and market size; (3) value attributable to a franchise's stadium/arena; and (4) value attributable to a franchise's brand management.[1] With respect to those four value components, all but the first are primarily intangible and difficult to approximate without a rigorous methodology. Accordingly, one frequent assessment is that, while the analysis serves as a useful tool in valuing franchises, the accuracy of the underlying individual team data limits the veracity of the analysis on a team-by-team basis.

At the same time, there is certainly something to be said for a valuation approach that is consistently applied over time. Regardless of the accuracy of any particular franchise valuation, a review of a set of the *Forbes* valuations over time can reveal trends for specific leagues, as well as across leagues. For example, the chart in Figure 5.1 shows that as of 1997, average franchise values for all four leagues were still relatively tightly grouped, whereas NFL valuations have spiked significantly since then, outstripping the growth in values of the other leagues fairly significantly. With respect to the growth rates of franchise values, all four leagues have demonstrated impressive results in the *Forbes* data. Since 1991, the average value of an NFL franchise has grown by 13.6 percent per year, which is closely trailed by the growth rate of the average franchise in the NBA at 11.6 percent. The other two leagues' average franchise values have also grown steadily since 1991, with the NHL at 9.8 percent and MLB at 7.8 percent per year.

DRIVERS OF FRANCHISE VALUES

From the *Forbes* data in Figure 5.1, the overall trends in franchise values can be understood. However, when valuing a particular franchise, factors that are specific to the league, city, and team in question must be taken into consideration.

League Issues

As seen in Figure 5.1, there is a clear disparity (which has become increasingly pronounced in recent years) in valuations of franchises in different leagues. It stands to reason that the league in which a franchise is a member is a highly significant driver of franchise value. Leagues can affect franchise value in three primary ways: labor situation; league-developed revenue streams; and league rules regarding ownership and debt. Among the most publicized areas of league rules are player salary constraints, which vary widely across leagues. It stands to reason that a league with tight controls on player salaries creates a greater degree of cost certainty for its franchises, which in turn should have a positive effect on franchise value. In practice, the NFL has a tight salary cap that is tied to a fixed portion of leaguewide revenues, and the NHL has gone to a similar system as of its latest collective bargaining agreement (CBA). Meanwhile, the NBA does have a salary cap, but there are exceptions that lead to a slightly higher degree of variance in player salaries. Finally, MLB does not have a salary cap. Its main salary constraint is a "luxury tax"—a tax on salaries over a certain level—which to date has directly impacted only a few franchises. Figure 5.2 shows that the

FIGURE 5.2
Average Percentage of Revenues Spent on Player Salaries by League

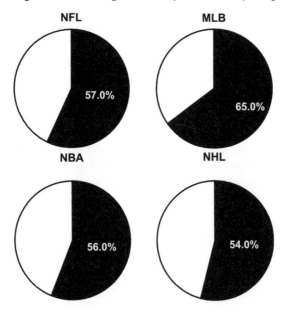

Source: MZ Sports LLC proprietary research.

FIGURE 5.3
CBA Term for Each League

League	CBA Starts	CBA Terminates	Extension/Early Termination Options
MLB	2007 Season	After 2011 Season	None
NBA	2005-06 Season	After 2010-11 Season	The League has the option to extend the agreement through the 2011-12 season
NFL	2006 Season	After 2012 Season	The Players Association and the League each have the option to end the agreement after the 2009 season
NHL	2005-06 Season	After 2010-11 Season	The Players Association has the option to end the agreement after the 2008-09 season, or extend it through the 2011-12 season

Source: MZ Sports LLC proprietary research.

average percent of revenues dedicated to covering player salary expenditures (including player development costs) is higher for MLB than for the other three leagues.

Labor stability, or lack thereof, is another important driver of franchise value. A league with no labor problems on the horizon is not likely to experience any value-depleting work stoppages. Noting the fact that the aforementioned issues with salary constraints are usually the primary cause of labor strife, an ideal situation from a franchise value perspective would be a CBA that is lucrative for franchise owners, yet still provides players with an acceptable level of compensation to ensure labor peace. Any deviation in either direction from this equilibrium can lead to potential work stoppages, which can be extremely damaging to franchise values in the short term. Figure 5.3 shows the current term of the active CBA for each league.

Revenue sharing can also significantly drive value. Leagues with a relatively high degree of local revenue sharing are likely to have smaller disparities in valuations between higher revenue franchises and lower revenue ones. The NFL has the highest degree of revenue sharing; a policy that has helped drive franchise value. MLB, in recent years, has increased revenue sharing in response to a growing gap in revenues between large- and small-market teams. The same can be said for the NHL, which determined that a higher degree of revenue-sharing was vital to the survival of many of its franchises during its CBA negotiations of 2004/05. The NBA also can have a significant degree of revenue-sharing, though it is not as clear-cut as the systems employed by the NFL and NHL. In the NBA, revenue-sharing is derived from a luxury tax on player salaries over a specific threshold. Depending on player compensation as a percentage of overall league revenues as well

FIGURE 5.4

Per-Team National Media Revenues by League

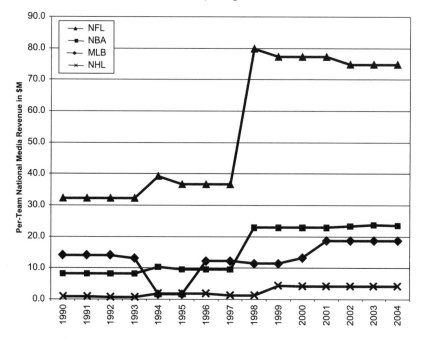

Source: Adapted and compiled from: Street & Smith's Sports Business Journal Research, "Sports Rights Fees," *Street and Smith's Sports Business Daily*, 2006, http://www.sportsbusinessdaily.com/index.cfm?fuseac tion=tdi.main&departmentId=24#sportsrightsfees (accessed January 2007).

as individual team spending, the luxury tax trigger may or may not be tripped in a given year.

It should also be noted that local revenue-sharing is one value driver that should be examined in conjunction with national revenues, as leagues that have a large amount of the latter will be able to lessen the relative importance of local revenues. The primary sources of national revenues, which are shared equally among all franchises within a given league, are national TV rights contracts. Figure 5.4 shows the average per-team national media revenue for each league from 1991 to 2006.

Figure 5.4 shows that per-team national media revenues in the NFL exceed those of the other three leagues. These figures depict why national TV revenues are a highly significant value driver. An NFL franchise starts out with nearly $80 million of guaranteed revenue without ever having to sell a ticket, or a sponsorship package, whereas an NHL franchise would only have roughly $5 million guaranteed from national TV rights.

FIGURE 5.5
Average Nielsen Ratings (1999–2005) by League

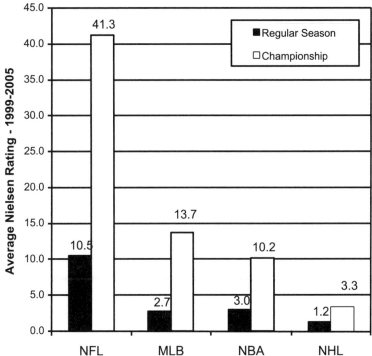

Source: Adapted and compiled from: Street & Smith's Sports Business Journal Research, "Final Nielsen TV Ratings," *Street and Smith's Sports Business Daily,* 2006, http://www.sportsbusinessdaily.com/index.cfm? fuseaction=tdi.main&departmentId=24#finaltvratings (accessed January 2007).

It is not surprising that the relative size of the rights fees received by each league is generally correlated to the average Nielsen ratings of their respective game broadcasts, as seen in Figure 5.5 for 1999–2005.

At the same time, these national TV revenues only tell part of the national media story for each league, and the remaining parts of that story are constantly evolving. The concept of "new media," a term intended to encompass Internet, wireless, and cellular-based revenue streams, has become more and more of a focal point for sports leagues. As the U.S. population becomes more attuned to new media entertainment opportunities, the leagues are positioning themselves to create heretofore-untapped revenue sources. MLB appears to be at the forefront of this initiative, with its creation and ownership of MLB Advanced Media (MLBAM), a venture focused on the delivery of MLB-related content over new forms of media. Thus far,

MLBAM has proven extremely successful, maintaining a position on the forefront of this type of technology while simultaneously managing to generate positive cash flows. While the other leagues are trailing behind MLB in these endeavors, they too are placing an increasing emphasis on the development of business models that capitalize on these newfound opportunities. All four leagues have formed partnerships with cutting-edge companies like YouTube and Google, along with cellphone service providers, for the delivery of for-sale content to consumers through all means other than the television set. While these business models are nowhere near being fully fleshed out, a key driver of franchise value into the future will be how prepared each league (and thus, each franchise) is for the next wave of media opportunities.

Even as new media revenue streams are still evolving, each league has become increasingly adept in recent years at generating significant nontelevision revenues on a national basis to be distributed to all of the member franchises. Specifically, each league has established marketing arms that generate a great deal of sponsorship and licensing revenues at the league level. With all of the diversified entertainment options available in today's society, association with powerful, established, highly relevant entities like the four major leagues has become extremely attractive to corporations. Accordingly, the leagues have not hesitated to capitalize financially on the attention they receive from the corporate world. With that in mind, it is clear that a significant portion of any franchise's revenues is being generated from a highly advantageous position by the leagues themselves, and the subsequent value-enhancing benefits are passed along to the franchises.

In addition to leaguewide revenues, each league has policies regarding debt and ownership that impact value. The limits on the amount of debt a franchise can carry is as follows:

- NFL: $150 million
- NBA: $115 million
- NHL: 50 percent of franchise value
- MLB: 10 × earnings before interest, taxes, depreciation, and amortization (EBITDA), or 15 × EBITDA in the case of a new ballpark

These rules are intended to ensure that each franchise has a limited amount of debt in the event of an economic downturn. The nature of the debt rules has caused debate within each league as to which method best drives value—a fixed-debt amount (NFL and NBA), a value-based test (NHL), or a profitability-based test (MLB).

Furthermore, the debt rules ensure that each franchise's owners have some "skin in the game," which incentivizes the owners to make decisions that should be at least partially driven by the franchise's best financial interests. Along these lines, the NFL and NBA each impose fixed minimum equity requirements on the franchise's controlling general partner (GP), or controlling owner of the franchise. One could surmise that debt limits, especially fixed debt limits, serve to limit growth in franchise value by reducing the universe of potential owners/acquirers. On the other hand, the tradeoff for this reduced franchise demand is increased franchise stability as poorly capitalized owners are less likely to be involved.

Another important league-related value driver is the potential availability of financial capital. Each league works to increase the value of each of its franchises; one example is in the leagues' willingness to establish leaguewide credit facilities to allow its franchises to access debt at below-market prices and terms. Due to each league's aggregate financial strength, the financial markets are often willing to provide extremely favorable lending terms, which the leagues can pass on to their respective franchises. This has been an important factor in franchises' ability to finance the construction of new/renovated facilities, which in turn potentially allows them to increase their revenues significantly, benefiting the league as a whole. League-wide credit facilities exist in the NFL, MLB, and the NBA. In addition to its league-wide credit facility, the NFL established a well-received program titled "G-3" in order to provide an additional source of favorably priced debt to be used specifically for new facility construction. Access to inexpensive debt is highly attractive for a team owner and thus drives franchise value.

Specific Team Issues

On a franchise-specific level, there are also numerous drivers of value. Within a given league, market size is the most important driver. A larger market translates to a larger potential fan base to purchase tickets and to watch or listen to games. Increased demand for tickets helps drive ticket prices as well. In addition, a larger market usually means a stronger corporate presence, resulting in increased demand for premium seating and sponsorships. While it would appear obvious that there would be a direct correlation between franchise size and franchise value, this is not always the case. Figure 5.6 shows the sale prices of franchises recently sold in each of the four major leagues in comparison to the market size of each of those franchises.

Figure 5.6 demonstrates that the correlation between franchise sale price and market size varies by league. For MLB franchises, there appears to be a clear relationship between market size and sale price. This also appears to ring true for NHL franchises. For NBA and NFL franchises, however, it

FIGURE 5.6
Franchise Sale Prices vs. Market Size

League	Franchise	Sale Price	Market Size Ranking
MLB	Los Angeles Dodgers	$421M	2
	Boston Red Sox	$375M	5
	Washington Nationals	$450M	8
	Milwaukee Brewers	$220M	33
	Cincinnati Reds	$260M	34
NBA	New Jersey Nets	$300M	1
	Boston Celtics	$360M	5
	Seattle Supersonics	$350M	13
	Cleveland Cavaliers	$375M	16
	Charlotte Bobcats	$300M	27
NFL	New York Jets	$635M	1
	Washington Redskins	$750M	8
	Atlanta Falcons	$545M	9
	Minnesota Vikings	$600M	15
	Baltimore Ravens	$600M	24
NHL	New Jersey Devils (1)	$175M	1
	Nerw York Islanders (1)	$195M	1
	San Jose Sharks (1)	$125M	6
	St. Louis Blues (2)	$135M	21
	Buffalo Sabres (1)	$75M	49

(1) Franchise was sold duiring the term of the 1994-2004 Collective
     Bargaining Agreement
(2) Franchise was sold duiring the term of the Collective Bargaining
     Agreement signed in 2005

Sources: MZ Sports LLC proprietary research; AR&D Television Branding, "Nielsen Media Research Local Universe Estimates," AR&D Television Branding website, www.ar-d.com/pdf/DMAListing_2005-2006. pdf (accessed January 2007).

appears as though market size is significantly less of a determining factor. This dichotomy is explained, at least in part, by the disparities between leagues. As mentioned earlier, leagues with a relatively high degree of local revenue-sharing and a large amount of national revenues inherently deem-phasize, at least partially, local revenues as a driver of franchise value. Of course, it is probably dangerous to attempt to draw a meaningful conclusion with any degree of confidence from the sample set detailed in Figure 5.6, as market size is only the starting point of the examination of the potential drivers of franchise value.

In addition to market size, a team's arena situation is a large driver of value. The most important question is the ability of the building to maximize revenues. A newer facility will generally be fully equipped with amenities that have been proven, in recent years, to be better revenue drivers than those of venues of the past. This is generally reflected in the quality and availability of premium seating and sponsorship opportunities, but also carries over into the quality and accessibility of concessions and merchandise sales points, on-site tertiary businesses (restaurants, lounges, and so on), and general fan-friendliness. A new facility is very likely to have been constructed with all of the aforementioned concepts near the top of the priority list, whereas franchises in outdated venues may be facing an uphill battle in one or more of those areas. Of course, merely examining the quality of the venue would be missing another huge component of this particular revenue driver—the franchise's lease arrangement.

While the facility quality may determine revenue potential, the lease will ultimately define how much of that revenue the team gets to keep. Most facilities are funded in part by the public sector, and franchises and their public partner negotiate the financial and operating arrangements. Some leases are fairly straightforward rental arrangements—the team pays a designated amount of rent to the public sector in exchange for the right to play at the facility and, in return, keeps all of the revenues and is responsible for all of the expenses associated with the facility. However, there is an entire continuum of lease arrangements that result in revenue- and/or expense-sharing between the franchise and the public sector. In these cases, the proportion of revenues and expenses that are directed to the franchise is just as important in terms of franchise value as the overall size of the revenue pool.

Furthermore, the notion of potential ancillary real estate opportunities on or near the facility's site and the division of any potential revenues from those possible ventures are other factors in the ultimate determination of how a franchise's facility can drive value. Numerous examples of development surrounding sports facilities exist, as team owners look for additional sources of income. For example, in Dallas, Texas, the Victory development is a $3-billion development project surrounding the arena that hosts the Dallas Mavericks and Dallas Stars.[2] Meanwhile, in Glendale, Arizona, the Westgate development, adjacent to the arena for the Phoenix Coyotes, features 6.5 million square feet of mixed-use property.[3] In Brooklyn, New York, the Atlantic Yards area will have 7.7 million square feet of mixed-use property that is on track to be developed around the new basketball arena for the Nets that is planned.[4] In these instances, the franchise owners have played and/or will play a large role in the development of this valuable real estate, as their respective franchises have served as the anchors for the surrounding areas.

FIGURE 5.7
Franchise-Owned Regional Sports Networks

Franchise(s)	Regional Sports Network	Market Size Ranking
New York Mets	Sportsnet New York (SNY)	1
New York Yankees	Yankees Entertainment and Sports Network (YES)	1
Chicago Blackhawks, Bulls, Cubs, and White Sox	Comcast SportsNet Chicago (CSN-Chicago)	3
Philadelphia Flyers and 76ers	Comcast SportsNet Philadelphia (CSN-Philadelphia)	4
Boston Bruins and Red Sox	New England Sports Network (NESN)	5
Baltimore Orioles and Washington Nationals	Mid-Atlantic Sports Network (MASN)	8 / 24
Cleveland Indians	SportsTime Ohio (STO)	16
Colorado Avalanche and Denver Nuggets	Altitude Sports and Entertainment Network (ASE)	18
Kansas City Royals	Royals Sports Television Network (RSTN)	31

Source: Adapted and compiled from AR&D Television Branding, "Nielsen Media Research Local Universe Estimates," AR&D Television Branding website, www.ar-d.com/pdf/DMAListing_2005-2006.pdf (accessed January 2007).

Local media opportunities also drive value. A franchise's territory determines the size of the viewer base in its local media market, which in turn dictates the potential revenues that teams can generate through local broadcast rights. An additional factor to be considered in the valuation of a franchise is the duration of its existing local media contracts. If a franchise is locked in to a long-term local media deal at rates which are or will be below market, franchise value would be impacted. On the other hand, a franchise that is at or near the end of an existing broadcast agreement has a great deal of flexibility. The franchise will be able to negotiate a new set of agreements, most likely under favorable terms, given the inevitable fight for local media rights among the various outlets. A strategy that has become increasingly desirable in recent years has been the formation of regional sports networks (RSNs). Under the traditional model, franchises would sell the broadcast rights to their games to local television networks in exchange for a rights fee. However, franchises have become more attuned to the idea of filling the role of their traditional broadcast partners themselves in order to directly access the consumers. Figure 5.7 shows a list of franchise-owned RSNs.

As demonstrated in Figure 5.7, RSNs are most prevalent in the largest markets—these are the locations in which the television rights are most valuable, and accordingly, the franchises have the most incentive to retain those rights themselves. Clearly, the existence or potential existence of an RSN has the potential to have a big impact on franchise value. At the same time, it is very important to note that the vast majority of franchises are not involved with RSNs, which adds complexity to any attempts to compare values between two or more franchises with different approaches to local media opportunities.

Another key driver is how a franchise has been operated in the past, as well as how it might be operated on a going-forward basis. If a franchise has been governed in such a way as to have created significant and unavoidable operating losses in the near future, then those losses need to be considered as a detractor from franchise value. For example, a franchise may have signed up to long-term below-market sponsorship and local media deals, or taken on significant long-term player salary commitments. These dynamics could lead to future operating losses that will need to be funded by the owner and should be factored into any valuation accordingly.

At the same time, a given franchise may have potential synergies that could create added value to a specific owner. For example, the owner of a local television network might need entertainment content for the network. In this case, franchise ownership would also increase the value of a related property, the network, as well. A similar example would be an individual who already owns one sports franchise in a specific market and is considering the acquisition of a second franchise in a different league in that market. In this scenario, that owner may be able to combine back-office and sales/marketing staffs, which would enable him or her to reduce consolidated operating expenses, creating added value.

In addition, the potential for unrealized upside in revenues and profit drives value. Often, team owners sell franchises that are underperforming in their market for any number of reasons, and a new owner can greatly enhance revenue performance. For example, a franchise may be located in a large market with a great deal of disposable income, but may also have a sales staff that is inefficiently incentivized and/or managed or have a ticket pricing policy that leaves substantial dollars on the table.

VALUATION METHODOLOGY—REVENUE MULTIPLES

It is clear that a wide variety of factors drive franchise valuation, factors that impact both revenues and expenses. Thus, like any other business, valuing a sports franchise must be undertaken with the requisite amount of rigor, focusing not only on a team's current state of affairs, but its potential future financial profile.

Taking into account profitability and future growth are staples in valuing assets in most industries. Whether one is looking to acquire assets in the real estate business, which often trade as a multiple of funds from operations (FFO—a cash flow measure) or media, which trade as a multiple of EBITDA or on price/earnings ratios, the basis for the analysis is profitability.

However, sports franchises are typically valued based on revenue multiples. This approach requires minimal information—franchise revenues along with historical revenue multiples for the league. For example, if a buyer and seller agreed on a set of comparable franchise sale transactions that ended up reflecting an average revenue multiple of 2.5×, and the franchise under consideration had annual revenues of $100 million, then the valuation dictated by this approach would be $250 million.

This approach is preferred due to several factors. First, this approach intentionally disregards cash flow variability. If a franchise is hypothetically on track to generate $10 million of net cash flow, when suddenly the owner decides to pour an additional $30 million into player salaries that year, then the projected $10-million profits instantly become $20 million of losses. It can be reasonably argued that the $30-million player salary expenditure was merely a one-off decision made unilaterally by the previous owner on a non-repeating basis and, as a result, should not have any effect on the true value of the franchise. Because sports franchises' profitability are so heavily dependent on discretionary owner-specific operational decisions, one might argue that it would not be fair to base a valuation on any metric that takes these decisions into account, as they will not reoccur in the future. In addition, a revenue-based multiple approach makes the assumption that all franchises could theoretically be operated with an identical expense structure, which would imply that the only differentiating factor between franchises would be their respective revenues.

Sellers of teams favor the revenue multiple approach for the very reasons described in the previous paragraph. By focusing the valuation on the revenue side of a franchise's financial statements, they are able to short-circuit any potential value-depressing issues with the franchise's actual operations. Furthermore, this approach is fairly easy to grasp, which makes it easier for the seller to try to keep the revenue multiple as the focal point of discussions and negotiations, which can further distract a potential buyer from a deeper investigation of the franchise's current state of operations. If the seller is successful in this endeavor, then the buyer will not spend time thinking about potential upside opportunities or ongoing operating losses, but, rather, will be focused on debating the fairness of the applicable multiple itself.

In order to derive the appropriate revenue multiple, the universe of comparable transactions should be as large as possible to minimize the impact of any particular off-market deal. Figure 5.8 shows historical revenue multiples for the eight most recent franchise sales in each league.

Figure 5.8 shows clear disparities in the average revenue multiple for each of the four major leagues. However, of equal importance is the wide variation of multiples within a given league. This variation hints at the fact that a revenue multiple-based valuation should be based on a carefully culled set of comparables. Numerous factors are used to narrow the pool of potential

FIGURE 5.8
Historical Revenue Multiples

League	Year	Franchise	Revenue Multiple at Acquisition (1)	Acquirer
MLB	2002	Boston Red Sox	2.4x	John Henry
	2002	New York Mets	2.5x	Fred Wilpon
	2003	Anaheim Angels	1.6x	Arturo Moreno
	2004	Los Angeles Dodgers	2.4x	Frank and Jamie McCourt
	2004	Milwaukee Brewers	1.9x	Mark Attanasio
	2005	Oakland Athletics	1.4x	Lew Wolff
	2005	Cincinnati Reds	2.0x	Robert Castellini
	2006	Washington Nationals	3.7x	Lerner Family
		Average MLB Multiple	**2.2x**	
NBA	2000	Vancouver Grizzlies	3.2x	Michael Heisley
	2001	Seattle Supersonics	2.7x	Howard Schultz
	2002	Boston Celtics	3.8x	Wyc Grousbeck and Stephen Pagliuca
	2003	Charlotte Bobcats	3.3x	Robert Johnson
	2004	Phoenix Suns	4.0x	Robert Sarver
	2004	New Jersey Nets	3.0x	Bruce Ratner
	2005	Cleveland Cavaliers	4.7x	Dan Gilbert
	2006	Seattle Supersonics	3.9x	Clay Bennett
		Average NBA Multiple	**3.6x**	
NFL	1998	Cleveland Browns	3.7x	Alfred Lerner
	1999	Houston Texans	3.7x	Robert McNair
	1999	Washington Redskins	5.3x	Daniel Snyder
	2000	Baltimore Ravens	5.0x	Art Modell
	2000	New York Jets	6.1x	Woody Johnson
	2002	Atlanta Falcons	4.9x	Arthur Blank
	2004	Baltimore Ravens	3.5x	Steve Bisciotti
	2005	Minnesota Vikings	4.2x	Steve Bisciotti
		Average NFL Multiple	**4.5x**	
NHL	2000	Phoenix Coyotes	2.0x	Steve Ellman
	2001	Florida Panthers	1.5x	Alan Cohen
	2002	San Jose Sharks	1.7x	Kevin Compton
	2003	Buffalo Sabres	1.5x	Tom Golisano
	2003	Ottawa Senators	1.3x	Eugene Melnyk
	2004	New Jersey Devils	1.7x	Jeffrey Vanderbeek
	2005	Anaheim Mighty Ducks	1.0x	Henry Samueli
	2006	St. Louis Blues	1.9x	Dave Checketts
		Average NHL Multiple	**1.6x**	

(1) Revenue Multiple at Acquisition is equal to the price paid for the franchise divided by the franchise's revenues. For example, a team with $100M of revenues and a sale price of $300M would have a revenue multiple of 3.0x.

Source: MZ Sports LLC proprietary research.

comparable transactions. CBA changes, market size, type of seller—all can impact whether or not a prior transaction is included.

Once an agreed-upon set of comparable transactions is established, the revenue multiple will be adjusted based on team- and league-specific value drivers as described earlier. This could include potential upside at the team or league level, inclusion of new media opportunities, local media opportunities, or long-term obligations to players or front-office staff. For example, assume that, based on comparable transactions (large market for example), both parties agree as a starting point on a revenue multiple of 2.5×. Then the negotiations regarding value will be based on adjustment factors to the 2.5× multiple. A buyer may argue, for example, that long-term player commitments should work to adjust the multiple to 2.3× revenues or that a long-term media deal that does not let the buyer take advantage of a potential RSN reduces the multiple to 2.0×.

The most notable shortcoming to this type of approach is that the adjustments are done at a very high level and are not based on a rigorous financial analysis, especially on the expense side. Existing team losses, high payroll, large front-office costs, inflexibility regarding local media are but a few examples that can dramatically impact value. Simple adjustments in revenue multiples cannot adequately replace rigorous financial analysis in determining the bottom line impact.

VALUATION METHODOLOGY–DISCOUNTED CASH FLOW

A valuation approach that should be more effective in incorporating the franchise specific drivers described above is the discounted cash flow (DCF) approach, which bases valuation on projected annual operating cash flows discounted at the buyer's hurdle rate. While comparable transactions provide a handy benchmark, DCF allows a franchise to be examined based on its own merits and unique attributes.

The DCF approach historically has been considered difficult to implement for the reasons listed above, including lack of profitability and dramatic swings in income due to player payroll. However, buyers who are spending multiple hundreds of millions of dollars on a franchise are taking the position that they will run the franchise as a business, in some cases targeting a specific cash-flow profit (net of debt service) and in the worst case, as a break-even proposition. This line of reasoning eliminates the concerns, on a DCF basis, of on-going losses. Clearly, the notion of a break-even or better bottom line must be grounded in reality. However, with the leagues reining in player costs, for the most part tying player payroll to a percentage of league revenues, owners are now better positioned to argue that future profits are achievable. In addition, numerous recent buyers have been able to increase revenues and profitability dramatically, again creating the argument for DCF. Finally, with increased information sharing among teams, franchise buyers can more effectively create business plans that tie to expenses to revenues.

In addition to annual operating cash-flow projections, a DCF analysis will include a projected exit value or terminal value, which can be calculated using either multiples or growth rates in conjunction with discount rates.

Typically, if a multiple is used for the exit value, the multiple will be based on an implied revenue multiple at the time of purchase, with sensitivity analysis to test various exit values.

DCF relies on numerous assumptions, both in terms of operating projection and exit value. Clearly, then, one has to have a high degree of confidence in the assumptions and significant knowledge and understanding of a franchise's operations. Testing for various operating and exit value scenarios helps greatly in this regard. While the assumptions in question are just that, assumptions, this approach, if undertaken with the appropriate level of rigor, should produce more appropriate results compared to a revenue multiple approach, which often fails to properly account for or measure certain operating factors and future profitability.

NOTES

1. Michael K. Ozanian and Kurt Badenhausen, "The Business of Baseball," *Forbes*, April 20, 2006, http://www.forbes.com/2006/04/17/06mlb_baseball_valuations_land. html (accessed January 2007).

2. Christine Perez, "Woods Takes Victory Park to New Level," *Dallas Business Journal*, December 29, 2006, http://www.bizjournals.com/dallas/stories/2007/01/01/ story1.html?t=printable (accessed January 2007).

3. Scott Wong, "Westgate Gears Up for Parties," *Arizona Republic*, December 27, 2006, http://www.azcentral.com/community/glendale/articles/1227gl-blockparty27Z18. html (accessed January 2007).

4. Matthew Schuerman, "Square Feet—2006 vs. 2003," *New York Observer Real Estate*, April 4, 2006, http://therealestate.observer.com/2006/04/square-feet-2006-vs-2003.html (accessed January 2007).

Six

Professional Sports Facilities, Teams, Government Subsidies, and Economic Impact

Xia Feng

DO PROFESSIONAL SPORTS ACT AS CATALYST FOR METROPOLITAN ECONOMIES?

In the past two decades, the United States experienced a boom in construction of sports stadiums and arenas. Sixty-four major-league stadiums and arenas were built for the four major professional sports: the National Football League (NFL), the Major League Baseball (MLB), the National Basketball Association (NBA), and the National Hockey League (NHL) from 1991 to 2006.[1] This trend shows no sign of stopping. Big cities compete to construct new stadiums to attract new teams or renovate old ones to retain their current teams. As of this writing six new stadiums for NFL teams are either currently under construction or proposed. One new arena for an NBA team is currently under construction in Charlotte, North Carolina. One new arena for NHL's Pittsburgh Penguins has been proposed. Seven new ballparks for MLB teams are either proposed or to be opened in 2008 or 2009.

Though the particular details of competition for sports facility construction and teams differ from city to city, the general motivation for investment in them is the same. City officials usually claim that sports facilities and teams can generate substantial economic impacts, in terms of income increases, job creation, and tax-revenue increases, because people who attend games from out of the city will spend money at the facilities and on many other related or unrelated activities in the cities, thus injecting new spending in the city. According to regional input-output models, this new spending will generate substantial multiplier effects on sports-related industries under the assumption of no leakage, that is, if spending only circulates within the host community. The multiplier effects work even with money leakages but with less magnitude. Furthermore, a major-league sports team reputedly makes a city a "major league city," and therefore attracts new businesses to locate in the city. Theses claims usually are supported by estimates provided by consulting firms who are commissioned and paid to quantify these economic impacts. Just by looking at the large numbers in consultants' reports, cities would regard sports facilities and teams as an engine of the community's economic development.[2]

However, debate arises over the economic impacts, mainly over the benefits, on the city or broader regional economies. A growing body of independent empirical research has shown that professional sports facilities and teams have little or no significant positive impacts or even negative effects on the metropolitan economy.[3] Different from the promotional economic impact studies from consulting firms, these independent studies usually employ a pooled time-series and cross-sectional regression model to examine the impact of sports facilities and teams on local economic development in terms of aggregate or per capita personal income and employment growth. These retrospective studies provide no significant evidence of positive effects when comparing metropolitan areas with a professional sports team to the ones without a team.

Despite the growing empirical evidence that there is little significant economic impact from the facilities and teams, cities continue to invest billions of dollars to construct new facilities. From a regional development policy point of view, this phenomenon raises several questions worth addressing: Do professional sports facilities and teams act as a catalyst to metropolitan economies or not? What are the relevant economic benefits and costs? What is the best way to finance the costs of construction? The differences between the results of the two types of studies also raise interesting questions: If there is little or even negative economic impact, as many empirical studies show, then what are the rationales for cities to compete to subsidize facilities and teams? What are the benefits beyond income, jobs, and taxes and how can they be appropriately quantified? Why do the two groups of studies have different results? These questions will be explored and discussed next.

PUBLIC FINANCING OF SPORTS AND ITS RATIONALE

Large metropolitan areas compete with each other to retain and attract professional sports teams. They have to compete because of the monopoly power implicitly and explicitly given to professional sports leagues. The main form of this competition is public subsidies for the construction of new

TABLE 6.1

Historical and Inflation Adjusted Costs on Sports Stadiums and Arenas for Professional Teams (By Decade)

		Stadiums				
		Nominal Dollars (US$ million)		**2006 Dollars (US$ million)**		**Public Share (%)**
Decade	**No. Built**	**Total**	**Average**	**Total**	**Average**	**Average**
Before 1961	18					
1961–1970	9	266.70	29.63	1921.61	213.51	88.01
1971–1980	11	827.20	75.20	3032.77	275.71	90.20
1981–1990	5	819.00	163.80	1409.14	281.83	67.20
1991–2000	20	5161.00	258.05	6878.54	343.93	70.85
2001–2006	13	4676.80	359.75	5390.42	414.65	61.89
1961–2006	58	11750.70	202.60	18632.49	321.25	74.86
		Arenas				
		Nominal Dollars (US$ million)		**2006 Dollars (US$ million)**		**Public Share (%)**
Decade	**No. Built**	**Total**	**Average**	**Total**	**Average**	**Average**
Before 1961	3					
1961–1970	3	180.50	60.17	1276.08	425.36	100.00
1971–1980	5	111.90	22.38	363.53	72.71	100.00
1981–1990	8	630.20	78.78	1113.24	139.15	57.92
1991–2000	27	4729.90	175.18	6381.36	236.35	45.07
2001–2006	4	1190.29	297.57	1190.29	297.57	83.50
1961–2006	47	6842.79	145.59	10324.50	219.67	59.88

Source: Compiled by John L. Crompton, Dennis E. Howard, and T. Var, "Financing Major League Facilities: Status, Evolution and Conflicting Forces," *Journal of Sports Management* 17 (2003): 156-18; and Ballparks Web site by Munsey and Suppes, http://www.ballparks.com/index.html.
Note: The construction cost index is from *Engineering News-Record,* March 20, 2006. Stadiums and arenas built before 1961 lack cost data.

sports facilities. Among all the professional sports facilities built from 1961 to 2006, many were fully or partially subsidized. In 2006 dollars, the total investment from 1961 to 2006 in sports facilities in use or under construction at that time was $28.96 billion, of which $19.5 billion was publicly subsidized. Table 6.1 provides some historical evidence on investment on new sports stadiums and arenas and the share of public financing.[4]

There has been a boom in construction of sports stadiums and arenas since the 1990s. Among the fifty-eight stadiums built during 1961–2006 thirty-three were built after 1990, and among the forty-seven arenas thirty-one were built after 1990. From 1961 to 1980 the average public subsidy for stadium and arena construction was very high, on average around 94.6 percent, especially in the 1970s. This might be because the popularity of professional sports grew substantially during that period in terms of the number of franchises, venue attendance, and television viewing. Also, funding was widely perceived to be the exclusive responsibility of public entities during this period. Later, even though the publicly funded share of construction costs decreased, it was still large, on average around 64.4 percent for all sports facilities over the period 1981–2006. Also note that although the percentage was lower in the later period, the total subsidy in dollars is actually higher since the average construction cost increased over time. For example, the highest average public share of stadium construction costs was 90.2 percent from 1961 to 1980, corresponding to $248.67 million in 2006 dollars. The lowest average public share was 61.89 percent from 1980 to 2006, corresponding to $256.63 million in 2006 dollars.

Constructing a major sports facility is costly. Often the cost includes not only the construction cost of the facility itself, but also many other costs associated with construction, such as buying the land, relocating businesses, and infrastructure such as enhanced roads, sewers, and parking lots. So why are state and local governments willing to subsidize costly stadium and arena construction? What is the rationale underlying this phenomenon, even though most evidence from academic research shows that the economic impacts claimed are not quite justified by the impacts they generate?

The answers to the above questions mostly lie in the economic impact and intangible benefits, such as improved quality of life, civic pride or community self-esteem, enhanced community image as a major-league city, and psychic income.[5] These benefits can be traced back to firm theoretical origins.

In public welfare economics, for a good to be publicly subsidized it must be a public or quasi-public good which generates positive externalities. In other words, if there is a market failure in the supply of a good, then the provision of that good should be subsidized fully or partially. Are sports facilities public or quasi-public goods? In economic theory, a public good must be nonrivalrous and nonexcludable. Economists have traditionally argued that, because of these characteristics, public goods will not be supplied by a profit-oriented market economy. If they are to be supplied at all, government must supply them. The first characteristic implies that once the good is produced one person can benefit from it without diminishing others' enjoyment. In other words, the marginal cost of an additional person consuming a nonrivalrous good, once it is produced, is zero. Clearly, an individual can view a sports facility without diminishing another's viewing. As to the games that take place in these facilities, one more person may be admitted into a stadium without diminishing others' enjoyment of the game and paying anything extra since the cost of the stadium is fixed.[6] So we may say that sports facilities are nonrivalrous. To be nonexcludable, viewing sports facilities must be free and open to the public. As to the games, although one has to pay for enjoying the game and it is feasible to exclude those who do not buy tickets from enjoying the benefit of the game, consumers may still enjoy the benefit of the contests through watching TV without attending the live game, if these events are substitutes for attendance. Even people who never follow the teams by any means can enjoy the intangible consumption benefits such as sports spirit, civic pride, and major-league status. These intangible benefits of sports facilities and teams are a source of social value that cannot be captured completely through ticket sales and other media revenues that lead to a partial market failure. This is because sports facilities and teams generate positive externalities and cannot exclude those who do not attend the game from enjoying the benefit of the game. Of course the extent of the benefit may be different among those who attend games, those who watch games via TV, and those who never watch games by any means.

Even more, the businesses in a city also enjoy intangible benefits from the presence of a sports facility and a professional sports team.[7] For example, the presence of a professional sports franchise may have a positive impact on business property values. It is impossible to exclude the businesses from this benefit. So sports facilities and their teams fulfill the definition of a public or quasi-public good if we strictly adhere to the second characteristic. Therefore the supply of sports facilities by the private sector will be certainly less than is desired by society. According to economic theory, the obvious solution is that the government must supply them fully or partially. This is one theoretical rationale for cities providing subsidies to construct stadiums and arenas to attract or retain a major league team.

Another theoretical rationale lies in the market structure of the sports industry. Often sports teams are organized as cartels. An entire book was recently devoted to the discussion of monopoly power exercised by professional sports leagues.[8] For example, MLB has a formal antitrust exemption. Other sports leagues have also been allowed to control many aspects of their leagues based on the unique negotiation involved in the bargaining game. For example, North America's four major professional sports leagues control the supply of teams, the placement of franchises in different markets, and the number of teams that may play in any region. The leagues also have some control over the location of teams, rules of ownership, and so on. However, in reality the United States has more possible host cities than sports teams.[9] In other words, demand for sports teams is much greater than the supply of the teams. There is ample evidence that the demand for sports would lead to the existence of many more teams if the four leagues were not profit-maximizing cartels.[10]

It is this characteristic of the sports market structure that determines the bargaining power of teams and cities. Often cities are faced with a choice between gaining or keeping a team with subsidies or losing it without subsidies. A subsidized team may appear to be a better choice due to the economic benefits claimed in a consulting firm's report. So cities are forced to compete to subsidize facilities in order to keep their current teams or attract a new team.

Creating competition in the sports industry is one way to improve the bargaining position of cities.[11] However, competition, in the case of free entry, would increase the number of teams and substantially reduce the size of subsidies, but it would not eliminate subsidies. Jeffrey Owen examined the role of market structure in determining league size and subsidies from cities to teams and developed a model in which teams attempt to capture social value through stadium subsidies. He concluded that the number of teams in the league, determined endogenously, increases when subsidies to teams are permitted. The size of the subsidy paid by a city depends on the threat point of teams based on the social value of a team to the largest city without a team.[12] Even a completely competitive market for teams would not put an end to subsidies as long as there exist some external benefits which cannot be captured by the teams or, in other words, as long as the social benefits exceed the private benefits. This is true because sports facilities are already public goods.

ECONOMIC IMPACT OF SPORTS FACILITIES AND TEAMS: EVIDENCE FROM EMPIRICAL STUDIES

Cities often justify the public financing of sports facilities by claiming large economic impacts that the facilities and teams will bring to the city. These claims are usually supported by economic impact studies that are performed by consulting firms using IMPLAN, an economic-impact-study software package. These studies are commissioned to justify the public subsidies for the facility. In doing so, they usually estimate large positive economic impacts in terms of personal income, jobs, and tax revenues by adopting unreasonable assumptions that bias the results. For example, in an economic-impact analysis of the proposed ballpark for the Boston Red Sox in 1999, it was estimated that the construction of the proposed ballpark, which took two and a half years, would generate a one-time total impact of $491.6 million in spending and 4,769 one-year, full-time-equivalent jobs in the state of Massachusetts. The projected annual attendance of close to 3.2 million fans would generate $502.5 million in total annual spending impact and 7,217 total annual full-time equivalent jobs in the state.[13] These big numbers are used by cities to justify their subsidies for the construction of sports facilities. A meta-analysis of thirteen impact studies using IMPLAN was performed to determine whether economic impact studies tend to overstate the teams' impacts and to investigate the causes of the wide variance of economic impact estimates in different studies.[14] This analysis showed that, although some of the variance of the estimates is due to observable differences in the size of the geographical region and sports team, differing assumptions about whether the nonsports-related expenditures of locals and tourists should be included accounted for a substantial variance in the estimated impact. In other words, the use of gross or net impacts accounted for a substantial variation in the impact estimates. This analysis concluded that the studies in the sample tended to adopt the methodologies that would inflate the economic impact of the sports team; thus their results are not reliable.

However, the positive economic impact reported in these prospective studies are not generally found in retrospective empirical studies by academic researchers.[15] These empirical studies typically employ econometric regression techniques using a combination of time-series and cross-section data to evaluate the past economic impacts in terms of the level or growth rate of personal real income and employment from sports on metropolitan economies.

The earliest research in this category of *ex post* studies, by Baade and Dye in 1990, used both cross-section time-series and pooled regression analysis.[16] This study evaluated the impact of NFL and MLB teams and new stadiums on metropolitan area income. The data was for nine metropolitan areas from 1965 to 1983. An empirical model of the determination of aggregate metropolitan area income shows an insignificant impact of the presence of a NFL team, presence of a MLB team, and presence of a new or renovated stadium, in nine areas and a significant positive effect on Seattle of the presence of a new stadium. Interestingly the pooled estimate shows a significant negative effect of a football team but a significant positive effect of a baseball team at the 10 percent level. This might be due to different scheduling patterns between football and baseball, for example, the fact that many more baseball games than football games are played in a season.

A second empirical model of the determination of the fraction of the income in multistate region as the dependent variable shows mixed results, but a pattern of potential negative effect of a new or renovated stadium. The pooled estimates again also show a significant negative effect of a new or renovated stadium and an insignificant effect of both a football and baseball team. This result is consistent with the hypothesis that stadium subsidies might bias local development toward low-wage jobs. This is because either the construction of stadiums or sports events mostly produce more temporary, part-time, and low-paid jobs than permanent, high-paid jobs, which might generate no significant effect on the local income or even lower the income level.

Two similar studies examined whether stadiums and professional sports have significant positive impacts on income and employment in cities. The sample included forty-eight cities, thirteen with no teams and others that hosted a team in at least one of the four major sports over the period from 1958 to 1987. Using regression techniques, the results from a reduced form model of income determination showed no significant effects from sports for all cities except a significantly positive effect in Indianapolis and a significantly negative effect in Baltimore. Results from a reduced form model of employment determination failed to support a positive correlation between sports and job creation, too, which suggests that sports just realign economic activity within a city's leisure industry rather than adding to it.

Baade and Sanderson investigated the relationship between professional sports and job creation using data for ten metropolitan areas over the period 1958–1993.[17] Again the study did not find a positive relationship. Further evidence showed that creating jobs through subsidies for sports is inefficient and costly since the jobs created are low-paid and the present value of the return on this investment is likely to be quite low in comparison with investment alternatives such as a subvention for the location of an industrial park or department store.

However, a common problem with this approach is that it does not contain control variables for regional income levels. Critics argue that other variables, such as race, education, and percent of poor, have too little year-to-year variation for each metropolitan area and instead used a time trend, which is assigned a value of 1 for the base year and goes up to the number of years of the period examined, to reflect general influences acting on metropolitan area personal income. Another potential problem is the potential endogeneity between income growth in the metropolitan area and the presence of the sports facility and team. A city with higher income growth will have greater financing ability, thus more chance to construct a stadium and to attract a sports team.

Along this direction, Coates and Humphreys extended Baade and Dye's method by using a larger sample size (thirty-seven standard metropolitan areas) and a longer and more recent sample period (1969–1994). They also expanded the sports environment variables to include entry and exit of franchise, stadium construction, and capacity, and controlled for more variables other than the sports environment that may affect income. Further they added structure to the disturbance term to control for region-specific and time-specific disturbances. They found that the overall impact of the sports variables was to reduce real per capita income (no impact on the growth of real per capita income and negative impact on the level). The other paper extending Baade and Sanderson, by Hudson, traced the literature on regional growth model and explicitly controlled for the effects of other attributes on an economy's employment growth, such as market size, labor costs, education levels, energy prices, and tax levels. Hudson's result, consistent with all the previous literature, was no significant effects from professional sports on a city's employment growth.[18]

All the above results are contrary to the claims by the proponents of subsidies for construction of sports facilities. Why do academic studies consistently find no positive economic impacts or even negative impacts from professional sports to local economies? Some research may provide some insights into this question.[19] These explanations are not mutually exclusive and may be parallel.

A first potential explanation for little positive effects or even negative effects is offered by Nelson who examined the role of stadium location in the economic effect of major league stadiums on regional economies.[20] The hypothesis is that a metropolitan area's share of regional income will rise when major-league stadiums are located in the central business district (CBD) but fall when located elsewhere. The paper argued that people attending games in the CBD are more likely to spend money before and after games than if they attended games at non-CDB locations. Using a sample of forty-three metropolitan areas over twenty-six years from 1969 to 1994, and controlling for demographic variables (such as percentage of college-educated residents and percentage in poverty), labor market characteristics (percentage employed and total employment), and local economic structure (percentage of labor force employed in construction, wholesale trade, and so on), this paper examined the effect of a stadium located within the CBD, at the CBD edge, elsewhere in the central city, and in the suburbs of a metropolitan area respectively. The author concluded that a stadium located in the CBD will probably generate greater economic benefits than one located in the suburbs. This result is robust to an agglomeration effect, such as when more than one team plays in the same stadium. Indeed, if a stadium is built elsewhere, it may lead to localized blight that dampens the metropolitan-area share of regional income. Though this gives a potential explanation to the lack of positive impact for Baade's article, "Professional Sports as Catalyst for Metropolitan Economic Development," it is not sufficient to justify the claim that stadiums located within CBD will cover the costs.[21]

A similar argument was made by Santo. The new generation of sports facilities would have more favorable economic impacts than their predecessors because they are built in the urban core with an emphasis on revitalization and tourist appeal and theoretically a retro-style ballpark in a downtown is more likely to attract visitors from a wider area and to induce longer stays and greater ancillary spending than its utilitarian suburban counterpart. Santo investigated the same problem as Baade and Dye with a more current set of data for the period 1984–2001 for nineteen metropolitan statistical areas (MSAs) using the same two regression equations as those by Baade and Dye, except for unique football and baseball stadium variables. Contradictory to the findings of Baade and Dye and Baade, Santo found mixed effects (both positive and negative) at the MSA income level and significantly positive impacts for many stadiums when using MSA income share to the region. In Baade the significantly positive impact on metropolitan income was found only in Indianapolis due to the fact that Indianapolis included sports as part of a larger development strategy in the 1980s. Santo pointed out that it is now far more common for cities to utilize this strategy to tie revitalization efforts to sports-related development, and thus cities should expect positive effects from sports stadiums in more and more cities, so context matters.[22]

A second explanation for the lack of positive impacts relates to the effect of the number of teams playing in one stadium. Contrary to the robust result from Nelson where he investigated the agglomeration effects when multiple teams play in one stadium, Gius and Johnson found that, while cities with a single major team did not have significantly different per capita income from cities without teams, cities with more than one team had statistically significant higher per capita income than cities without teams, which is inconsistent with prior research. A possible explanation for this inconsistency is that previous research mostly focused on the impact of a single team. Also this study is different from many existing studies in that the unit of analysis is cities while most existing studies use MSAs, a larger geographic area. So it is possible that cities may be drawing business away from suburbs, thus leaving the entire MSA unaffected. We may not expect the impacts from sports stadiums and games on cities to spill over to the entire MSA. Future research may examine the impacts on cities and their associated suburbs within MSAs where stadiums are located in cities to confirm this hypothesis that location and unit of study area matter.[23]

Quite different from the above two potential explanations, which focus on the geographic features such as location, several other explanations from economic theory have been proposed, and some are confirmed by empirical studies.[24] Coates and Humphreys proposed several possible explanations for their observed negative effect based on economic theory. One is that there are compensating differentials from sports stadiums and teams to the residents of the MSA. They argued that residents in a MSA with major sports teams are willing to pay for the presence of sports teams in the form of accepting a lower real per capita income because of large positive nonpecuniary or intangible benefits derived from sport.[25] This is true, but only a partial explanation, because those nonpecuniary benefits cannot be measured directly through econometric analysis, and it is well known in the environmental economics literature that they are usually captured in the form of higher land rents and lower wage rate in the area. The effects on land rent or wage rates are often evaluated using a hedonic model.[26] So their argument ignored the effects on land rent or housing values. Carlino and Coulson used a hedonic model to measure the compensating wage and rent differentials from NFL teams. Their results are consistent with this explanation that wages in MSAs with a NFL team fall approximately by 2 percent.[27] The underlying idea comes from consumer theory. Residents in MSAs with a sports team and in MSAs without one should have the same utility level and be equally happy when given the choice of living and working in MSAs with a team but with higher housing prices and lower income level or living and working in MSAs without a team but with lower housing prices and higher income level. Otherwise residents would migrate among MSAs until reaching the equilibrium.

The second explanation is that the public subsidies to sports stadiums and teams reduce public spending on local infrastructure, education, and other determinants of economic development. This is the opportunity cost of public subsidies to stadiums and teams. The universal debate between the proponents and opponents of public financing to stadiums should not focus on whether sports stadiums and teams bring any economic impacts to the community, but whether the economic impact from sports is the highest among the economic impacts from all the alternative investments. Therefore, future research should focus on economic-impact studies of alternative public investments including sports stadiums. We may also view this phenomenon as another type of "crowding-out" effect of any general public investment. The public investment in sports stadiums crowds out other, maybe more efficient in terms of productivity, public investments so that it reduces the income level of the community.

The third explanation relates sports events to unobservable productivity growth in a MSA. They posit the same hypothesis about the relationship between productivity and professional sports in a review paper.[28] This hypothesis can be tested empirically. Based on model and using the same data in Coates and Humphreys, Davis and End found that winning percentage of local sports teams has a significant positive impact on real per capita wage income.[29] If an increase in real per capita wage income implies an increase of productivity, then their finding implies winning percentage has a significant positive impact on productivity, which, albeit indirectly, supports the idea that increase in personal income may be partially result of increased productivity posited by Coates and Humphreys.[30] Davis and End explained this finding from a psychological perspective that if a sports team's performance influences judgments of personal competencies, mood, and self-esteem, for example, it is possible that the outcome of a sporting event may influence one's performance at work. Interestingly, another paper by Berument and Yucel found a similar result for the Turkish football team Fenerbache. They claimed that when someone's favorite team is successful then that person gets in a better mood and becomes more productive. Using the success of a popular football team as a proxy for the workers' mood or morale, they found a positive feedback from Fenerbache's success to economic performance such that the monthly industrial growth rate increased by 0.26 percent with the number of games won by Fenerbache in European cups, regardless where the game was played.[31]

While criticizing the approach of those promotional studies by consulting firms using regional input-output models, Siegfried and Zimbalist pointed out that substitution effects are generally ignored in the promotional studies when measuring the income and employment multipliers.[32] According to consumer theory, consumers are faced with an exogenous budget constraint and they choose their consumption bundles to maximize their utility constrained by a budget. So if they choose to go to sports games, then they have to consume less of other goods given their income level. While it is obvious that this substitution effect exists if the empirical evidence shows no positive or even negative effects on the MSA income, this hypothesis was not tested until Coates and Humphreys's study focused on the impact of professional sports stadiums and teams on employment and earnings only in specific sectors, namely the services and retail sectors, in the U.S. cities. They used the model in a previous study and data from thirty-seven MSAs over the period 1969–1996. Their results showed that although professional sports has a small positive effects on earnings per employee in the Amusement and Recreation sector (SIC 79), this positive effect is offset by a decrease in both earnings per employee in the Eating and Drinking Establishments sector and employment in the larger Services and Retail Trade sectors.[33] This suggests that the direct spending on sports does not add new money in other sectors like restaurants and hotels but switches money from these sectors to sports-related sectors, which implies sports and other amusements and related activities appear to be substitutes. Therefore the net effect on the spending in a whole MSA is left to be zero or very close to zero. So there is no significant positive effect on a MSA in terms of employment and income.

NONPECUNIARY IMPACTS: EVIDENCE BEYOND INCOME, JOBS, AND TAXES

The previous section discussed direct economic impact from sports facilities and teams in terms of income increase, jobs creation, and tax revenues. Almost all empirical studies show no positive or even negative impact of sports teams and facilities of these variables.[34] As mentioned, one of the explanations for this evidence is that significant nonpecuniary or intangible benefits accrue to the residents which are not captured directly by the teams. It is these intangible benefits that most advocates of sports subsidies label as an alternative rationale to justify for the public subsidies to the facilities. In this section we will examine the nonpecuniary impacts from professional sports: What benefits exist beyond income, jobs, and taxes?

There are quite a few studies discussing intangible benefits, but most are descriptive.[35] In the earliest argument for this intangible value of a sports team to the city, Rosentraub pointed out that Baade's work failed to measure the real value of a team to a city and its economic development. Rosentraub admitted that while sports may have little economic impact, their importance to society means that "any city without a team and a first rate facility is outside the mainstream of Western culture." He considered sports a cultural icon and coalition glue. Noll and Zimbalist also pointed out that the cultural importance of major-league team sports in American society most assuredly exceeds its economic significance as a business. Though professional sport is simply too small a component of any region's economy to be an engine or a propulsive industry, this does not mean sports is not important to the life and vitality of a city and its economy. Even Baade, who consistently found little evidence of positive impacts of sports, also admitted in his rejoinder to his own paper and one to Rosentraub that the reason he did not include intangible benefits is not they are unimportant but proponents of sports subsidies justified the rationale based on economic grounds.[36]

The noneconomic impact can be roughly divided into the following five nonexclusive types:

1. Public consumption benefits or consumer surplus (Noll and Zimbalist; Siegfried and Zimbalist) enjoyed by the attendees;
2. External benefits to the nonattendees through media and daily conversation (Siegfried and Zimbalist);

3. Public-image enhancement from "major-league city" status or community self-esteem (Crompton; Eckstein and Delaney; Siegfried and Zimbalist);

4. Community collective conscience, which refers to the shared values, beliefs, and experiences that bind community members together (Eckstein and Delaney). This is the same as what Rosentraub called "coalition glue," what Crompton called "psychic income," and what Groothuis, Johnson, and Whitehead called "civic pride"; and

5. Increased community visibility (Crompton).[37]

In a review paper about the benefits of hosting a major-league sports franchise, Rappaport and Wilkerson used improved quality of life to represent all the intangible benefits.[38]

Nonpecuniary impact generated from sports facilities and teams is long recognized, but few studies measure it. Noll and Zimbalist pointed out its importance, and they also admitted that "the practical significance of the preceding argument (public consumption benefits) is, of course, extremely difficult to quantify" and "these benefits may be large enough to offset the subsidy, even if the team has no net effect on local economic activity, although quantifying them is extremely difficult. Most likely, these consumer benefits presumably are the real reason that cities are willing to spend so much on attracting and keeping a team."[39] However, academic researchers are making efforts in this direction toward measuring these noneconomic benefits.. Irani first estimated an attendance (demand for tickets) function using data on annual attendance for MLB teams and ticket prices. Then he estimated the consumer surplus, which is the difference between the maximum that consumers would be willing to pay for a good and what they actually do pay, from attendance for each MLB team. His results suggested that public subsidies of professional sports teams can often pass the cost-benefit test. However, estimates of the price of attending a game ignored some costs incurred by consumers, such as transportation costs, including the cost of the time of transportation, the opportunity cost of attending a game, and so on. Ignoring these components of the total price will reduce the reliability of his estimated consumers' surplus, and the reliability of his cost-benefit test. To avoid this problem and to correct this measurement error, Alexander, Kern, and Neil offered a second set of estimates of the private consumption benefits from attending games. They also evaluated the consumption benefits through the traditional welfare economics method: consumers' surplus. But their approach was based on the team's annual revenues from ticket sales and the price elasticity of attendance rather than ticket prices. The results of this benefit-cost test show that the magnitude of consumers' surplus depends substantially on the demand elasticity. Only if the demand elasticity is very inelastic, 0.5 or less, can the private consumption benefits justify the construction of baseball parks or football stadiums in the $300- to $400-million range. Though a number of demand studies have produced price elasticities less than 1, there are also estimates substantially greater than 1. So they concluded that for most franchises in the four major professional sports, the consumers' surplus may be insufficient to justify building a facility at public expense on benefit-cost grounds.[40]

Note their results are based on the cost of a facility between $300 and $400 million, which implies that we might have different results if the cost is below $300 million. In fact, according to Crompton, Howard, and Var, among fifty-three stadiums built between 1961 and 2003 eighteen stadiums cost more than $300 million and only five out of forty-seven arenas cost more than $300 million in real 2003 dollars.[41] So more research is needed focusing on a set of parallel ranges of facility costs and demand elasticities.

Another effort to measure intangible benefits uses the contingent valuation method (CVM) in a series of case studies.[42] All these case studies reach a consensus that the value of the public goods (one of the direct benefits, e.g., so-called civic pride, fan loyalty, or community spirit as a direct result form the presence of a team) is not sufficient to support the frequently made claims by the advocates of the sports stadiums. However, Johnson, Groothuis, and Whitehead raised some qualifications for these results.[43] For example, in the case study of Pittsburgh Penguins of the NHL, they argued that hockey remains the least popular of the four major league sports, even though Pittsburgh enjoys a reputation as a good hockey city. Also the results may not be representative of other cities.

Much like the evidence from economic-impact studies where positive impacts were found in some MSAs and sports while not in others, it is very possible that different sports in different cities may produce public good values large enough to justify the public subsidies. Nevertheless, using all major professional sports in Michigan and Minnesota, Owen argued that while aggregate willingness-to-pay (WTP) values are somewhat less than typical stadium subsidies, they are large enough to be considered an important factor in public funding for stadiums.[44]

A third approach to quantify intangible benefits applies hedonic models to real estate values.[45] It is a stylized fact that many nonmarket values from environmental amenities and disamenities, or demographic disamenities (e.g., crime), will be reflected in the local housing and labor markets. By using a hedonic model applied to the housing market, one can derive the demand for a particular attribute such as number of bathrooms, fireplace, or clean air or water. One can also measure the effect of each attribute on house prices through the coefficient estimate of each observable attribute in the hedonic model. Carlino and Coulson employed a hedonic model to measure the nonpecuniary benefits from the presence of NFL team in central cities and MSAs.[46] With two separate equations, one for rent and the other for wages, they controlled for city-fixed effects, time-fixed effects, a large number of time-varying city characteristics, and a large number of individual housing characteristics in the housing equation and individual demographic and employment characteristics in the wage equation. Their data are for the sixty largest MSAs over the period 1993–1999. The analysis was performed at three different levels of geographic aggregation: the city, the MSA, and the consolidated MSA (CMSA). Despite all of these controls, their results showed that the presence of an NFL team raises annual housing rents by approximately 8 percent in central cities; this effect is robust to any respecification of the model by adding or removing certain variables. Annual housing rents increase by approximately 4 percent over the entire CMSA but the increase was not statistically significant. When many different specifications of the model were estimated using MSA and CMSA level data as they did for city level data, the NFL effects on rents were positive and significant at both MSA and CMSA levels. None of their regressions has an R^2 more than 0.3, which indicates poor model explanatory power; therefore one should be careful when drawing conclusions from their results as they may not be useful for justifying public subsidies. Coates, Humphreys, and Zimbalist found that Carlino and Coulson's results are sensitive to both sample and model specifications.[47] For example, after dropping only six zero-log-rent observations none of the coefficients on the NFL indicator variables were significant under five alternative model specifications. Also Carlino and Coulson failed to consider the spatial heterogeneity in their cross-sectional metropolitan data. To correct on this, one needs to use a smaller unit of observation, such as census tracts or block groups. One also needs to incorporate spatial information into the model.

Tu used a hedonic housing price model to investigate the impact of FedEx Field, home of the NFL's Washington Redskins, on housing values for houses in Prince George's County, Maryland.[48] Although a traditional hedonic model seemed to show that FedEx Field had a negative impact on property values within a one-mile and two-mile radius of the stadium, the lower values in the impact area may have been the cause, not the effect, of the location selection of FedEx Field. This assertion was justified by a difference-in-difference approach that the value of a property inside the impact area was lower than that of a comparable unit outside the area even before the site was selected for this stadium. By comparing the price differentials between properties in and out of the impact area over the predevelopment, development, and postdevelopment periods, the difference-in-difference approach showed that the price differentials were narrowed after the announcement of site selection and further reduced after the stadium was completed. This indicated that the construction of the stadium actually improved the housing prices in the surrounding area. The impact was minimal when the property was more than 2.5 miles away from the stadium. Tu estimated that the aggregate increase in property value after the completion of FedEx Field was approximately $42 million based on the average home price in Prince George's County, but failed to incorporate spatial dependence, which exists in cross-sectional data, into the model. Also the aggregate increase in property value is only a part of the intangible benefits that residents might enjoy from the stadium. To get a more precise estimate of the intangible benefits, one needs to calculate the total WTP for all households in the sample. More case studies along this direction will provide more insights into the literature of measuring intangible benefits.

Dehring, Depken, and Ward investigated two sets of stadium announcements about a new stadium for the NFL's Dallas Cowboys. One was a proposal to build a new stadium in Dallas Fair Park, which was ultimately abandoned. The other was a proposal to build a stadium in Arlington, which was confirmed. They employed a standard hedonic housing price model to estimate the effects of these announcements. For the Dallas Fair Park case, they found that property values increased near Dallas Fair Park after the announcement of the new stadium proposal. However, in Dallas County, which would have paid for the stadium with a sales tax increased of 0.5 percent, residential property values decreased after the announcement. These patterns were reversed when the proposal was abandoned. The three announcements concerning the stadium proposal in Arlington all had a negative impact on property values but each was individually insignificant. However, the aggregate impact of the three announcements was negative and statistically significant. The accumulated net impact corresponded to a 1.5 percent decline in property values in Arlington, which is almost equal to the anticipated household sales tax burden. Their results differ from Tu, who found a positive amenity effect for properties located within three miles of FedEx Field. Again, both models may be misspecified due to spatial auto-correlation in the individual housing data, thus their estimates may be biased.[49]

Although nonpecuniary impacts from sports facilities and teams attract increased attention from both policymakers and academic researchers, most studies focusing on these benefits are descriptive. Still, efforts are being made to quantify them. The traditional welfare economic analysis and the CVM approach have been used to perform cost-benefit analyses to justify the public financing of the sports facilities construction.[50] Their results show that the intangible benefits alone are not large enough to justify the public subsidies. Using a hedonic price model, both Carlino and Coulson and Tu showed that the presence of a NFL team and its stadium will increase the housing value. But they did not calculate the total WTP for all the households to perform a cost-benefit.[51] As discussed previously, some other problems exist in these two papers. We will discuss the methodological issues in detail in the next section.

METHODOLOGY MATTERS

Why do researchers reach different conclusions when estimating the economic and noneconomic impacts from the same sports teams and facilities? Despite differences in data and scope, such as type of sports, number of MSAs studied, or time periods, the key reason is that the methodology matters and contributes to the differences in the results. Economic impact studies can be broadly divided into two categories. One is prospective and *ex ante,* using regional input-output models carried out using IMPLAN. The other is retrospective and *ex post,* using econometric models with past data. The same reason applies when evaluating the economic impacts of sports facilities and events. While regional input-output models are frequently used when identifying crucial industries in an area and quantifying the economic impact of policies in the regional science literature, these models are often criticized for restrictive assumptions, for example, constant proportions between inputs and output, between labor and output, and between value added and output. In the application to sports facilities and events, the input-output model is often misused. A review paper identified eleven frequently committed misapplications in an attempt to bring them to the attention of sports managers who may be responsible for commissioning, interpreting, or evaluating the economic studies.[52] It is these misapplications, and unreasonable assumptions underlying the methodologies, that lead to different results between the prospective studies generating substantial positive economic impacts and retrospective studies providing little or even negative impacts. In their recent survey paper, Siegfried and Zimbalist also discussed some methodological problems found in a number of "economic impact studies" that claim large positive economic benefits from sports facilities.[53] The following misapplications contribute to the discrepancy between the two literatures:

1. *Misrepresentation of the employment multiplier.* Employment multipliers show the number of full-time equivalent (FTE) jobs attributable to visitor expenditure. But in reality many of the jobs created are short-term or part-time. In some cases additional labor demand can be met by greater

utilization of the existing labor force, especially in the case of "one-off" sports events, so they are unlikely to generate permanent employment increases due to their short-term nature. This also provides an explanation for the lack of empirical evidence supporting employment growth in the academic literature. These part-time or short-term jobs are usually low paid. This might answer the question how sports facilities and teams can reduce the per capita income level in a MSA. Careful implementation in IMPLAN with detailed data on the number of jobs created and labor income will produce a good estimate of the size of this effect. For example, a large portion of total employment impact from sports events is in the services and restaurant and bar sectors. However, earnings per worker in these sectors are usually low, which might drag down the average income per worker. So it is not accurate to treat both full-time and part-time jobs as the same in IMPLAN.

2. *Failure to define the study area accurately.* Crompton pointed out that changes in geographic boundaries of the study may lead to changes in multiplier size because the magnitude of a multiplier depends on the economic structure of the host community. Conventional wisdom holds that the larger the defined area's economic base, the larger the value added from the original expenditures and the smaller the leakage that is likely to occur. Most professional sports are located in large MSAs, and the revenues the franchise receives tend to stay in the MSAs.[54] Because of this, IMPLAN will generate large income and employment multipliers. However, the empirical studies using MSA income and employment data generally fail to support the results from IMPLAN studies. This is because IMPLAN ignores the nature of the assumption about the relationship between multiplier magnitude and the size of geographic area. On one hand, the larger the study area, the less leakage. On the other hand, it is not expected that spillover effects generated from sports facilities and events located in central cities will spread over to the distant suburbs, because the spillover effects are distance decaying. Sometimes, instead of net spillover effects from urban city to suburbs, there might be net backwash effects from central city to suburbs.[55] In the case of net backwash effects, central cities grow while the suburbs decline because cities draw business and employment away from the suburbs. Therefore, as a whole we might observe a net zero effect from the presence of a professional sports franchise in the MSA. This may explain why empirical studies with MSA as their geographic unit of analysis generally do not find any positive impacts from stadiums and teams. As mentioned earlier, future empirical research on economic impact of sports facilities and teams can explore ways to separate the effects of sports on the city and the effects on the suburbs within a MSA to test this hypothesis.

3. *Inclusion of local spectators.* Many IMPLAN studies include local expenditures because the multipliers become unacceptably small to those commissioning the studies if local expenditures are excluded. However, this inclusion is incorrect. Only new spending that is added into the economy can be counted when implementing an economic impact analysis, that is, only expenditures by visitors from outside of the host community can be included. The expenditures by local spectators are just a recycling of existing expenditure because of the substitution effect discussed above. This is also what academic researchers use to explain their results of little or even negative direct impacts from sports. By excluding these local expenditures, the multiplier effects should not be as large as most prospective studies report and this is consistent with the findings from academic studies. The meta-analysis by Hudson showed that including local expenditures had a significant positive effect on the estimated economic impact in IMPLAN-based studies.[56]

4. *Inclusion of "timeswitchers" and "casuals."*[57] This is also a large source of misuse in IMPLAN. Including these consumers is statistically significant in the meta-analysis by Hudson, which implies it is a major source of variation in the results in impact studies.[58] While this could be controlled for by collecting data through surveys when conducting an impact study using IMPLAN, it would be difficult in empirical studies to control for the variables that also induce visitor expenditures besides the presence of a sports event, for example, visitor spending due to a business trip.

5. *Omission of opportunity cost.* The most criticized drawback of regional input-output models is the omission of costs and focus only on economic benefits: no benefit-cost analysis or mention of the opportunity cost.

Noneconomic impact studies also can be grouped into two categories based on the methodology employed. Generally there are two basic methods to quantify the intangible benefits or nonmarket values of public goods. One is the stated preference approach (e.g., CVM), and the other is the revealed preference approach, which includes the standard hedonic approach. Both Rappaport and Wilkerson and Crompton suggest CVM as an appropriate approach for measuring the improved quality of life or intangible benefits generated by a professional sports franchise.[59] But one should be very careful when employing this method because there are quite a few sources of bias in the responses to CVM surveys, such as interviewer bias, information bias, instrument bias, scope effect, embedding effect, sequencing effect, and other biases in sample selection.

Johnson, Mondello, and Whitehead applied CVM to the case of keeping an NFL team and attracting an NBA team to Jacksonville, Florida, using both a temporal embedding effect and an ordering effect. Temporal embedding exists if survey respondents do not differentiate between payment-period lengths and leads to unrealistic implicit discount rates.[60] This study elicited annual payments over two different periods, five and ten years, for the NFL team and potential NBA team in Jacksonville. Their research shows that the total WTP in the ten-year period is less than twice the total WTP in the five-year payment period, which implies that WTP estimates from respondents are sensitive to the length of payment period. They find no evidence of temporal embedding effect. Ordering effects exist if WTP varies widely with the order in which the question appears on the survey.[61] Their study finds no ordering effects in the NFL models but possible ordering effect in the NBA model in that the probability of a positive WTP is greater when the NBA team and or arena appears first in the valuation sequence. This might be due to lack of experience with an NBA team, leading to an increased WTP when aggregated to total WTP. This calls attention to various bias issues inherent in CVM-based measures of intangible benefits from sports facilities and teams.

To avoid the potential problems with the CVM approach, one could employ a standard hedonic price model to measure intangible benefits. The hedonic model is a well-established approach in environmental evaluation. It has been employed to investigate the effects of natural amenities such as open space and green belts, disamenities such as air or water pollution, the presence of nuclear power plants, or an event such as the cleanup of a toxic waste site, as well as neighborhood characteristics such as crime or school quality.

The intangible benefits provided by sports facilities and teams as public goods have been discussed above. Rappaport and Wilkerson also suggested the hedonic method to measure the improved quality of life, but to date it has only been used by Carlino and Coulson, Tu, and Dehring, Depken and Ward.[62] But, as discussed above, the results from these three studies are mixed. The most important drawback in this approach, and most other hedonic applications, is the neglect of spatial autocorrelation. It is well established that spatial effects (spatial dependence and spatial heterogeneity) exist in most cross-sectional geographic data. Ignoring these spatial effects in econometric modeling will lead to model misspecification and biased estimates.[63] Some studies have shown that there is significant spatial autocorrelation in the housing market.[64] Future research in measuring non-economic impacts using hedonic model should explicitly incorporate spatial effects.

CONCLUSION

This chapter reviewed economic impact studies using both regional input-output methods and econometric methods to evaluate the effects of sports facilities and teams. The assumptions and methodologies underlying these two approaches matter in that they lead to different conclusions about the economic impact of sports facilities. This is why the two streams of literature produce different results. Prospective studies conducted by consulting firms using input-output models usually generate large multiplier effects while retrospective studies by academic researchers provide little evidence of positive effects and even negative effects. Some explanations from both econometric studies and studies of methodology were discussed.[65] The conclusion from both is that the large impacts generated by the prospective studies may not be correct due to misapplication of regional input-output models, so local communities may not receive large, significant, positive economic impacts from sports in terms of income and employment. This finding implies that using sports as the engine of local economic development may not be a sound policy.

So why do cities compete to subsidize the sports-facility construction if there are no or little positive effects? Cities still compete to subsidize sports because of the monopoly power explicitly or implicitly given to professional sports leagues. When cities are faced with a choice of gaining or keeping a team with subsidies or losing it without subsidies, often a subsidized team may be a better choice. The threat of moving to an alternative city gives professional sports bargaining power in the negotiation for facility construction subsidies. So it has to be subsidized.

Professional sports facility construction may also be subsidized because professional sports facilities are public goods or quasi-public goods that generate nonmarket values to the public. Finally, professional sports obviously generate important noneconomic benefits. "Major-league city" status, civic pride, community collective conscience, and increased community visibility are all the important noneconomic benefits enjoyed by the residents of hosting communities. These intangible benefits are assumed to be capitalized into property values and may outweigh the costs. Finally, sports as a business alone can never be an engine of local economic development. However, its cultural importance and the intangible benefits it generates can be more important than its economic importance to residents of American cities.

NOTES

1. This number does not include the facilities currently under construction and the ones currently proposed as of 2006.

2. For example, in an economic impact study prepared for the proposed NFL stadium in Arlington, Texas, they claim that construction alone would create 2,222 new jobs for Tarrant County and the annual ongoing operations would create 983 jobs. Economic Research Associates, "Economic and Fiscal Impacts for the Proposed NFL

Stadium in Arlington, Texas," ERA Project No. 15652, Prepared for City of Arlington, 2004.

3. Robert A. Baade and Richard F. Dye, "The Impact of Stadiums and Professional Sports on Metropolitan Area Development," *Growth and Change* (Spring 1990): 1–14; Robert A. Baade, "Professional Sports as Catalyst for Metropolitan Economic Development," *Journal of Urban Affairs* 18, no. 1 (1996): 1–17; Dennis Coates and Brad R. Humphreys, "The Growth Effects of Sports Franchises, Stadiums, and Arenas," *Journal of Policy Analysis and Management* 18, no. 4 (1999): 601–624; Dennis Coates and Brad R. Humphreys, "The Effect of Professional Sports on Earnings and Employment in the Services and Retail Sectors in U.S. Cities," *Regional Science and Urban Economics* 33 (2003): 175–198; John Siegfried and Andrew Zimbalist, "The Economics of Sports Facilities and Their Communities," *Journal of Economics Perspectives* 14, no. 3 (2000): 95–114.

4. The numbers provided here are as of April 2006. The nominal dollars for each stadium and arena from 1961 to 2003 are from John L. Crompton, Dennis E. Howard, and T. Var, "Financing Major League Facilities: Status, Evolution and Conflicting Forces," *Journal of Sports Management* 17 (2003): 156–184. The nominal cost for stadiums and arenas after 2003 is from the Ballparks Web site maintained by Munsey and Suppes, http://www.ballparks.com/index.html. The construction cost index is from *Engineering News-Record,* March 20, 2006, with the base year 1913 = 100.

5. John Crompton, "Beyond Economic Impact: an Alternative Rationale for the Public Subsidy of Major League Sports Facilities," *Journal of Sports Management* 18 (2004): 40–58; Rick Eckstein and Kevin Delaney, "New Sports Stadiums, Community Self-esteem, and Community Collective Conscience," *Journal of Sports and Social Issues* 26, no. 3 (2002): 235–247; Peter A. Groothuis, Bruce K. Johnson, and John C. Whitehead, "Public Funding of Professional Sports Stadiums: Public Choice or Civic Pride?" *Eastern Economic Journal* 30, no. 4 (2004): 515–528; Roger G. Noll and Andrew Zimbalist, "The Economic Impact of Sports Teams and Facilities," in *Sports, Jobs, and Taxes*, ed. Roger G. Noll and Andrew Zimbalist (Washington, D.C.: Brookings Institution Press, 1997); Jordan Rappaport and Chad Wilkerson, "What Are the Benefits of Hosting a Major League Sports Franchise?" *Economic Review (Federal Reserve Bank of Kansas City)* (2001); Mark S. Rosentraub, "Does the Emperor Have New Clothes? A Reply to Robert J. Baade," *Journal of Urban Affairs* 18, no. 1 (1996): 23–31.

6. Of course, the admission of more persons into a stadium is up to the seating capacity of the facility. Beyond the seating capacity, the admission of one more person into a stadium would induce negative effects on other persons. This case is similar to the case of highway, which is viewed as a public good.

7. Usually business enjoys a tremendous economic benefit from the presence of a professional sports team, especially the industries like retail and services. But some businesses enjoy noneconomic benefits, too.

8. James Quirk and Rodney D. Fort, *Pay Dirt: The Business of Professional Team Sports* (Princeton, N.J.: Princeton University Press, 1992).

9. There are currently thirty-two NFL teams, thirty NBA teams, thirty MLB teams, and thirty NHL teams playing in sixty-one cities.

10. James Quirk and Rodney D. Fort, *Hard Ball: The Abuse of Power in Pro Team Sports* (Princeton, N.J.: Princeton University Press, 1999).

11. Robert A. Baade and Allen R. Sanderson, "The Employment Effect of Teams and Sports Facilities," in *Sports, Jobs, and Taxes*, ed. Noll and Zimbalist.

12. Jeffrey G. Owen, "The Stadium Game: Cities vs. Teams," *Journal of Sports Economics* 4, no. 3 (2003): 183–202. The subsidy in Owen's model is the difference between the largest profit a team could earn in a city without a team minus the operating profit a team earns in its current city. So larger cities pay smaller subsidies and may not pay anything because as their size gives teams larger profit potential such that the profit a team can earn there exceeds the threat point.

13. C. H. Johnson Consulting, Inc., "Economic Impact Analysis of the Proposed Ballpark for the Boston Red Sox," prepared for the Greater Boston Convention and Visitors Bureau and the Greater Boston Chamber of Commerce, 1999.

14. Ian Hudson, "The Use and Misuse of Economic Impact Analysis: The Case of Professional Sports," *Journal of Sport and Social Issues* 25, no.1 (2001): 20–39.

15. John P. Blair and David W. Swindell, "Sports, Politics, and Economics: The Cincinnati Story," in *Sports, Jobs, and Taxes*, ed. Noll and Zimbalist; Ian Hudson, "Bright Lights, Big City: Do Professional Sports Teams Increase Employment?" *Journal of Urban Affairs* 21, no. 4 (1999): 397–407; Bruce K. Johnson and John C. Whitehead, "Value of Public Goods from Sports Stadiums: The CVM Approach," *Contemporary Economic Policy* 18, no. 1 (2000): 48–58; Bruce K. Johnson, Peter A. Groothuis, and John C. Whitehead, "The Value of Public Goods Generated by a Major League Sports Team: CVM," *Journal of Sports Economics* 2, no. 1 (2001): 6–21; Mark Gius and Donn Johnson, "An Empirical Estimation of the Economic Impact of Major League Sports Teams on Cities," *Journal of Business & Economic Studies* 7, no. 1 (2001): 32–38l; Phillip A. Miller, "The Economic Impact of Sports Stadium Construction: The Case of the Construction Industry in St. Louis, MO," *Journal of Urban Affair* 24, no. 2 (2002): 159–173.

16. Baade and Dye, "Impact of Stadiums and Professional Sports."

17. Baade and Sanderson, "Employment Effect of Teams and Sports Facilities."

18. Coates and Humphreys, "The Growth Effects of Sports Franchises, Stadiums, and Arenas"; Hudson, "The Use and Misuse of Economic Impact Analysis."

19. Arthur C. Nelson, "Prosperity or Blight? A Question of Major League Stadiums Locations," *Economic Development Quarterly* 15, no. 3 (2001): 255–265.

20. Ibid.

21. Baade's "Professional Sports as Catalyst" suggests the pattern that in those MSAs where MSA income rose with respect to the number of stadiums, stadiums usually were located in the CBD, e.g., Indianapolis, Cincinnati, and Pittsburgh. In other MSAs where the correlation was negative, stadiums were located outside of the CBD.

22. Charles Santo, "The Economic Impact of Sports Stadiums: Recasting the Analysis in Context," *Journal of Urban Affairs* 27, no. 2 (2005): 177–191; Baade, "Professional Sports as Catalyst"; Baade and Dye, "The Impact of Stadiums and Professional Sports". Baade and Dye used only one stadium variable and made no distinction between football stadium and baseball stadium.

23. Nelson, "Prosperity or Blight?; Gius and Johnson, "Empirical Estimation of the Economic Impact."

24. Gerald A. Carlino and N. Edward Coulson, "Compensating Differentials and the Social Benefits of the NFL," *Journal of Urban Economics* 56, no. 1 (2004): 25–50;

Dennis Coates and Brad R. Humphreys, "Professional Sports Facilities, Franchises and Urban Economic Development," *Public Finance and Management* 3, no. 3 (2003): 1–23.

25. There should be several ways to express and measure people's willingness to pay for the presence of a major professional sports stadium and team in their community. They can pay it in the form of city tax, bonds, or directly through the purchase of season tickets, or indirectly through an increased willingness to accept a lower wage level. The nonpecuniary benefits will be discussed in detail in the next section as noneconomic impacts.

26. The core idea of the hedonic model is that the price of any differentiated good will be determined by the combination of its characteristics. It is called "hedonic" because it is determined by both the different qualities of the good and the "pleasure" (in economic terms, "utility") from these qualities. A house is a differentiated good; the price of a house is then determined by a number of housing characteristics and intangible characteristics associated with the house, such as environmental quality of the neighborhood the house is located in and so on.

27. However, their wage effect is not statistically significant. Carlino and Coulson, "Compensating Differentials and the Social Benefits of the NFL," also found that the presence of an NFL team raises annual house rents by approximately 8 percent. The effect on housing values will be discussed next since here we only address the reduced income level from the empirical studies.

28. Coates and Humphreys, "Professional Sports Facilities."

29. Coates and Humphreys found that a Super Bowl victory has a positive effect on the real per capita personal income in the city that is home to the winning team from the Super Bowl, perhaps reflecting a link between winning the Super Bowl and the productivity of workers in cities. See Dennis Coates and Brad R. Humphreys, "The Economic Impact of Postseason Play in Professional Sports," *Journal of Sports Economics* 3, no. 3 (2002): 291–299. M. C. Davis and C. M. End, "A Winning Proposition: The Economic Impact of Successful NFL Franchises," Working paper, Department of Economics and Finance, University of Missouri–Rolla, 2006.

30. Coates and Humphreys, "Economic Impact of Postseason Play"; Coates and Humphreys, "Professional Sports Facilities."

31. Davis and End, "Winning Proposition"; H. Berument and E. M. Yucel, "Long Live Fenerbache: The Production Boosting Effects of Football," *Journal of Economic Psychology* 26, no. 6 (2005): 842–861.

32. Siegfried and Zimbalist, "Economics of Sports Facilities."

33. Coates and Humphreys, "Growth Effects of Sports Franchises"; Coates and Humphreys, "Effect of Professional Sports on Earnings and Employment." They tested the effects of sports on the employment and employment share of one-digit sectors Services (SIC 7) and Retail Trade (SIC 5), earnings of two-digit sectors Amusements and Recreation (SIC 79), Hotels and Other Lodging Places (SIC 70), and Eating, Drinking Establishments (SIC 58).

34. Note tax revenues are discussed only in the prospective studies by the consulting firms. The academic research mostly focuses on income and employment.

35. Crompton, "Beyond Economic Impact"; Eckstein and Delaney, "New Sports Stadiums"; Groothuis, Johnson, and Whitehead, "Public Funding of Professional Sports

Stadiums"; Noll and Zimbalist, "Economic Impact of Sports Teams and Facilities"; Rappaport and Wilkerson, "What Are the Benefits of Hosting a Major League Sports Franchise?"; Rosentraub, "Does the Emperor Have New Clothes?"; Siegfried and Zimbalist, "Economics of Sports Facilities."

36. Rosentraub, "Does the Emperor Have New Clothes?" 27; Baade, "Professional Sports as Catalyst"; Noll and Zimbalist, "Economic Impact of Sports Teams and Facilities"; Robert A. Baade, "Stadium Subsidies Make Little Economic Sense for Cities, a Rejoinder," *Journal of Urban Affairs* 18, no. 1 (1996): 33–37.

37. Noll and Zimbalist, "Economic Impact of Sports Teams and Facilities"; Siegfried and Zimbalist, "Economics of Sports Facilities"; Crompton, "Beyond Economic Impact"; Eckstein and Delaney, "New Sports Stadiums"; Rosentraub, "Does the Emperor Have New Clothes?"; Groothuis, Johnson, and Whitehead, "Public Funding of Professional Sports Stadiums."

38. Rappaport and Wilkerson, "What Are the Benefits of Hosting a Major League Sports Franchise?"

39. Noll and Zimbalist, "Economic Impact of Sports Teams and Facilities," 58, 97.

40. D. Irani, "Public Subsidies to Stadiums: Do the Costs Outweigh the Benefits?" *Public Finance Review* 25, no. 2 (1997): 238–253; Donald L. Alexander, William Kern, and Jon Neil, "Valuing Consumption Benefits from Professional Sports Franchises," *Journal of Urban Economics* 48 (2000): 321–337.

41. Crompton, Howard, and Var, "Financing Major League Facilities," 156–184.

42. Bruce K. Johnson, Michael J. Mondello, and John C. Whitehead, "Contingent Valuation of Sports: Temporal Embedding and Ordering Effects," *Journal of Sports Economics* 6, no. 2 (2005): 1–23. The contingent valuation method (CVM) involves directly asking people, in a survey, how much they would be willing to pay for specific goods and services. In some cases, people are asked for the compensation they would be willing to accept to give up specific goods and services. It is called "contingent" valuation because people are asked to state their willingness to pay, contingent on a specific hypothetical scenario and description of the goods and services. We will only discuss the empirical results and evidence from these studies here. The CVM methodology will be discussed in the next section on methodology.

43. Johnson, Groothuis, and Whitehead, "Value of Public Goods Generated by a Major League Sports Team."

44. Owen, "The Stadium Game."

45. Charles C. Tu, "How Does a New Sports Stadium Affect Housing Values? The Case of FedEx Field," *Land Economics* 81, no. 3 (2005): 379–395; C. A. Dehring, Craig A. Depken, and M. R. Ward, "The Impact of Stadium Announcements on Residential Property Values: Evidence from a Natural Experiment in Dallas–Fort Worth," Working Paper, Department of Economics at University of Texas at Arlington, 2006.

46. Carlino and Coulson, "Compensating Differentials and the Social Benefits of the NFL."

47. Dennis D. Coates, Brad R. Humphreys, and Andrew Zimbalist, "Compensating Differentials and the Social Benefits of the NFL—A Comment," *Journal of Urban Economics* 60, no. 1 (2006): 124–131; Carlino and Coulson, "Compensating Differentials and the Social Benefits of the NFL."

48. Tu, "How Does a New Sports Stadium Affect Housing Values?"

49. Dehring, Depken, and Ward, "Impact of Stadium Announcements on Residential Property Value"; Tu, "How Does a New Sports Stadium Affect Housing Values?"

50. Irani, "Public Subsidies to Stadiums"; Alexander, Kern, and Neil, "Valuing Consumption Benefits from Professional Sports Franchises."

51. Carlino and Coulson, "Compensating Differentials and the Social Benefits of the NFL"; Tu, "How Does a New Sports Stadium Affect Housing Values?"

52. We will not discuss all of the eleven sources of misapplications here but just several most criticized misuses. For a full reference, please refer to John L. Crompton, "Economic Impact Analysis of Sports Facilities and Events: Eleven Sources of Misapplication," *Journal of Sports Management* 9 (1995). The eleven sources are (1) using sales instead of household income multipliers; (2) misrepresentation of employment multipliers; (3) using incremental instead of normal multiplier coefficients; (4) failure to define the area of interest accurately; (5) inclusion of local spectators; (6) failure to exclude "time-switchers" and "casuals"; (7) use of "fudged" multipliers coefficients; (8) claiming total instead of marginal economic benefits; (9) confusion of turnover and multiplier; (10) omission of opportunity cost; and (11) measurement only of benefits: omitting costs.

53. Siegfried and Zimbalist, "Economics of Sports Facilities."

54. Crompton, "Economic Impact Analysis of Sports Facilities and Events." But there might be cases that the owners may not be from the MSA, and the players may not live in the city too. So when implementing IMPLAN, it is best to define the study area case by case. There is no general rule.

55. In the regional growth literature, there are two types of spillover effects, namely spread effects and backwash effects. The former exists when we observe the growth in urban core stimulate the growth in the suburbs within a MSA. The latter exists when we observe the growth in urban core lead to a decline in the suburbs. Usually there are mixed effects of these two types when investigating their economic growth. If the former dominates the latter, then we say there is a net spread effect from urban core to suburbs, otherwise a net backwash effect.

56. Hudson, "Use and Misuse of Economic Impact Analysis."

57. "Time-switchers" refer to visitors at a sports event who may have been planning a visit to the community for a long time but changed the timing of their visit to coincide with the event. So their spending cannot be attributed to the event, because it would have been made without the event at a different time of the year. "Casuals" refer to visitors at a sports event who may already have been in the community, attracted by other features, and may have elected to go to the sports event instead of doing something else. Their spending also cannot be attributed to the event, because it would have occurred without the event, too.

Opportunity cost has been discussed earlier when explaining why we have little or even negative impacts.

58. Hudson, "Use and Misuse of Economic Impact Analysis."

59. Rappaport and Wilkerson, "What Are the Benefits of Hosting a Major League Sports Franchise?"; Crompton, "Beyond Economic Impact."

60. Johnson, Mondello, and Whitehead, "Contingent Valuation of Sports." Embedding effect occurs when comparing the values of two goods with one of which is embedded in the other. Studies find that the good is assigned a smaller value if the question

asking WTP for this good is embedded in a question asking WTP for a more inclusive good. The same good is assigned a higher value if WTP for it is evaluated independently.

61. Generally, WTP for a particular good valued at the end of a long sequence is less than WTP for the same good values independently or at the top of a sequence.

62. Rappaport and Wilkerson, "What Are the Benefits of Hosting a Major League Sports Franchise?"; Carlino and Coulson, "Compensating Differentials and the Social Benefits of the NFL"; Tu, "How Does a New Sports Stadium Affect Housing Values?"; and Dehring, Depken and Ward, "Impact of Stadium Announcements."

63. Luc Anselin, *Spatial Econometrics: Methods and Models* (Boston: Kluwer Academic, 1988).

64. S. Basu and T. G. Thibodeau, "Analysis of Spatial Autocorrelation in House Prices," *Journal of Real Estate Finance and Economics* 17, no. 1 (1998): 61–85; C. W. Kim, T. T. Phipps, and L. Anselin, "Measuring the Benefits of Air Quality Improvement: A Spatial Hedonic Approach," *Journal of Environmental Economics and Management* 45, no. 1 (2003): 24–39.

65. Coates and Humphreys, "Effect of Professional Sports on Earnings and Employment"; Gius and Johnson, "An Empirical Estimation of the Economic Impact of Major League Sports Teams on Cities"; Hudson, "Use and Misuse of Economic Impact Analysis"; Nelson, "Prosperity or Blight?"; Crompton, "Economic Impact Analysis of Sports Facilities and Events."

Seven

Pay and Performance of Players in Sports Leagues: International Comparisons

Bernd Frick and Rob Simmons

This chapter will analyze the relationship between pay and performance of professional sports players on teams located in Europe and in North America. Among the sports that we will survey will be American football (the National Football League, henceforth NFL), Major League Baseball (henceforth MLB), and European soccer. We shall examine the relationship between salary and performance at individual player level, in which we seek to isolate the main economic and sporting determinants of salary. We shall also show how player salaries have evolved in relation to revenue growth in major sports, especially broadcasting revenues.

The chapter will reveal some critical differences between professional player labor markets in North America and Europe. North American labor markets are characterized by closed structures with few imports from overseas. They are also highly regulated, a feature that generates market power for team owners and helps hold down salaries of many players below their contributions to team revenues. The small number of professional franchises in major North American leagues (generally just over thirty in any league) also contributes to buyer power in the player labor market.

In contrast, labor markets in European football have much fewer restrictions, and opportunities to move between leagues are much greater, especially with the European Union (EU) countries where freedom of labor to move is a central tenet.

The chapter unfolds as follows. We begin by establishing some basic theory to show how salaries of professional team players might be determined. We then compare labor market structures in Europe and North

America. Given these analytical foundations, we can assess the now considerable empirical evidence on player earnings. The last three sections look at particular issues in player labor markets. We examine the role of player transfers for cash in European football. We assess the evidence on relationships between career duration, contract length and player salary in an occupation that is inherently risky, since players can be cut from their teams and may also suffer long-term injuries. The last issue to consider is the extent to which forms of discrimination against ethnic minorities persist in modern sports leagues.

THEORY

A convenient starting point for an analysis of pay determination of team sports players is the *marginal productivity theory*, which is the workhorse of modern labor economics. In this theory, firms (teams) demand (hire) labor to produce output (team wins). Players are then workers who supply labor services. These players produce team wins in conjunction with other inputs (coaches, training facilities). Players participate in games, viewing of which is purchased by spectators at the stadium or through media broadcasting. Marginal productivity theory predicts that profit-maximizing teams will pay players a salary equal to their marginal revenue product.

Hence the marginal revenue product of an extra player is the marginal revenue of one more win to the team multiplied by the marginal contribution of the player to wins. Note that this makes revenues a function of wins and not matches; losses do not count toward revenue.

Conventional economics assumes diminishing returns in production. Adding extra players will generate more wins but at a decreasing rate. Then, if the market for players is perfectly competitive without restrictions, market forces will ensure that the wage paid to a player will equal his marginal revenue product. From this principle, it can be deduced that professional sports players are highly paid because their marginal revenue products are high. In contrast, teachers are paid much less because, although they are more productive, the prices of the output they produce are low. Alternatively, teachers may have high output prices, for example, in private schools, but their marginal product of labor could be low. Equivalently, for sports stars, high salaries could be a reflection of high product prices (high marginal revenue product of wins) rather than high ability to convert playing effort into wins. This raises the question of whether celebrity players can generate high salaries from their marginal revenue product, independent of their ability to generate wins. For example, a Chinese footballer on an English Premier

League team's roster might generate high levels of merchandise sales in Asia. However, it is unlikely that players would be selected for teams just because they have high celebrity appeal in mass markets. High marginal physical product (impact of players on wins) is a prerequisite for high marginal revenue product. Moreover, celebrity appeal would diminish if the player was revealed to be unsuccessful in helping his team win matches.

It is not surprising that high potential earnings in major sports such as soccer, baseball, and American football induce many youngsters to try to gain entry into leagues. Even in minor-league baseball and lower-division soccer, typical earnings will exceed what players might earn in their next best occupations. In general, increased player earnings will encourage more potential candidates to attempt to join the professional ranks. It is worth noting, though, that some players can substitute between different sports. In the 1990s the West Indies cricket team lost their high-ranking status in Test cricket as potential cricketers turned to more lucrative sports such as baseball and basketball.

At this point, the term "supply" needs further clarification. The number of players on the field at any time in a given sport will be fixed, and team rosters will be fixed in size, either by league rules (as in the NFL) or by convention (as in soccer). The treatment of supply in sports economics then switches from number of players to the less easily measured concept of "talent." Many players are available to play professional sports but few have the requisite talent. In some sports and in some specialist positions on sports teams, size becomes an important factor. Basketball players need to be tall while linemen in American football need to be strong and bulky. David Berri, Stacey Brook, Bernd Frick, Aju Fenn, and Roberto Vicente-Mayoral point to the "short supply of tall people" in basketball as a key factor driving up player earnings in the National Basketball Association (NBA).[1]

In a competitive market, the supply of talent should be upward sloping or vertical in wage-talent space while the demand for talent is downward sloping. In market equilibrium, demand for players should match supply and the resulting salaries should reflect this.

The competitive theory does deliver some sensible predictions. If there is an increase in available talent due, for example, to more lenient rules governing work permits for foreign-born players, the supply of talent schedule shifts to the right in wage-talent space. Player salaries will fall and units of talent (player quality) will increase, which will be more attractive to fans. If there is an increase in value of broadcasting rights, then the demand for talent schedule, derived from marginal revenue product, will shift to the right. Player salaries will increase and units of talent will also rise. Again this will attract bigger audiences but clubs will face increased player costs.

In major sports leagues, the number of teams or franchises will typically be limited. In North America, there are only thirty-two MLB and thirty-two NFL franchises. Entry into these leagues requires large payments by incoming teams and approval by incumbent clubs, which will be concerned about loss of profits as the league expands. Premier divisions of European soccer leagues contain eighteen or twenty clubs, although some entry is assured by the system of promotion and relegation. Typically, three clubs are promoted and three are relegated each season. Germany has thirty-six professional clubs in two divisions with a semiprofessional league of two divisions below this. England's soccer league is unusually large with a hierarchy of ninety-two teams in four divisions. Overall, this means that the number of professional clubs is fairly small and this confers some buying power for teams in the player labor market. But players themselves have some specialized ability. Players are neither completely homogenous nor completely specialized. This creates a situation of bilateral monopoly in which players and teams share a surplus or economic rent. Only a few players who are sufficiently differentiated can shift surpluses (rents) completely into salaries; these players will tend to be the "superstars" of their sports. With bargaining over salaries between team owners and players (or rather their agents), wages will generally fall between marginal revenue product and lowest wage that would induce players to remain professionals. The greater the bargaining power for players, the closer salaries will move toward marginal revenue products. But restrictions on entry into leagues, and a small number of professional teams, will ensure that salaries lie below marginal revenue product.

One plausible rationale for underpayment of players relative to marginal revenue product is that players enjoy rising salaries over their careers as they establish themselves as professionals. But teams may incur costs of training and development. Training tends to be fairly common in style and methods across teams, and only a small proportion could be thought of as specific to the team. An example of *firm-specific training* is the playbook used by NFL teams. This playbook has plays that are specific in design to a team. But most training is transferable. Actually, the team playbook is also transferable as players can memorize the plays and translate them into other teams' game strategies. In the early years of player careers, players implicitly pay for some of the costs of training with salaries that are below marginal revenue product. In later years, assuming they survive in the league, players receive salaries in excess of marginal revenue product both as compensation for earlier underpayment and as an incentive to reject bids for services from rival teams. But this theory of seniority does not match some sports leagues too well. NFL teams rely on the college football system to generate player talent and allocate this talent to teams through the reverse-order draft system in which the worst-performing teams get first picks of the crop of emerging college talent.

MLB teams rely on minor-league teams to develop their players. Anthony Krautmann, Elizabeth Gustafson, and Lawrence Hadley found that, although restricted players received pay below marginal revenue product, MLB team owners could only recover around 50 percent of their training costs.[2] Unfortunately, estimates of training costs and associated comparisons of salary and marginal revenue product are not available for European football. It is notable, though, that top-division teams have expanded their training facilities over the last decade and have simultaneously begun to use "nursery teams" in a manner similar to the use of minor-league teams by MLB.

The theory of bilateral monopoly seems particularly well suited to the NFL, which is a closed league of thirty-two teams. This league has a "thin" labor market and the properties of such a market are clearly explained by Michael Leeds and Sandra Kowalewski.[3] Bilateral monopoly is less relevant for European soccer leagues because players are potentially mobile across many leagues, the number of potential buying teams is much greater than for NFL and MLB, and players can sort themselves into hierarchical divisions on the basis of ability. In North American leagues, some buyer power is observed partly because the number of teams is small but also because, as the next section shows, there are considerable restrictions on free agency. In European soccer, free agency is much more advanced and the barriers to mobility that persist are largely due to culture and language.

An advantage enjoyed by researchers investigating labor market issues is that a wealth of performance and salary data are readily available, especially for North American sports, where salaries are comprehensively reported by *USA Today* and posted on Web sites. Gerald Scully developed a pioneering method for comparing salaries of baseball players to their marginal revenue products.[4] This method modeled the relationship among team performance, team revenues, and players' contribution to team performance.

Anthony Krautmann notes several problems with this method and proposes an alternative.[5] Essentially, the player's contribution to the team's performance is assumed to be separable from other inputs. Even if we accept that, for baseball, the primary action is well defined with one batter facing one pitcher at any time (although not for the whole game), so individual performances are clearly measured, it remains the case that teammates and coaches can raise player performance. This complementarity means that marginal revenue product will be estimated with upward bias (since the contribution of other players and coaches is ignored). Krautmann's alternative method is to assume that free agents in baseball receive their marginal revenue product and then use this as a benchmark to assess the shortfall of restricted players' salaries from their marginal revenue product. Thus, Kraut-mann's method assumes that free agents are paid correctly according to marginal revenue product while players who are tied to their teams are paid below their marginal revenue product.

Although an improvement upon Scully's method, Krautmann's alternative assumes what needs to be proved, namely, that free agents are actually paid according to marginal revenue product. A recent contribution by John Burger and Stephen Walters suggests that some MLB free agents may actually be overpaid, that is, receive salaries *greater* than marginal revenue product.[6] This is due to a winners' curse in which teams systematically overbid for free agents. As they point out, this overbidding ought to be eradicated over time as teams learn from their mistakes. Also, the lack of commercial judgment inherent in overbidding is at odds with the example of the Oakland A's baseball team highlighted in a famous popular book by Michael Lewis, *Moneyball*.[7] In this example, Oakland hired specialist baseball analysts to improve their performance. Their chosen strategy was to emphasize more selective hitting and "walks" by batters. Basically, this means leaving the ball alone unless there is a strong enough chance that it can be hit. This strategy successfully raised Oakland's performance but only temporarily. Other teams copied Oakland's strategy. In the process the initial salary advantage for batters practicing the skills utilized by Oakland was eroded fairly quickly by market forces, as shown by Jahn Hakes and Raymond Sauer.[8] The *Moneyball* experience stands in sharp contrast to the apparent irrational behavior implied by overbidding in the winners' curse.

Many European soccer fans will readily identify with an application of the winners' curse to their leagues. Teams often seem to hire players without extensive research into their background, attributes, lifestyles, and ability to complement existing team members. This is especially the case for imports of players from far-off countries in South America and Africa. Players are sometimes hired largely on the basis of recommendations of agents and video clips. Perfect information on player ability cannot be taken for granted and asymmetric information may have important effects on player salaries and team performance. Mistakes in hiring are often associated with "panic-buying" behavior by teams fearing impending demotion and hence substantial losses of revenues. Such vulnerable teams are precisely those that lack the resources and infrastructure to conduct efficient searches for new player talent. But overpayment following panic-buying is largely due to asymmetric information rather than a winners' curse. Although players' agents like to promote the notion of multiple bidders for player services, the reality is that at most three clubs, and usually just one or two, will be involved in active negotiations over a player's contract.[9]

MARKET STRUCTURE

The structure of sports labor markets is shaped by the restrictions imposed by the various leagues. In North America these restrictions include:

- A *player draft* where initial entry into the league is through the organized recruitment of a pool of available players, usually from college;
- A *reserve clause* where players are tied to their teams until they qualify for free agency; under *restricted free agency* in NFL, players with three years experience can only negotiate new contracts with rival teams if their existing team has not made an appropriate matching offer comparable to rivals' terms;
- A long period before *free agency* (the freedom to move to any club that makes a suitable salary offer) is achieved—this period is four years in NFL and six years in MLB;
- A *salary cap* that imposes a ceiling on total payroll allowed for a team, usually as a percentage of designated revenues. This is applied to teams in NBA, NFL, and NHL. Baseball does not have a salary cap and its primary tool for redistributing revenues is currently a luxury tax on high-revenue teams (such as New York Yankees and Boston Red Sox). The proceeds of this tax are then redistributed through the league.

None of these restrictions apply in European soccer, although the English Football League (comprising tiers two through four) operates a voluntary restraint on ratios of payroll to turnover of less than 70 percent while a hard salary cap is imposed in English Rugby League and Rugby Union.

The history of the reserve clause in MLB, originating in 1879, is documented by Stefan Szymanski and Andrew Zimbalist.[10] They make clear that, although this measure was cited as a mechanism to sustain an appropriate level of competitive balance in the league, in practice team owners saw an opportunity to hold down player labor costs and raise profits. Moreover, conventional theory of sports leagues (with profit-maximizing teams) shows that a reserve clause will not affect competitive balance.[11] Players will migrate to teams where their marginal revenue product is highest, regardless of a reserve clause, and the allocation of player talent, and therefore competitive balance in a league, will be independent of specific labor market restrictions. This is the *invariance proposition*, essentially an application of the Coase theorem of property rights in economics and much-cited within sports economics following its first statement and application to baseball by Simon Rottenberg.[12]

In baseball, the reserve clause restricted a player to a club for the length of contract plus one additional year, if the team renewed the existing contract. Crucially, owners interpreted renewal of contract "on the same terms" to imply renewal of the reserve clause itself.[13] This meant that a team could employ a player for as long as it wished.

The reserve clause and associated restrictions were preserved by an exemption from antitrust legal prosecution. The reserve clause was only successfully challenged in 1976, and even then the move to free agency was partial. The subsequent explosion of MLB player salaries was as predicted, giving a hint of what was to follow when full free agency was earned in European football.[14]

The length of time taken to get to free agency together with a small number of teams combine to confer buyer (monopsony) power on team owners in MLB and NFL. Recent estimates of salary shortfall for restricted players in MLB and NFL are provided by Anthony Krautmann, David Berri, and Peter von Allmen, following the "free-market" method of Krautmann for computing marginal revenue product, discussed above.[15] The marginal revenue products of baseball free agents were estimated from data over 1997 to 2002. Then the shortfalls of restricted player salaries, that is, players with less than four years of experience who were not eligible for salary arbitration, were computed for 2002 and 2003. For this subset of 165 players wages were on average 34 percent of free agent marginal revenue product. Similarly, NFL free agent marginal revenue products were computed for 2004 and 2005. Taking 198 restricted NFL players in 2004 and 2005, defining "restricted" as players with less than three years experience playing under the reserve clause, Krautmann et al. find that average salaries were 64 percent of unrestricted free agents' marginal revenue product. Taken together, these results from MLB and NFL show strong evidence of substantial monopsony power; the reserve clause remains binding and important in these leagues.

Stefan Szymanski and Andrew Zimbalist show that the English Football League initiated its version of a reserve clause in the 1880s shortly after its first application in North American baseball.[16] The authors regard the timing as not a coincidence, although they cannot prove any collusive arrangement. This English version became known as the "retain and transfer" system. At the end of a football season, teams were obliged, by league rules, to decide which players to retain and which to release. Retention had to cover a salary no less than a league-wide agreed minimum. If players were released, then clubs could still demand compensation (a monetary *transfer fee*) for loss of player services from rival teams prepared to hire the newly available players, even if players' contracts had expired.[17]

A further restriction imposed in English soccer was the *maximum wage*. This was a simple ceiling on weekly earnings of footballers. Set at £20 per week in the 1950s, this sum was not much greater than skilled engineers or teachers earned at this time. The maximum wage was enforced by penalties on clubs that paid more. Not surprisingly, clubs offered side payments to star players in the form of house renovations, fitted kitchens, and luxury cars.

In North America, the attack on the reserve clause was led by players' unions. Collective bargaining between team owners and players' unions, at the league level, became an integral part of employment contract negotiations and such bargains became especially important in the latter part of the twentieth century. This is rather ironic given the low levels of union membership and union bargaining recognition in the U.S. economy as a whole. Breakdown of negotiations between unions and team owners has led to periodic strikes and lockouts, such as the 1987 strike in NFL (in which striking players were replaced by substitute labor in a shortened season) and the loss of the entire 2004/05 NHL season as players were locked out by owners.

In contrast to North America, players' unions in European soccer have been less effective in bargaining over salaries and employment terms. John Harding documents the general weakness of the English Professional Footballers' Association (a players' union) over the twentieth century.[18] The English players' union did, however, under the leadership of Jimmy Hill, mount an effective campaign to abolish the maximum wage in 1961. This was followed by a High Court legal challenge to the retain-and-transfer system in 1963, which ruled that this constituted a "restrictive practice." By 1978 players in England and Scotland could negotiate a move to other clubs upon expiration of contracts provided that a transfer fee was agreeable between clubs. If an agreement was not reached, then a tribunal would arbitrate on the size of the transfer fee. But this was a peculiarly English result and the rest of Europe still had elements of the old retain-and-transfer system. In the early 1990s an out-of-contract Belgian footballer, Jean-Marc Bosman, tried to secure a transfer from RC Liege in Belgium to FC Dunkerque in France. Liege insisted on receiving a transfer fee from Dunkerque, which refused to pay. Bosman mounted a legal challenge that eventually went to the European Court of Justice and its verdict of December 1995 became known as the *Bosman ruling*.

The Bosman ruling affirmed the principle of free movement of labor throughout the European Union. Players whose contracts expired would now be able to accept employment offers from any club, without any exchange of transfer fee between clubs. Previously the player's surplus (excess of market value over value of earnings in next-best occupation) would have been divided between teams and players. Under the new arrangement, the players could capture all the surplus for themselves as transfer fees would be zero for out-of-contract footballers. Transfer fees were still retained for players who were hired within contracts at other clubs. The second innovation in

FIGURE 7.1
The Development of Player Salaries in the German Bundesliga, 1995/96–2005/06

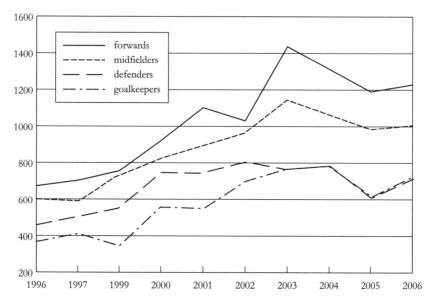

Source: Courtesy of the *Scottish Journal of Political Economy*.
Note: Figures in nominal Euros.

the Bosman ruling was to declare illegal any restrictions on foreign-born EU nationals in domestic teams. Prior to 1995, several European leagues had restricted the number of foreign-born players to three per team. Although work-permit restrictions were still enforceable for non-EU players the market for footballers became genuinely international and teams in England, Germany, Italy, and Spain began to acquire multinational playing squads.

As with free agency in baseball, player salaries in European football rose dramatically following the Bosman ruling. Figure 7.1 shows the development of player salaries in the German Bundesliga since 1996. Isolating the impact of the Bosman ruling on player salaries is difficult since dramatic growth in values of football broadcasting rights occurred in Germany (and other European countries) at roughly the same time as the move to free agency. In the graph, the dip in player salaries around 2003/04 is attributable to the collapse of the major football broadcaster, Kirch, and the delay while a new buyer of TV rights was sought.

The recent history of English Premier League TV broadcasting is documented in Volume 1 by Babatunde Buraimo and Rob Simmons. Several top footballers playing in the Premier League managed to secure lucrative new

TABLE 7.1
Top Annual Salaries in English Premier League, 2007/08

Player	Club	Salary (US$m)
John Terry	Chelsea	13.5
Andriy Shevchenko	Chelsea	12.1
Michael Ballack	Chelsea	12.1
Steven Gerrard	Liverpool	12.0
Cristiano Ronaldo	Manchester United	11.9
Wayne Rooney	Manchester United	11.0
Michael Owen	Newcastle United	11.0
Frank Lampard	Chelsea	10.0
Rio Ferdinand	Manchester United	10.0
Fernando Torres	Liverpool	9.0
Didier Drogba	Chelsea	9.0
Jamie Carragher	Liverpool	8.0
Michael Essien	Chelsea	8.0
Kieron Dyer	West Ham United	8.0

contracts with existing or new clubs in the close season of 2007, in anticipation of increased broadcast revenues. Some figures were collated by *The Guardian* newspaper and reveal numbers on a par with stars in major North American leagues. Recall that European footballers' contracts are guaranteed and the figures reported are for basic salary and exclude bonuses. What is immediately striking about Table 7.1 is the preponderance of the biggest clubs, Chelsea, Manchester United, and Liverpool, in the list.

SALARY DETERMINATION

Measures of player salary in North American sports are now widely available. Some care needs to be taken in converting these measures for statistical analysis. NFL salary data comprise base salary, signing bonus, other bonuses, and a "salary cap" measure used to assess a team's total payroll against the prescribed NFL salary cap. Signing bonuses can be large as NFL teams have an incentive to load salary into the bonus component to circumvent the salary cap. At the same time, though, the signing bonus is guaranteed while base salary is not. Salary cap management is a delicate skill for an NFL team's management. For salary cap purposes, the signing bonus is pro-rated over the life of a contract and use of this measure smoothes out salaries to give a more consistent measure of player value in any season. Thus, most statistical analysis of NFL salaries uses the measure that contains the pro-rated bonus measure.[19]

In Europe, measures of player salary are less readily available. The data used in the study of players in Italy's Serie A by Lucifora and Simmons were taken from a unique newspaper publication.[20] Some German Bundesliga salary data have been published by *Kicker* football magazine and these have been used by Frick to analyze salaries.[21] The Transfermarkt.de Web site offers a pan-European "market value" measure that can be used as a proxy for salary. Using the German subset of actual salaries, Frick finds a correlation coefficient between the two measures of 0.8, which is high enough to suggest that the proxy is useful for analysis.

In most occupations, salaries have a skewed distribution with a thin right-hand tail as only a few workers earn very high salaries. For professional team athletes, this tendency is further exaggerated, with a small number of players earning far more than their teammates, giving rise to suggestions of "superstar" effects. For analysis, this means that standard statistical estimation methods, such as ordinary least squares, are inappropriate as (log) salary does not follow a normal distribution. Hence, some researchers have adopted more sophisticated procedures such as quantile regression.[22] In this approach effects of independent variables on (log) salary are allowed to vary across the salary distribution.

Figure 7.1 shows the development of average player salaries by position in the Bundesliga. This makes clear that there is a robust ordering of salaries by position: forwards, midfielders, defenders, and goalkeepers in descending order. Of course, forwards have the more glamorous and crowd-pleasing association with goal-scoring, needed to win games, while defenders have more prosaic and also less well-measured functions in stopping opponents from scoring. This salary ranking seems quite plausible and has been supported in various empirical studies.[23]

Econometric models of player salary determination typically follow the same approach as used in other labor markets. This adopts the Mincer human capital formulation in which salary depends on measures of experience, tenure with team, performance, and measures of reputation. The basic idea is that players enhance their own, and their team's, productivity through experience, but this accumulation of experience adds to team revenues at a decreasing rate. Hence, it is usual to include experience squared as variable alongside experience. However, the conventional economic interpretation of experience as contributing to accumulated knowledge and productivity needs modification for sports players. Although knowledge and experience are indeed valued by head coaches, longevity in team sports is largely due to selection. Players compete for starting positions and their sustained presence in teams denotes ability to perform better than rivals for their positions. Appropriate team selection—when to drop an experienced player and when to bring in a younger, less experienced player—is a critical feature of good team management. Over time players lose some components of ability, such as speed and athleticism, and eventually any extra benefits to teams from greater experience are offset by the extra costs associated with depleted speed and physical condition. In regressions of European footballer salaries, it appears that the age at which players maximize earnings potential is around twenty-eight.[24] For the NFL Berri and Simmons find that peak earnings of running backs are achieved (for the median player) at eight years' experience, which for a typical drafting age of twenty-one implies an age of twenty-nine.[25] Thus the two types of football are similar in peak earning age.

Lucifora and Simmons found goals scored to be an important determinant of forwards' salaries in Italy's Serie A in the 1995/96 season. They found a convex relationship between salary and goals; more goals raised salary at an increasing rate, *ceteris paribus*. Assists by other players (final passes leading to goals scored) were also statistically significant but one extra assist had a smaller impact on salary than one extra goal.

It is customary for sports economists to invoke Lawrence Kahn on the virtues of extensive sports pay and performance data with which to analyze labor economics problems.[26] But reality is more complicated. For defenders in European soccer and defensive and offensive linemen in the NFL, suitable performance metrics are not available. For European soccer, the basic measures available are goals scored and assists. A higher weight for more recent performance seems plausible, and is supported by available evidence. Berri, Schmidt, and Brook stress that performance in NFL teams is very inconsistent, largely due to injuries although inconsistent performances of teammates (and play-calling by offensive and defensive coordinators) also play a part.[27]

For the NFL it makes little sense to use touchdowns as a performance measure as these are end-products of sophisticated plays executed by many, if not all, offensive team members. Berri and Simmons model running-back salaries using rush and pass-reception yards as key performance measures. This raises the tricky question of team complementarities, which also applies to European football. The rushing yards earned by running backs will be due not just to the player's own effort but the successful blocking of teammates. One rigorous approach to modeling team production effects was applied to ice hockey (NHL) by Idson and Kahane.[28] They derived performance measures for teammates minus the contribution of the subject player in the database and found strong evidence of complementarities. An alternative approach, followed by Berri and Simmons, is to assume that total payrolls of team units (such as other skill positions and offensive line in NFL) are suitable proxies for team quality in these complementary units. The prediction is that a running back playing with a more expensive offensive line will have his marginal revenue product, and hence salary, augmented as this complementary unit will be more effective in helping the running back rush and catch the football.

Two objections to this procedure are, first, that NFL teams are subject to a salary cap and so a fully competitive market does not apply (and extra payroll for offensive line might mean that the team has to hire running backs on lower pay) and, second, that some members of the offensive line will not be free agents and will have pay set below marginal revenue product, in turn implying that payroll is not a good proxy for offensive line productivity. Nevertheless, David Berri and Rob Simmons find that extra total salary spent on both offensive line and skill positions other than running back are each associated significantly with higher running-back salary, at all quantiles of the salary distribution. So despite the salary cap, and despite the lack of free agency, complementary inputs are effective in raising running-back salaries in NFL. It would be interesting to see if similar effects can be found in European soccer.

In addition to performance measures, analysts sometimes use measures of peer reputation. For European football, this could include the number of appearances for representative national teams or a simple dummy variable to denote contemporary selection to national teams.[29] This raises the question of which matches to include (just World Cup and European Championship or a broader scope including ad hoc friendly matches?) and the quality of opposition. For the NFL, a suitable measure of peer esteem is selection to the end-of-season Pro Bowl teams, which is made by a poll of players, coaches, and fans. Berri and Simmons assume that once gained, Pro Bowl selection produces a permanent salary premium and find some empirical support for the idea. A novel approach to fan esteem of soccer players is taken by Garcia-del-Barrio and Pujol who use number of Google hits to capture fan interest in particular players in the top division of Spanish soccer.[30] In their best fitting model, a 10 percent increase in Google hits leads to a 3.2 percent increase in player market value. This estimate controls for a set of impacts on Google hits themselves.

Overall, there is now extensive evidence that player salaries depend on experience and its square, on individual performance and on reputational measures. The primary tasks for the next generation of player earnings studies are to uncouple impacts of complementary inputs (other players and coaches) and then to assess market efficiency for specific team labor components.

EUROPEAN TRANSFER MARKETS

One big difference between player labor markets in North America and Europe is the presence of player trades for cash in Europe. Some cash transfer fees can be spectacularly large, as shown in Table 7.2. This reveals a

TABLE 7.2
Top Ten All-Time Transfer Fees Involving European Clubs

Name	From	To	Fee (US$m)	Year
Zinedine Zidane	Juventus	Real Madrid	91.2	2001
Luis Figo	Barcelona	Real Madrid	74.0	2000
Hernan Crespo	Parma	Lazio	71.0	2000
Gianluigi Buffon	Parma	Juventus	65.2	2001
Christian Vieri	Lazio	Inter Milan	64.0	1999
Andriy Shevchenko	AC Milan	Chelsea	60.0	2006
Rio Ferdinand	Leeds	Manchester Utd	58.2	2002
Gaizka Mendieta	Valencia	Lazio	58.0	2001
Ronaldo	Inter Milan	Real Madrid	57.0	2002
Juan Sebastian Veron	Fiorentina	AC Milan	56.0	2001

hectic period of activity for big Italian and Spanish clubs around 2000–2002, as these teams aimed to dominate not just their own leagues but also the Union of European Football Associations (UEFA) Champions' League. Italian clubs, in particular, were beset by a series of financial problems after 2002, including revenues that were lower than expected, substantial losses, and a corruption scandal involving referee selection to particular games that led to stripping of a title and demotion for Juventus and a large points penalty for AC Milan, who nevertheless won the Champions' League in 2006/07.

Since 2002, the largest transfer fees have hovered around the $30–40 million mark with Thierry Henry moving from Arsenal to Barcelona for $33 million in the 2007 season. Some apparent anomalies remain; for example, the much less well-known forward Darren Bent transferred from Charlton to Tottenham for the same fee as Thierry Henry at around the same time. Since the Bosman ruling, it has become apparent that transfer fees depend on the amount of time left outstanding on a player's contract. Many players now invoke the Bosman ruling to run down their contracts and negotiate new ones at alternative clubs for zero transfer fee, known within the industry as "moving on a Bosman." For this to happen, the player must be at least twenty-four years old. For age below twenty-four, an independent arbitration panel decides on an appropriate level of compensation for the original club. Clubs then face a decision on whether to let a free transfer happen, or whether to capitalize on their asset, since a player contract should be the property of the club, and claim a transfer fee before the contract expires.[31] The result of the Bosman ruling has been a bipolar structure of transfer fees with many players switching clubs for zero fees and another, still substantial, group moving for transfer fees of over $5 million. Figure 7.2

FIGURE 7.2
The Development of Transfer Fees in the German Bundesliga,
1981/82–2006/07

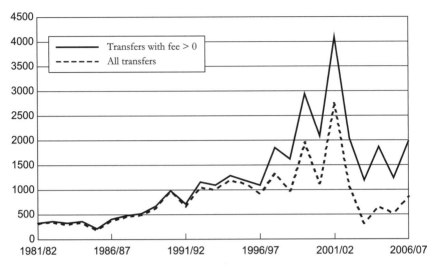

Source: Courtesy of the *Scottish Journal of Political Economy.*
Note: Nominal figures in 1,000 €.

shows that average transfer fees in the Bundesliga fell from €4 million in 2001/02 to €2 million in 2006/07. Bernd Frick also points out that the percentage of player moves involving payment of a transfer fee fell from 95 percent in the 1990s to less than 40 percent after 2000. Again, this reflects the influence of the European Union's Bosman ruling.

Bernd Frick shows a consensus among studies of observed transfer fees in Europe, which indicates that key determinants are player age, career games played, and number of international appearances.[32] Characteristics of the buying club, usually recent success or size, have also been found to affect transfer fees.

It is worth asking what purpose is served by cash transfer fees. In England Lord Stevens was appointed by the Premier League to launch a high-level investigation into possible forms of corruption involving transfer fees paid by some English clubs. Among the allegations were claims that some player agents were taking cash inducements from clubs to facilitate some transfers of players between clubs. It appeared that some agents were working on behalf of both clubs and players, leading to a possible conflict of interest. A further problem arose in 2007 when the transfer of Argentinian World Cup star Carlos Tevez from Boca Juniors in Argentina to West Ham in England led to the player's contract being owned by an offshore third-party company, contrary to Premier League rules. This external ownership then caused problems later when Tevez wanted to accept an offer of employment from Manchester United. This raised questions of whether Manchester United should pay a transfer fee to West Ham, and if so how much. In Italy it is sometimes the case that two clubs can jointly own the contract of a player. Such legal complications are, of course, absent in North American sports.

In submissions to the European Court of Justice over the Bosman case, some national football associations, notably the French, claimed that transfer fees were payments designed to reflect the expenditures incurred by selling clubs in training and developing players. Moreover, it was claimed, transfer fees were also a "solidarity" mechanism that enabled small-market teams to develop players for sale to bigger teams and for revenues to be redistributed through the league. But Advocate-General Lenz correctly dismissed both claims in his verdict on the Bosman case. First, the larger transfer fees bore no relation to any conceivable figure for costs of training and development. Second, if leagues really wanted to redistribute revenues from big teams to small teams, then the transfer market was far from an ideal means to do so since it would rely on the lottery of finding star players for sale, which is a highly uncertain process. Furthermore, since 1995, bigger clubs have considerably expanded their facilities for training and developing young players so that they now have considerable surpluses of talent.

Marco Tervio offers a simple rationalization of the transfer market.[33] He argues that cash-transfer payments help teams reallocate playing resources to strengthen squads. This reallocation requires prices to be attached to player moves and the transfer market does precisely this. But this poses the unanswered question of why North American leagues, believed to be more profit-oriented and more commercially aware than European leagues, have retained what is essentially a barter mechanism for player trades. Economists would normally propose that barter is a less efficient trading mechanism than a set of market-driven prices. One answer is that disputed ownership of player registrations, as in the Carlos Tevez transfer, might too readily arise, causing excessive litigation and possible loss of trust and integrity in the league.

CAREER DURATION AND CONTRACT LENGTH

Witnauer, Rogers, and Saint Onge report that average career length in MLB, for a sample of players in the twentieth century, was 5.7 years.[34] In the more violent and injury-prone NFL, the players' association reports a current career length of 3.2 years. Bernd Frick shows that soccer player career length in the German Bundesliga is 3.4 years. Low average career length in the two types of football reflects impacts both of injury and of wastage as players are discharged by teams. NFL players lack guaranteed contracts, although signing bonuses are guaranteed. Players can be "cut" at will by team owners. Turnover of players with similar and substitutable skills (backup linemen, for example) is considerable. Likewise, in European soccer, teams have large numbers of fringe players who are hired on short-term contracts or on terms that are highly contingent (e.g., on set numbers of first team appearances). Hence, across sports leagues player careers are risky. This is partly due to physical risk of injury but also because teams are not prepared to overly inflate roster sizes. In NFL roster sizes are fixed (at fifty-three players), while in European soccer clubs will find excessive squad sizes too costly to manage. In all sports, players compete for starting places. In baseball such competition is lessened by the fact that player rotation is an integral part of the long schedule of 162 games per season. In European football, only the very biggest clubs can afford the luxury of rotation of players between domestic league matches and UEFA Champions' League games.

Career lengths vary considerably by specialization of skill and position across teams and within positions. In the NFL a quarterback who remains healthy and productive (e.g., Brett Favre) can amass a career length of over ten seasons. In European football, starting goalkeepers typically have longer career lengths than outfield players. As noted above, the Bosman ruling of 1995 liberalized player labor markets in European football. The average career duration of Bundesliga players rose rather than fell after 1995. Actually, what emerged was essentially a dual labor market. One set of highly productive players secured longer careers in top divisions, not necessarily at the same club, while another set joined a pool of temporary labor, moving frequently on short-term contracts before joining clubs in lower divisions or lower-status leagues. A recent innovation in Europe is the "loan transfer." Under this arrangement, a soccer club will "lend" a player to another team. The player's contract, including salary, must still be honored. Usually, the borrowing club takes over the player's salary commitment for the duration of the loan, which can be between one month and a full season. Sometimes, the lending club will continue to pay a player's salary for the loan spell if the borrowing club is cash-strapped and the sending club feels that the player's market value will increase through greater playing exposure at another club.

Over the post-Bosman period, it is also the case that growing revenue disparities within and between divisions have increased risk for teams, which means that teams make greater efforts to secure the services of players with proven performance records. But we should note that teams also widened player searches into previously untapped territory such as Africa and Asia, and this is not so consistent with an explanation of longer careers based upon team risk aversion. A further consideration is that advances in physical conditioning and improved player fitness and diet became more important in the 1990s as management and coaching practices became more scientific. The improvement in player conditioning is not exogenous. Top European football players became increasingly aware, sometimes through deselection from their teams, that bohemian lifestyles and substance abuse were incompatible with effective performance at the highest level.

From 2002 MLB introduced tighter rules on disability insurance on players, which allowed insurers to place a two- or three-year limit on insurance coverage. This gave franchises a strong incentive to reduce contract lengths. Keith Dobkowski finds that the average length of a free agent MLB contract fell from 2.7 years in 2001 to 1.8 years in 2002.[35] Rookie contracts will typically be of longer duration. Hence, baseball players manage to survive in MLB on a sequence of short-term contracts spread over a career that is somewhat longer on average than in other North American sports.

Player careers in European professional soccer are of a rather short duration. Average career duration (defined as the total number of years an individual has been playing in the German Bundesliga, ignoring exits and re-entries) is 4 years, while average spell length (defined as the number of consecutive years played without any interruption) is 3.4 years. As Figure 7.3 shows for the Bundesliga, nearly half of all spells and more than one-third of the careers last for just one season.

FIGURE 7.3
The Duration of Football Players' Careers in the German Bundesliga, 1963/64–2002/03

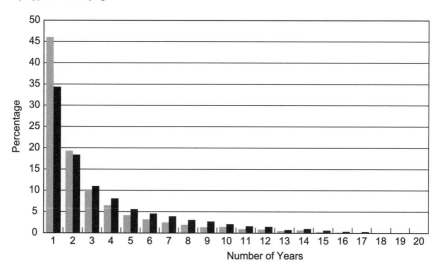

Source: Courtesy of the *Scottish Journal of Political Economy.*

In European soccer, it appears that average contract length increased after the Bosman ruling of 1995 from 2.5 years to over 3 years.[36] This, in turn implies that in every single season about one-third of the players are negotiating a new contract. Again, this conceals a dual labor market outcome. One group of players exists on a sequence of short-term contracts of one year or less while another group enjoys guaranteed contract duration of three or more years. This latter group comprises promising young players and experienced players with proven performance. For MLB, Joel Maxcy argues that better players would earn longer contracts because they are less risky than inferior players and something similar seems to operate in European soccer.[37] Note that in European soccer and baseball, unlike American football, salary contracts are fully guaranteed in that teams are obliged to pay the full amount outstanding on a contract if they wish to remove a player from their roster, with the exception of course of gross misconduct on the part of the player. European footballers can, and sometimes do, buy themselves out of their own contracts if they wish to move without the need for a host team to pay a transfer fee. This practice will be worthwhile for the player if there is a sufficient salary and bonus package on offer at a rival club.

Eberhard Feess, Bernd Frick, and Gerd Muehlheusser use a large data base of German Bundesliga players to show that various measures of player performance, both objective and subjective, significantly increase in the last year of a player's contract.[38] They also find that the variance in player performance is lower in the final year of contract. This is consistent with strategic incentive-based behavior. Players raise their effort levels in the hope and expectation of securing contract renewal (at existing club or elsewhere). Such strategic behavior is also observed in some investigations of player contracts in North American sports. As Kevin Stiroh puts it in his study of the NBA, long-term contracts are good for team owners when players are competing for renewal but they are less good when workers have them and reduce effort once the contract is locked in.[39]

DISCRIMINATION

Salary discrimination in sports can be defined as unequal pay for two types of player with similar attributes other than race, ethnicity, or nationality. In North American sports, black (African American) players constitute the majority of players in NBA and NFL. There are three possible sources of discrimination: *employer,* where team owners impose their preferences for or against particular groups; *co-worker,* where players exercise their preferences; and *customer,* where fans signal disapproval of particular groups. Employer discrimination raises the problem that if a team owner refuses to hire a particular type of player, or equivalently offers insufficient salary terms, then the team may not win as many games as it could, particularly as these players could move elsewhere to teams whose owners are not prejudiced. The same outcome can occur via co-worker discrimination, but not through customer discrimination. Employer or co-worker discrimination will damage team performance, independently of whether owner objectives are to maximize profits or wins. This suggests that discriminatory behavior in team sports by team owners or players is fundamentally irrational.

The literature on salary discrimination and customer discrimination in North American sports is concisely surveyed by Lawrence Kahn.[40] Customer discrimination is typically addressed by analysis of gate attendance or TV audiences. Evidence is mixed, with some studies finding evidence of discrimination, but it is not clear that this evidence is robust over time.[41] Orn Bodvarsson and Mark Partridge present a rigorous encompassing model of the three types of discrimination applied to NBA salaries.[42] Controlling for player skills and their substitutability, they find evidence in favor of (white) co-worker and (black) fan discrimination, but not employer discrimination. But the proxy measure used to identify fan discrimination is the share of African Americans in the local population. To the extent that the proportion of African Americans in stadium attendance differs from the proportion in the local population (and it also matters how wide a definition of "local" is used), then this proxy measure loses its validity.

In the United States in 2005, a media debate emerged over whether some black quarterbacks were worth their place as starters on NFL teams, following controversial on-air comments by (subsequently fired) conservative pundit Rush Limbaugh alleging "favorable" treatment to black players. Until recently, starting NFL quarterbacks tended to be predominantly white but a growing number of black players has broken through into this high-profile (and potentially high-earning) position. Berri and Simmons analyzed salary determination for NFL quarterbacks over 1995 to 2006.[43] They draw two main conclusions from their quantile regression estimates. First, on average, black quarterbacks tend to run with the ball more than white quarterbacks, but there appears to be no salary reward for this function even though running by quarterbacks adds to team productivity. Second, white quarterbacks receive increased salary for numbers of yards gained by successful pass completions. This performance-related component, as an implicit determinant of player salary, is substantially reduced for black quarterbacks. Hence, controlling for ability and experience and also controlling for positions in the salary distribution, Berri and Simmons do find evidence that black quarterbacks receive lower salaries than white quarterbacks with similar characteristics.

A further aspect of discrimination that has received attention in NFL is the tendency for head coaches to be white. Although there are many black players and assistant coaches in the NFL, promotion to head coach is, on the surface, disproportionately weighted toward white coaches. This problem was recognized by the NFL and a rule was imposed by Commissioner Rooney (the "Rooney rule") that at least one black candidate should be interviewed for any head coach vacancy. An analysis of NFL hiring decisions over 1970 to 2005 by Ben Solow, John Solow, and Todd Walker finds that race does not influence NFL head coach hiring decisions.[44] They argue that the NFL should attempt to increase the number of qualified minority candidates. Arguably, there may soon be a demonstration effect following Tony Dungy's achievement as the first African American head coach to win a Super Bowl (in 2007 for the Indianapolis Colts).

In the English Football League, black players were a rarity until the 1978–1979 season, when West Bromwich Albion had the novelty of three black players in the same team. The arrival of black players into the English Football League lagged well behind the large-scale immigration of Caribbean, African, and Asian families into Britain in the 1940s and 1950s. Similarly, up to the 1990s, ethnic minorities, and indeed women, were underrepresented in stadium attendances as English soccer was predominantly a sport watched and played by young white blue-collar males.[45] It was as late as 1979 that the first black player (Laurie Cunningham) represented the national team in a competitive match. Now black players are integrated into professional teams throughout Europe.

The question of racial discrimination in English soccer has been addressed in a novel approach by Stefan Szymanski.[46] Conventional estimates of extent of salary discrimination use statistical analysis of individual salaries, distinguishing between white and black subsamples. These studies ask whether black players are paid less than similarly able and experienced white players. A big problem for these studies is that unobserved player productivity may be correlated with racial or ethnic characteristics and this may result in biased estimates of discrimination. This is especially the case where available performance measures are limited to broad indicators such as goals scored and assists. These measures do not adequately account for the performance of defenders or midfield players.

Szymanski proposes a "market test" for discrimination. He assumes that a competitive market for footballers prevails (and restrictions on player mobility are certainly much less than in North America) and that team relative payrolls, scaled by league average, are strongly correlated with team performance, measured by league points divided by maximum possible (to allow for ties). This correlation has much empirical support.[47] Suppose a team adds more to its payroll, relative to league average, for a particular ethnic or racial group. If team performance is shown to increase, then this is evidence of discrimination. The method suggests that a team could raise its points total, and hence league position, either by hiring more of a particular group at a given market wage or by improving quality by acquiring players of this group at higher salary. Applying this principle to all four divisions of English soccer over the period 1977/78 to 1992/93, Szymanski finds evidence of discrimination. In a sequel, Ian Preston and Stefan Szymanski used Census of Population and attendance data to reject the hypothesis of customer discrimination as a source of discrimination in English football.[48] With co-worker discrimination also ruled out, they were led to propose employer discrimination as the dominant type. It would be useful to repeat the discrimination market test for the post-Bosman period. Since 1995 European teams have become multinational and multiracial and now contain a wide variety of ethnic groups. For example, Figure 7.4 shows the sharp decline in German-born players appearing in the Bundesliga since the mid-1980s. Also

FIGURE 7.4
The Percentage of German-Born Players in the Bundesliga, 1963/64–2005/06

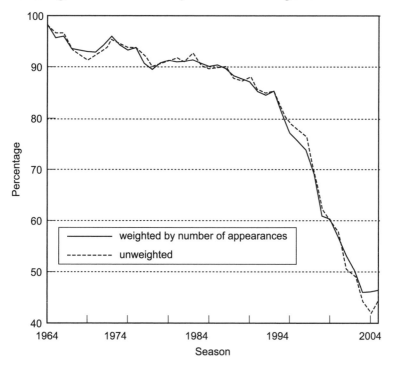

Source: Courtesy of the *Scottish Journal of Political Economy.*

revenues have become less equally distributed across teams, with increased financial penalties for relegation from the top divisions. We would expect that discrimination should have been eradicated as a result.

Pedace adopts Szymanski's market test to examine the extent of nationality discrimination in English football.[49] Pedace finds that players from South America enjoy a substantial salary premium in English soccer; teams would perform better if they spent less on salaries of South Americans. Although this result is based on a rather small number of South American players, some empirical corroboration is offered by Bernd Frick.[50] Using a conventional statistical earnings function, he finds that South American players receive a salary premium of 50 percent. There are several possible reasons for this result. First, South American players are noted for high levels of skill and excitement and will attract fans to a greater extent than players from other regions. This may be a case where salaries reflect marginal revenue product rather than marginal physical product as South American players attract greater viewership at the stadium and on TV, and therefore increased team revenues, as Pedace finds. Second, the best South American players are already located in the Spanish and Italian leagues, partly through preferences for culture, climate, and language, but also because teams in these leagues have playing styles that can accommodate South American talent. This leaves a residual pool of talent available for the English Premier League and the Bundesliga. This residual talent is likely to be more uncertain in quality and teams, and their head coaches may have overpredicted their abilities to convert such talent into team wins. Note that such an explanation is distinct from the "winners' curse" phenomenon that we discussed above.

CONCLUSIONS

There is now considerable evidence on the relationship between performance and earnings in professional sports leagues. Although many fans may believe player pay to be arbitrarily determined, statistical studies have shown that player salaries in team sports on both sides of the Atlantic depend on age, experience, and ability. Ability is the most fundamental determinant of earnings since, by construction (and sometimes by league rules), only a limited number of players can appear on team rosters. Appearance on a roster denotes successful selection, which in turn depends on ability. Given selection, player earnings typically rise with age to a peak at age twenty-eight in the NFL and in European soccer and then decline as players' physical attributes are depleted. Additional determinants of player earnings are on-field performance, as measured by goals in soccer or yards gained in the NFL, for example. Peer recognition is also a factor determining player salaries, for example, by selection for national representative teams in European soccer or for the Pro Bowl in the NFL.

Labor market structures differ significantly between North American sports and European soccer. The former exhibit high levels of regulation with player drafts, reserve clauses, and salary caps combining to confer buyer power (monopsony) on team owners. Players who do not qualify for free agency are then underpaid compared to their contributions to team revenues. To combat this, player unions have been forceful in North America in pursuit of minimum salary levels and industrial disputes, with strikes and lock-outs sometimes occurring, as in 2004/05 when the entire NHL season was abandoned. In contrast, European labor markets for soccer players are more fluid with few restrictions on mobility between EU countries.

A further important source of difference between North American and European player labor markets can be seen in the treatment of player trades. In North America, player trades for cash are rarely observed. Trades are conducted by player exchange and by bargaining over future draft picks. In European soccer, teams often exchange players for transfer fees; these can be substantial. However, many players now exercise the option to move clubs on expiration of contract, without a transfer fee being paid. The Bosman ruling of 1995 led to an increasing number of player moves occurring without a transfer fee.

From the point of view of team owners, player trades (whether for cash or by player exchange or exchange of draft picks) serve to reallocate team playing talent. Some trades are successful, while others are spectacular flops. Players who look good in one team may not perform so well in others. It is here that interaction with teammates is so important. The role of player and coaching interactions in team sports is an underresearched area in both North America and Europe and this is primarily where more analysis is needed.

Other personnel issues investigated by sports economics include the effects of employment contract design on player effort and persistence of discrimination. On the former, some studies show that player effort rises just before a contract is expected to be renewed but falls shortly after the contract is signed. In European soccer, recognition of this feature has led to greater use of contingency and performance-related contract clauses. Some evidence suggesting existence of discrimination against ethnic minorities has also been found and recent research shows that black quarterbacks in the NFL receive lower pay for their efforts relative to similarly endowed white quarterbacks. In European soccer, evidence of employer racial discrimination against black players was found for the 1970s and 1980s but is unlikely to be present now as barriers to player mobility have broken down.

NOTES

1. David Berri, Stacey Brook, Bernd Frick, Aju Fenn, and Roberto Vicente-Mayoral, "The Short Supply of Tall People: Competitive Imbalance and the NBA," *Journal of Economic Issues* 39 (2005): 1029–1041.

2. Anthony Krautmann, Elizabeth Gustafson, and Lawrence Hadley, "Who Pays for Minor League Training Costs?," *Contemporary Economic Policy* 18 (2000): 37–47.

3. Michael Leeds and Sandra Kowalewski, "Winner Takes All in the NFL: The Effect of the Salary Cap and Free Agency on the Compensation of Skill Position Players," *Journal of Sports Economics* 2 (2001): 244–256.

4. Gerald Scully, "Pay and Performance in Major League Baseball," *American Economic Review* 64 (1974): 915–930.

5. Anthony Krautmann, "What's Wrong with Scully-Estimates of a Player's Marginal Revenue Product," *Economic Inquiry* 37 (1999): 369–381.

6. John Burger and Stephen Walters, "The Existence and Persistence of a Winner's Curse: New Evidence from the (Baseball) Field," *Southern Economic Journal* (forthcoming).

7. Michael Lewis, *Moneyball: The Art of Winning an Unfair Game* (New York: W. W. Norton, 2004).

8. Jahn Hakes and Raymond Sauer, "An Economic Evaluation of the *Moneyball* Hypothesis," *Journal of Economic Perspectives* 20 (2006): 173–186.

9. For example, when Thierry Henry transferred from Arsenal to Barcelona in June 2007, for a fee of $33 million, Barcelona was the only credible bidder for his services.

10. Stefan Szymanski and Andrew Zimbalist, *National Pastime: How Americans Play Baseball and the Rest of the World Plays Soccer* (Washington, D.C.: Brookings Institution Press, 2005).

11. Rodney Fort and James Quirk, "Cross-Subsidization, Incentives, and Outcomes in Professional Team Sports," *Journal of Economic Literature* 33 (1995): 1265–1299.

12. Simon Rottenberg, "The Baseball Players' Labor Market," *Journal of Political Economy* 64 (1956): 242–258.

13. See Michael Leeds and Peter von Allmen, *The Economics of Sports*, 2nd. ed. (Boston: Addison-Wesley, 2005), 268–269.

14. For an evaluation of baseball salary growth immediately following new rules of free agency, see Paul Sommers and Noel Quinton, "Pay and Performance in Major League Baseball: The Case of the First Family of Free Agents," *Journal of Human Resources* 17 (1982): 426–436.

15. Anthony Krautmann, Peter von Allmen, and David Berri, "The Underpayment of Restricted Players in North American Sports Leagues," paper presented to Western Economic Association International, Seattle, June 2007.

16. Szymanski and Zimbalist, *National Pastime*.

17. See Robert Sandy, Peter Sloane, and Mark Rosentraub, *The Economics of Sport: An International Perspective* (Basingstoke: Palgrave Macmillan, 2004), 79.

18. John Harding, *For the Good of the Game: The Official History of the Professional Footballers' Association* (London: Robson Books, 1991).

19. For example, Leeds and Kowalewski, "Winner Takes All in the NFL"; and David Berri and Rob Simmons, "Does It Pay to Specialize? Evidence from the Gridiron," *Review of Industrial Organization*, forthcoming.

20. Claudio Lucifora and Rob Simmons, "Superstar Effects in Sport: Evidence from Italian Soccer," *Journal of Sports Economics* 4 (2003): 35–55.

21. Bernd Frick, "Salary Determination and the Pay-Performance Relationship in Professional Soccer: Evidence from Germany," in *Sports Economics after Fifty Years: Essays in Honour of Simon Rottenberg*, ed. Placido Rodriguez, Stefan Késenne, and Jaume Garcia (Oviedo: Ediciones de la Universidad de Oviedo, 2006), 125–146.

22. See Leeds and Kowalewski, "Winner Takes All in the NFL"; Berri and Simmons, "Does It Pay to Specialize?" for NFL; and Barton Hughes Hamilton, "Racial Discrimination and Professional Basketball Salaries in the 1990s," *Applied Economics* 29 (1997): 287–296.

23. Lucifora and Simmons, "Superstar Effects in Sport"; Frick, "Salary Determination and the Pay-Performance Relationship."

24. Lucifora and Simmons, "Superstar Effects in Sport"; Frick, "Salary Determination and the Pay-Performance Relationship."

25. Berri and Simmons, "Does It Pay to Specialize?"

26. Lawrence Kahn, "The Sports Business as a Labor Market Laboratory," *Journal of Economic Perspectives* 14 (2000): 75–94.

27. David Berri, Martin Schmidt, and Stacey Brook, *The Wages of Wins* (Stanford, Calif.: Stanford University Press, 2006).

28. Todd Idson and Leo Kahane, "Team Effects on Compensation: An Application to Salary Determination in the National Hockey League," *Economic Inquiry* 38 (2000): 345–357.

29. Frick, "Salary Determination and the Pay-Performance Relationship"; Lucifora and Simmons, "Superstar Effects in Sport."

30. Pedro Garcia-del-Barrio and Francesc Pujol, "Hidden Monopsony Rents in Winner-Take-All Markets: Sport and Economic Contribution of Spanish Soccer Players," *Managerial and Decision Economics* 28 (2007): 57–70. A paper on German soccer, similar both in design and results, is Erik Lehmann and Günther Schulze, "What Does It Take to Be a Star? The Role of Performance and the Media for German Soccer Players," mimeo, Max Planck Institute for Research into Economic Systems, Jena, 2005.

31. Bernd Frick, "The Football Players' Labor Market: Empirical Evidence from the Major European Leagues," *Scottish Journal of Political Economy* 54 (2007): 422–446.

32. Ibid.

33. Marco Tervio, "Transfer Fee Regulation and Player Development," *Journal of the European Economic Association* 4 (2006): 957–987.

34. William Witnauer, Richard Rogers, and Jarrod Saint Onge, "Major League Baseball Career Length in the Twentieth Century," *Population Research and Policy Review* 26 (2007): 371–386.

35. Keith Dobkowski, "Disability Insurance 3, Baseball Fans 1," Sports Business Simulations, 2007, www.sbs-world.com.

36. Eberhard Feess, Bernd Frick and Gerd Muehlheusser, "Legal Restrictions on Outside Trade Clauses—Theory and Evidence from German Soccer," IZA Discussion Paper no. 1140, Bonn, 2004.

37. Joel Maxcy, "Motivating Long-Term Employment Contracts: Risk Management in Major League Baseball," *Managerial and Decision Economics* 25 (2004): 109–120.

38. Eberhard Feess, Bernd Frick, and Gerd Muehlheusser, "Contract Duration and Player Performance: Empirical Evidence from German Soccer," mimeo, Witten/Herdecke University, 2007.

39. See Kevin Stiroh, "Playing for Keeps: Pay and Performance in the NBA," *Economic Inquiry* 45 (2007): 245–261. See also David Berri and Anthony Krautmann, "Shirking on the Court: Testing for the Incentive Effects of Guaranteed Pay," *Economic Inquiry* 44 (2006): 536–546.

40. Lawrence Kahn, "A Level Playing Field? Sports and Discrimination," in *The Economics of Sports*, ed. William Kern (Kalamazoo, Mich.: W. E. Upjohn Institute for Employment Research, 2000), 115–130.

41. See, for example, Lawrence Kahn and Peter Sherer, "Racial Differences in Professional Basketball Players' Compensation," *Journal of Labor Economics* 6 (1988): 40–61, and Mark Kanazawa and Jonas Funk, "Racial Discrimination in Professional Basketball: Evidence from the Nielsen Ratings," *Economic Inquiry* 39 (2001): 559–608.

42. Orn Bodvarsson and Mark Partridge, "A Supply and Demand Model of Co-worker, Employer, and Customer Discrimination," *Labour Economics* 8 (2001): 389–416.

43. David Berri and Rob Simmons, "Race and the Evaluation of Signal Callers in the National Football League," mimeo, Lancaster University Management School, 2007.

44. Ben Solow, John Solow and Todd Walker, "Moving on Up: The Rooney Rule and Minority Hiring in the NFL," paper presented to Western Economic Association International, Seattle, 2007. See also Janice Fanning Madden, "Differences in the Success of NFL Coaches by Race, 1990–2002," *Journal of Sports Economics* 5 (2004): 6–19.

45. Phil Vasili, *Colouring Over the White Line: The History of Black Footballers in Britain* (London: Mainstream, 2002). Note that representation of Asians in English professional football is very low while, even more surprisingly, take-up in English professional cricket is also low.

46. Stefan Szymanski, "A Market Test for Discrimination in the English Professional Soccer Leagues," *Journal of Political Economy* 108 (2000): 590–603.

47. For example, Rob Simmons and David Forrest, "Buying Success: Team Salaries and Performance in North American and European Sports Leagues," in *International Sports Economics Comparisons*, ed. Rodney Fort and John Fizel (Westport, Conn.: Praeger, 2004), 123–140.

48. Ian Preston and Stefan Szymanski, "Racial Discrimination in English Football," *Scottish Journal of Political Economy* 47 (2000): 342–363.

49. Roberto Pedace, "Earnings, Performance and Nationality Discrimination in a Highly Competitive Labor Market as an Analysis of an English Professional Soccer League," *Journal of Sports Economics* (forthcoming).

50. Frick, "Salary Determination and the Pay-Performance Relationship in Professional Soccer."

Eight

Salary Caps and Luxury Taxes in Professional Sports Leagues

Michael Leeds

Freedom of contract would be fatal to baseball.

Clark Griffith, player, coach,
and owner of the old Washington Senators

What right has the League to say to any player where he shall play next year? The days of slavery are over.

Cincinnati Enquirer (1880)

From the beginning of organized sport in the United States, teams have tried to gain an advantage over their competitors by bidding away their best players. Even before the first openly professional team, the Cincinnati Red Stockings, took the field in 1869, teams regularly enticed players with gifts or high-paying jobs.[1] To keep the bidding from getting out of hand, leagues have tried to impose limits on the degree to which teams compete for players. Few aspects of professional sports have caused more controversy. Strikes, lockouts, even the appearance of rival leagues have resulted from leagues' attempts to limit player salaries and from player resistance to those attempts.

Those who favor the attempts to rein in salaries view them a noble defense of the fans who root for teams located in small markets. Without limits, teams from Edmonton, Green Bay, or Kansas City would stand little chance of attracting the best players because they cannot afford to pay salaries that match those offered by teams from New York, Los Angeles, or Chicago. This, in turn, would endanger competitive balance, as teams from large cities would regularly win more games and more championships than teams from small cities. A league that lacks competitive balance would endanger teams from large and small cities alike, as fans ultimately lose interest in games whose outcome is a foregone conclusion.[2] Finally, ever-increasing payrolls drive up the cost of operation for all teams, further endangering their financial status.

Those who oppose limits on salaries see them as a naked grab for profits by wealthy team owners at the expense of players. They see the sports labor market as a "bilateral monopoly" in which a few players with unique skills bargain with a limited number of teams that demand such skills. In such "thin" labor markets, the salary is subject to bargaining between the two parties. This uncertainty stands in stark contrast to "thick" competitive markets with many employers and many workers, in which the impersonal forces of supply and demand determine salaries. Opponents of salary limits believe that teams continually try to limit players' ability to sell their talents freely. At times, players have referred to the limits on their mobility as a form of enslavement. In 1887 the star baseball player John Montgomery Ward wrote an article titled "Is the Ballplayer a Chattel?" for *Lippincott's Monthly*. Over eighty years later, star player Curt Flood wrote to baseball commissioner Bowie Kuhn, "I do not feel I am a piece of property to be bought and sold against my wishes."[3]

In this chapter, I first examine five ways in which teams in the four major North American Sports Leagues—Major League Baseball (MLB), the National Basketball Association (NBA), the National Football League (NFL), and the National Hockey League (NHL)—have tried to limit the salaries that they pay players. I begin by describing how these restrictions—the reserve clause, the player draft, the salary cap, the luxury tax, and revenue sharing—all operate. I then evaluate how these restrictions have affected competitive balance and profitability in the sports that have advocated them. After this, I describe the single-entity league and the transfer system, methods used by Major League Soccer (MLS) in North America and European soccer leagues belonging to the Union of European Football Associations (UEFA) to restrict salaries.

THE RESERVE CLAUSE AND FREE AGENCY

For a century, labor relations in professional sports were dominated by the reserve clause. Over this time period, the restrictions the reserve clause imposed on athletes was reviled as un-American, yet praised as the cornerstone of our "national pastime," often in the same breath: "The reserve rule is, on paper, the most unfair and degrading measure . . . ever passed in a free country. Still . . . it is necessary for the safety and preservation of the national game."[4]

The Nature and Origin of the Reserve Clause

For such a controversial document, the reserve clause appears rather innocuous. Read literally, it merely binds a player to the team that holds his contract—it *reserves* him—for the length of that contract plus one year. The power of the reserve clause came from teams' interpreting the phrase "renew this contract for the period of one year on the same terms" to mean they had the right to renew the entire contract—including the reserve clause—for the next year as well. This recursive system allowed a team to bind a player for his entire career. Indeed, many players believed that the reserve clause was actually a lifetime contract.[5] The reserve clause thus gave teams monopsony power over their players. Monopsony, a market structure containing only one buyer, tilts bargaining power strongly in favor of team owners, as the players cannot sell their talents to any other team. They can play for the team that owns their contract or not play at all.

When the MLB's National League was formed in 1876, team owners agreed to insert a reserve clause into the contract of five players on each team. Until they recognized the impact of the clause on their salaries, players were proud of being reserved. They regarded this clause as recognition of their star status. The owners quickly recognized the power that the reserve clause gave them over salaries. By 1887 the reserve clause had become a standard portion of every player's contract.[6] As other sports formed professional leagues, they adopted baseball's reserve clause, often word for word.

Players responded to the reserve clause in several ways. Starting in 1885 with the Brotherhood of Professional Base Ball Players, players in all leagues tried to create a countervailing power to the owners by forming professional organizations. Such attempts, however, were uniformly unsuccessful, in part because of manipulation by the owners and in part because of the players' own unwillingness to recognize their organizations as unions. The current players' associations were not formed until the 1950s and did not engage in serious collective bargaining until the 1970s.

The End of the Reserve Clause

Because it gives leagues monopsony power over players, the reserve clause has been the subject of numerous antitrust lawsuits. Free agency, the ability of a player to sell his services freely, came to football, basketball, and hockey as a direct result of successful antitrust lawsuits by players. Unlike the other three sports, baseball players could not bring antitrust suits against MLB because a 1922 Supreme Court decision gave MLB blanket exemption from antitrust laws. The Court ruled that baseball was a "public exhibition," not commerce, and hence was not subject to antitrust laws. While the court repeatedly upheld MLB's exemption (e.g., *Toolson v. New York Yankees* in 1953 and *Flood v. Kuhn* in 1971), it consistently refused to extend the exemption to any other sport or industry. Still, baseball players were the first to achieve free agency when the Major League Baseball Players Association (MLBPA) convinced an arbitration panel that the reserve clause applied for only one year and did not restrict player mobility indefinitely.[7]

The NFL was the first to lose a major court decision, though, ironically, it was the last of the four leagues to experience free agency. In 1946 George Radovich left the Detroit Lions after his contract expired to play with the Los Angeles Dons of the All American Football Conference (AAFC). After the AAFC folded, Radovich found himself blacklisted by the NFL and sued the league for antitrust violations. In 1957 the Supreme Court ruled in Radovich's favor and rejected the NFL's right to reserve players. The decision, however, did not bring free agency to the NFL. Instead, the owners engaged in a "gentlemen's agreement" not to pursue each other's players. When the agreement began to break down in the early 1960s, NFL commissioner Alvin "Pete" Rozelle unilaterally imposed restrictions on player movement. While the "Rozelle rule" explicitly recognized the rights of players to be free agents, it required the team signing a free agent to compensate the team that lost the free agent. If the two teams could not reach an agreement, the commissioner himself would impose one, which Rozelle hinted would generously compensate the team losing a player. A form of the Rozelle rule survived until 1992, when a U.S. District Court ruled in *McNeil et al. v. NFL*, that the Rozelle rule violated antitrust laws.[8]

The NHL and NBA both faced challenges to the reserve clause in the 1970s as a direct result of challenges by rival leagues. When several NHL players attempted to sign contracts with the new World Hockey Association (WHA), the NHL tried to stop them by citing the reserve clause. In 1972 the WHA successfully sued the NHL for violations of antitrust law. The lawsuit struck down the reserve clause, with which the NHL tried to keep its players from signing with WHA teams. While the WHA's suit was aimed at allowing players to sign with a rival league, the principle also applied to players seeking to change teams.

Free agency in the NBA resulted from the league's settling an antitrust lawsuit brought by Oscar Robertson, a star player and president of the National Basketball Players Association (NBPA). The lawsuit challenged the NBA on a number of issues, including its attempt to merge with the rival American Basketball Association (ABA), the player draft, and the reserve clause. Desperate to settle what had been a costly war with the ABA, the NBA ceased its appeal of the Robertson case in 1976 and agreed to phase in free agency over the next several years.

The Impact of Free Agency on Team Finances

Sports leagues defended the reserve clause by claiming that free agency would allow the richest teams to dominate the sport and would bankrupt the rest. On the surface, it appears that such dire financial claims were not justified, as no team in MLB, the NBA, NFL, or NHL has declared bankruptcy since the advent of free agency, and three leagues appear financially sound.

According to *Forbes* magazine, which provides annual analyses of team finances, the median NBA team had an operating income of over $9 million in 2005/06.[9] There was some disparity in operating income, as eleven of thirty NBA teams had negative operating income. Of these, however, one supposedly unprofitable team—the Dallas Mavericks—is owned by billionaire Mark Cuban, who has made little secret of his willingness to spend lavishly on his team, and another—the New Orleans Hornets—effectively lost its home city in the aftermath of Hurricane Katrina.

Thanks to its lucrative television contracts, the NFL is extremely profitable. Its median team had an operating income of over $35 million in 2005, over four times the NBA level. Moreover, all teams had positive operating income; the least profitable team had operating income of almost $8 million.

Unlike the NFL and NBA, which implemented salary caps soon after granting free agency, MLB moved quickly to unfettered free agency after it lost the reserve clause in 1976. Players were free to sign with new teams once they had logged six years of service in the major leagues. According to *Forbes,* the median baseball team made an operating income of over $16 million in 2005, with only five teams operating in the red. Moreover, four of those five teams—the New York Yankees and Mets, Boston Red Sox, and Los Angeles Dodgers—were also the four teams with the highest revenues and highest estimated market values. These teams' poor financial performance has two likely causes: either the teams have understated their revenues and inflated their costs or they do not care about profits and pursue other goals instead.

Of the four major sports, hockey appears to be on the thinnest ice. *Forbes* reports that more than half the thirty teams in the NHL lost money during the 2003/04 season (the last season for which *Forbes* data are available) and that the median level of operating income was −$0.85 million.[10] While one could (and the owners did) attribute these losses to rising labor costs, one should bear in mind that hockey had by far the lowest revenue stream. This, in turn, was due largely to declining income from television broadcasting rights. Whatever problems hockey might have with its cost structure, much of the NHL's financial trouble can therefore be blamed on mismanagement of its revenues. Moreover, even before the current collective bargaining agreement (CBA) imposed a salary cap, hockey players were the least free of free agents, not becoming unrestricted free agents until they were thirty years old.[11]

The Impact of Free Agency on Competitive Balance

This section focuses on the impact that free agency had on competitive balance in baseball because baseball made the clearest move to free agency. The impact of free agency on the NFL and NBA was obscured by their rapid adoption of salary caps. The many limitations on free agency in the NHL also reduced its impact on player movement. Only baseball allowed free movement of players without any form of restriction, at least until the 2002 CBA imposed a luxury tax on teams with high payrolls.

Empirical evidence from MLB and economic theory also cast doubt on the claim that the reserve clause was needed to preserve competitive balance. Table 8.1 shows the World Series Champions for the twenty-nine seasons since players gained free agency in 1976 (there was no World Series in 1994 due to the strike) and for the twenty-nine seasons before the advent of free agency.

Table 8.1 shows that a few teams, most notably the New York Yankees, dominated both eras, but it does not show clearly whether championships were more concentrated before or after free agency. To get a precise measure of concentration, I use the Herfindahl-Hirschman index (HHI).[12] The HHI starts with the number of championships (c_i) each team has won over a period of T years. Each era in Table 8.1 is twenty-nine years long, so $T = 29$ for both eras. Next, calculating HHI requires calculating the share of the total number of championships won by each team, squaring this share, and summing across all teams in the league. If every team took turns winning the World Series, over this period, each team's share would equal one for twenty-nine teams and zero for the thirtieth, so HHI would equal $29*(1/29)^2 = 1/29 = 0.034$.[13] If one team won every year, the index would equal $(29/29)^2 = 1.0$. Thus, a lower HHI means that championships are more evenly divided.

The HHI for the post–free agency period (1977–2006) is 0.082, precisely half the value of the HHI for the pre–free agency period (1948–1976), which is 0.164. The HHI thus tells us that World Series championships have been more evenly spread since the end of the reserve clause. Contrary to the predictions of team owners, big-market teams like the Yankees and Dodgers have not grown more dominant with the advent of free agency.

The failure of rich teams to win championship after championship supports an economic theory known as the Coase theorem.[14] In its original

TABLE 8.1
World Series Champions Pre– and Post–Free Agency

Pre–Free Agency		Post–Free Agency	
Year	Champion	Year	Champion
1948	Indians	1977	Yankees
1949	Yankees	1978	Yankees
1950	Yankees	1979	Pirates
1951	Yankees	1980	Phillies
1952	Yankees	1981	Dodgers
1953	Yankees	1982	Cardinals
1954	Giants	1983	Orioles
1955	Dodgers	1984	Tigers
1956	Yankees	1985	Royals
1957	Braves	1986	Mets
1958	Yankees	1987	Twins
1959	Dodgers	1988	Dodgers
1960	Pirates	1989	Athletics
1961	Yankees	1990	Reds
1962	Yankees	1991	Twins
1963	Dodgers	1992	Blue Jays
1964	Cardinals	1993	Blue Jays
1965	Dodgers	1995[a]	Braves
1966	Orioles	1996	Yankees
1967	Cardinals	1997	Marlins
1968	Tigers	1998	Yankees
1969	Mets	1999	Yankees
1970	Orioles	2000	Yankees
1971	Pirates	2001	Diamondbacks
1972	Athletics	2002	Angels
1973	Athletics	2003	Marlins
1974	Athletics	2004	Red Sox
1975	Reds	2005	White Sox
1976	Reds	2006	Cardinals

[a]No World Series was played in 1994 due to the strike.

form, the Coase theorem showed how society could resolve negative externalities, such as pollution. In the context of professional sports, it says that
players go to the teams that value their services most highly, regardless of
the contractual relationship between players and owners. The Coase theorem thus predicts that the end of the reserve clause should not have affected
the distribution of talent.

Under free agency, it is no surprise that players move as predicted by the
Coase theorem. The Yankees were able to obtain Alex Rodriguez and his $25
million per year contract because they were willing to pay more than other

teams. They were willing to pay more because they believed that Rodriguez would have a greater impact on their revenue than other teams did.[15]

While the Yankees were able to attract Alex Rodriguez in 2004 by offering him a more lucrative contract than other teams did, the reserve clause prevented them from making a similar offer to Babe Ruth in 1920. However, they still managed to acquire Babe Ruth because of one crucial similarity between the two situations: both players were more valuable to New York than to any other team. This, in turn meant that the Yankees were willing and able to pay more for their services. Unlike Alex Rodriguez, Babe Ruth did not control his own destiny. He effectively belonged to the Boston Red Sox, who owned his contract. By 1920, however, Ruth was worth much more in New York than in Boston, so the Yankees could compensate the Red Sox for his loss and still profit from Ruth's services. The change in property rights brought by free agency thus transferred income from team owners to players. However, as predicted by the Coase theorem, players moved to the Yankees, regardless of the constraints on players.

THE DRAFT

While the reserve clause effectively linked a player to the team that held his contract, players who had not yet signed a contract retained the right to bargain freely with teams. This source of free agency occasionally resulted in bidding wars between teams. In 1935 one such war broke out between the Philadelphia Eagles and the Brooklyn Dodgers for the services of Stan Kostka, a star fullback for the University of Minnesota.[16] The two teams drove the salary offer to $5,000 per year, the salary paid to Bronko Nagurski, the NFL's reigning superstar.

At the next league meeting, Eagles owner Bert Bell proposed a draft to prevent such conflicts in the future. The draft allowed teams to claim the rights to players who had not yet entered the league, conferring monopsony power on the team even before it had signed the player to a contract. As a *reverse-order* draft, Bell's proposal specified that teams would draft players in reverse order of their finish the previous season.

All the major professional leagues now have some form of draft. The number of rounds is specified in each league's CBA and varies with such factors as the number of roster slots, the existence of minor leagues that develop talent for the major-league teams, and the degree of certainty that the teams have about the ability of the players they draft. Because NBA rosters are so small and teams are relatively sure about the talents of the players they draft, the NBA draft lasts only two rounds. The NHL draft has five rounds, while the NFL, with its larger rosters, has a draft that lasts seven rounds. MLB, which faces the greatest uncertainty regarding the ability of the players it drafts, has no set number of rounds, with teams selecting until they no longer wish to select any more players. Any player who is not selected in the draft and who meets the league's eligibility requirements is allowed to negotiate freely with any team.

Sometimes the leagues have used the draft to limit what players may enter the league. In the NFL's early years, when it was afraid to offend officials in the more popular college game, the league refused to draft players until they (or at least the class they would have belonged to) graduated from college. More recently, the NBA has required that players be at least twenty years old before teams can draft them. The player associations in each league have occasionally challenged the draft as a violation of antitrust laws.

It is easy to dismiss the draft as a grab by team owners. That is how most player unions now regard it. They point out that no other profession has such restrictions on a new entrant's choice of employment. Certainly no economics instructor would submit to a system whereby schools got to pick new economics Ph.D.s in reverse order of the schools' SAT scores.

While it did contribute to teams' monopsony power, creating a reverse-order draft was a selfless act by some NFL team owners. The Chicago Bears and New York Giants, two dominant teams in the NFL's early years, had a great deal to lose in a system that might spread talent more evenly. Instead, the teams put the greater good ahead of their own self-interest and supported the proposal because, in the words of Giants' owner Tim Mara, "People come to see a competition. We could give them a competition only if the teams had some sort of equality."[17] Mara believed that a draft promoted competitive balance and that competitive balance was important for the long-term health of the NFL.

One drawback of a reverse-order draft is that it can actually worsen competition late in the season. Because the draft rewards poor performance with a high draft pick, teams that do not have a reasonable chance of making (or advancing in) the playoffs could lose intentionally in order to secure a higher spot in the draft. As a result of this perverse incentive, the NBA instituted a draft lottery in 1985. The lottery gives the teams with the worst records a better chance at a top draft pick, but it does not guarantee them one.[18] Because all four major leagues have long had player drafts, there is no way to evaluate whether competitive balance and team finances have been improved by the draft.

SALARY CAPS

The four major North American sports leagues have long regarded the salary cap as a panacea that would cure all worries about competitive balance

TABLE 8.2
Salary Cap Figures for Basketball, Football, and Hockey
(In Million US$)

Season	NBA	NFL	NHL
1984/85	$3.600		
1985/86	$4.233		
1986/87	$4.945		
1987/88	$6.164		
1988/89	$7.232		
1989/90	$9.802		
1990/91	$11.871		
1991/92	$12.500		
1992/93	$14.000		
1993/94	$15.175		
1994/95	$15.964	$34.600	
1995/96	$23.000	$37.100	
1996/97	$24.363	$40.777	
1997/98	$26.900	$41.450	
1998/99	$30.000	$52.388	
1999/2000	$34.000	$58.353	
2000/01	$35.500	$62.172	
2001/02	$42.500	$67.400	
2002/03	$40.271	$71.100	
2003/04	$43.840	$75.007	
2004/05	$43.870	$78.780	
2005/06	$49.500	$85.500	$39.000
2006/07	$53.135	$102.000	$44.000

and profitability. The NBA regards it as having saved the league in the 1980s and locked out its players for half a season in 1998/99 in order to tighten it. The NHL went even further and locked out its players for the entire 2004/05 season for the sake of a salary cap. MLB endured almost a quarter century of labor unrest in the owners' unsuccessful attempt to impose a salary cap, though it did manage to install a luxury tax (described below) in 2002. As with so much else, all three sports look longingly at football, wishing that they could have as successful a cap on salaries as the NFL has. The upper limits of team payrolls for the NBA, NFL, and NHL appear in Table 8.2.

Most people believe that the salary caps shown in Table 8.2 form an absolute limit to what teams may pay. In fact, salary caps are complex mechanisms for controlling payrolls that have features unique to each sport that uses them.

All caps, however, share several important features. First, with one important exception, salary caps do not *cap* salaries at all. Instead they impose limits on overall team payrolls. Second, salary caps are more accurately termed "salary bands." All impose minimum levels on team payrolls. In the NBA all teams must have payrolls that are at least 75 percent of the annual cap. NFL teams must pay at least 56 percent of designated league revenue, while NHL teams pay a minimum of 40 percent. Finally, salary caps do not limit what teams actually pay in a given year. When one looks at team payroll data from *USA Today*, one would believe that salary caps are more honored in the breach than the observance.[19] In 2005 nine of thirty-two NFL teams had payrolls that exceeded the league's official 2005 salary cap of $85.5 million, with the Seattle Seahawks going about $15 million over the cap. In the NBA twenty-three of thirty teams exceeded the official 2005/06 cap of $49.5 million, with the New York Knicks going more than $43 million over the cap. Even in the NHL, which lost the 2004/05 season to a dispute over salary caps, eight of thirty teams had payrolls exceeding the cap in 2005/06. The highest payroll in the NHL belonged to the New Jersey Devils at about $45 million. In this section, I explore what salary caps have and have not done to curb the rise in salaries and how salary caps have affected competitive balance in professional sports.

Just as MLB's reserve clause created the template for all other sports, the NBA set the precedent for all other sports' salary caps. As Table 8.2 shows, it predates all other salary caps by at least ten years. This early adoption is less a reflection of forward thinking by the NBA than it is a sign of the league's desperation in the early 1980s. Over the previous decade, the league had lost the reserve clause, and, thanks in part to the competition for players with the ABA, salaries had risen to 70 percent of gross revenues.[20] Desperate to restrain the pressure on team finances, the NBA convinced the players to accept a salary cap by guaranteeing the players a percentage of league revenues. That formula formed the basis for the first salary cap in the 1984/85 season and has been the basis for all other salary caps in professional sports.

The NBA's Salary Cap

Since the 1999 CBA that followed the lockout of 1998/99, the NBA salary cap has had two components: a team cap and an individual cap.[21] The team cap for the 2006/07 season is set at 51 percent of the league's projected basketball-related income (BRI). BRI comes from a wide variety of sources, including:

- Gate revenue from preseason, regular season, and playoff games
- Broadcast rights
- Concessions, parking, and pouring rights

- 40 percent of proceeds from signage and luxury suites
- 45–50 percent of proceeds from naming rights

The league divides this figure by the number of teams to get the limit on each team's payroll.[22] For the NBA in 2006/07, this came out to:

$$CAP = 0.51*\$3.125B \div 30 = \$53.135M \text{ per team}$$

Unlike a "hard cap," which cannot be exceeded under any circumstances, the NBA maintains a "soft cap," which has a number of exceptions, of which the best known are the "Larry Bird rule," the rookie exception, and the disabled-player exception.

The motivation for the Larry Bird rule was to allow teams to keep a core of players together. It is so named because the first application of the exception allowed the Boston Celtics to re-sign their star player, Larry Bird, without having to disband the rest of the team. To be eligible for the Larry Bird rule, a player must have been with the team for three consecutive years and may sign a contract for no more than six years. In addition, a player signed under the Larry Bird rule may not receive raises of more than 10.5 percent per year. The rookie exception allows a team to sign players it has drafted (according the limits on signing rookies) even if doing so pushes the team over the cap. The disabled-player exception allows a team to violate the cap in order to replace players who will miss the rest of the season due to injury.[23]

As a result of its lockout of the players in 1998/99, the NBA was able to add two new features to its salary cap. The first is a cap on individual salaries that effectively imposes a salary scale on players. The second is effectively a tax on player salaries.

As with the overall team cap, the individual salary cap is actually a band within which individual salaries must lie. For example, a rookie who entered the NBA in 2006/07 had to be paid at least $427,163 and at most $12.455 million. Similarly, a player with seven years' experience in 2006/07 had to be paid between $998,967 and $12.455 million.[24]

After the lockout of 1998/99, the NBA also instituted an escrow system to further tighten the salary cap. Under the escrow system, the league sets aside 9 percent of each player's salary.[25] If player salaries and benefits—regardless of exceptions—exceed 57 percent of BRI (6 percentage points over the limit set by the cap), then the league receives some of the funds in escrow to bring salaries and benefits down to the 57 percent limit. If salaries and benefits are below 57 percent to begin with, then the players receive all the money held in escrow. Players may not be penalized more than the 9 percent escrow payment, even if it is not enough to bring salaries and benefits below 57 percent.

The NFL's Salary Cap

The NFL negotiated a salary cap in 1994 with the National Football League Players Association (NFLPA).[26] The league's desire for a salary cap grew out of court rulings that had granted players free agency. Unlike the NBA, the NFL has a hard cap, in which there are no exemptions and almost all payments to players count against the cap. Still, almost one-third of all NFL teams' payrolls exceed the cap.

The formula for the NFL's salary cap closely resembles the NBA's formula, but the two differ in several important ways.[27] For the 2006 season, the NFL set aside 59.5 percent of its designated gross revenues (DGR) for player salaries and benefits. DGR includes:

- Gate revenue from preseason, regular season, and postseason games
- Broadcast rights
- Other licensing agreements
- The ticket revenue portion of income from luxury boxes and premium seating

The NFL's salary cap is based on the difference between the DGR and the nonsalary benefits received by players. One divides this figure by the number of teams (thirty-two) to get each team's payroll limit. In 2006 the limit was $102 million.

$$CAP = 0.595^*(DGR - B) \div 32 = \$102M \text{ per team.}$$

The computation of the NFL's cap differs from the computation of the NBA's cap in several important ways, of which I shall note three. First, while the NFL pays a higher percentage of its designated income than the NBA does, the higher percentage is more than offset by the second difference: the NFL counts less luxury-box revenue in DGR than the NBA counts in BRI. BRI includes all luxury-box revenue while DGR includes only the ticket revenue portion of luxury-box revenue. Teams share ticket revenue from luxury boxes with other teams as well as with players.[28] As a result, one of the primary reasons for the NFL teams' preoccupation with luxury boxes is that ticket revenue is only a small portion of luxury-box revenue. Most of the revenue from luxury boxes is typically listed as concession revenue, reflecting the food and amenities that make luxury boxes so luxurious. Teams do not share concession revenue with other teams, and the CBA explicitly excludes it from DGR. Second, the NFL further reduces payrolls by deducting its contribution to a league-wide benefit pool before computing the salary cap.

In theory, the NFL's hard cap is very simple: the sum of all players' salaries must fall within the band defined above. The reality, however, is more complicated. First, while NFL teams have fifty-three players on their active rosters, the salary cap applies only to the fifty-one highest-paid players. Second, bonuses create a difference between a team's actual payroll and its official payroll for salary cap purposes.

Bonuses have become an important part of player contracts in the NFL because, unlike the other major North American sports leagues, the NFL generally does not have guaranteed contracts. A multiyear contract is valid only if the player makes the team's active roster. Star players have gotten around the lack of guaranteed contracts by insisting on "signing bonuses," payable when the player signs his contract or on easily obtained "incentive bonuses" as a reward for performance. While such bonuses count against the salary cap, the NFL allows teams to prorate the bonus over the length of the contract rather than at the time they are paid. Thus, for cap purposes, a contract that pays a player $35 million dollars in equal $7 million increments over five years is indistinguishable from a contract that pays the player a $15-million signing bonus and $4 million over five years.[29]

Not all bonuses count against the cap. Signing bonuses, roster bonuses (paid if a player makes the team roster), and workout bonuses (paid if a player attends off-season team workouts) all fall into the category of "likely to be earned" (LTBE) bonuses and count against the salary cap. Similarly, any bonus paid for meeting standards that the player satisfied the previous year counts as LTBE and counts against the salary cap. Bonuses for meeting previously unmet goals (e.g., a running back running for more yards than he has before) count as "not likely to be earned" (NLTBE) and do not count against the cap.

The NHL's Salary Cap

The NHL's salary cap, enacted in the wake of the lockout that resulted in the cancellation of the 2004/05 season, sets the players' share of league revenue according to a sliding scale. The scale starts at 54 percent of "hockey-related" revenue when revenues are below $2.2 billion and reaches 57 percent of league revenues when revenues exceed $2.7 billion. The cap is a hard cap, including all salaries, signing bonuses, and performance bonuses. The NHL cap also includes individual player limits, with no player allowed to receive more than 20 percent of the team's allowable payroll.

Like the NBA, the NHL uses an escrow system to enforce its cap. For 2006/07, players paid 10 percent of their pay into an escrow account. They received funds from the account as long as the payments kept payrolls within the salary cap limits.

FIGURE 8.1

Team Payrolls in North American Sports Leagues, 2006

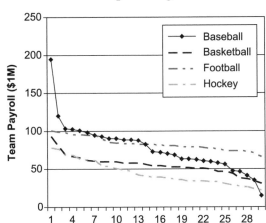

The Impact of Salary Caps

Salary caps have clearly affected the level and the dispersion of team pay-rolls. Figure 8.1 shows the payrolls of all MLB, NBA, NFL, and NHL teams for the 2006 or 2005/06 season. Baseball, the one sport that does not have a salary cap, had by far the highest payrolls. Six baseball teams (the Yankees, Boston Red Sox, Los Angeles Angels, Chicago White Sox, New York Mets, and Los Angeles Dodgers) all had higher payrolls than any team in the other three major sports. The variance of payrolls in MLB is also far wider than in any other sport. The thirteen MLB teams with the highest payrolls paid more than correspondingly ranked teams in every other sport. MLB teams with payrolls ranked fifteen to thirty all paid less than the corresponding NFL teams. The Florida Marlins, the MLB team with the lowest payroll, paid less than *any* other team in any of the four major sports.

Because hockey switched from not having a salary cap in 2003/04 to hav-ing a strict cap in 2005/06, comparing payrolls in those two years shows how the cap affected payrolls. Figure 8.2 compares team payrolls from the two years. The lower, flatter graph for 2005/06 shows that the salary cap reduced the mean and variance of payrolls. After averaging double-digit growth in the three seasons before the lockout, the average payroll fell by almost one-third in the year following the lockout. The decline was most pronounced among the highest payrolls. In 2005/06, the highest team payroll was more than 40 percent lower than the highest payroll in 2003/04. At the opposite end, how-ever, the five lowest payrolls were virtually unchanged in the two years.

FIGURE 8.2
Team Payroll for NHL Teams in 2003/04 and 2005/06

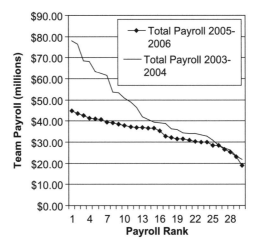

Whether salary caps promote competitive balance remains an open question. Because both salary caps and free agency began simultaneously in the NFL and almost simultaneously in the NBA, one cannot determine the impact of either factor alone by looking at each sport individually.[30] Instead, I compare how championships have varied in these two sports with championship turnover in baseball, which has had free agency but no salary caps over this period. By this standard, the NFL has had the least concentrated championships. The NFL's HHI for Super Bowl winners since 1995, the first season in which the NFL had a salary cap, is 0.138, while the HHI for MLB since 1995 is 0.181. NBA championships are even more concentrated. Its HHI since the 1985/86 season, the first season of its salary cap, is 0.198, while baseball's HHI for the same period is 0.083.[31]

Another way to see whether salary caps have affected competitive balance is to look at the correlation between teams' payrolls and winning percentages. A high correlation means that even if there is significant turnover in champions, the teams with high payrolls perform better over the course of the season than teams with low payrolls. Because salary caps compress team payrolls, they should also reduce the correlation between payrolls and within-season performance. As one might expect, in the 2006 season, MLB had the highest correlation between payroll and winning percentage (0.538), while the NFL, which has the smallest variation in payroll, had the lowest correlation in 2005/06 (0.156). This difference suggests a strong relationship between winning and payrolls. However, the NBA and the NHL do not fully support this conclusion. The NBA, which, by some standards has a stricter cap than the NFL does, had a correlation almost exactly in between the two extremes (0.368) in 2005/06. The correlation for the NHL in 2005/06 was roughly the same as for the NBA (0.330). Interestingly, NHL's correlation in 2005/06 was somewhat *higher* than in 2003/04, the year before limits were imposed (0.319).

LUXURY TAXES AND REVENUE SHARING

Intuitively, luxury taxes and revenue sharing appear to have little in common. Luxury taxes, the term applied to penalties imposed on teams whose payrolls exceed a given threshold, seem clearly aimed at limiting salary growth. Revenue sharing, however, seems to be a way for teams to promote competitive balance but seems to have nothing to do with players. In fact, both can place significant restrictions on team payrolls.

Luxury Taxes

While MLB has no explicit salary cap, the 2002 CBA imposed the sport's first luxury tax. In 2006, all teams with payrolls in excess of $136.5 million were subject to the tax. A team received a warning if its payroll exceeded the threshold for the first time. It paid a tax equal to 30 percent of its "overspending" if its payroll exceeded the threshold for the second time, and it paid a 40 percent tax for a third or successive violation. George Steinbrenner, the owner of the New York Yankees, has called the luxury tax a "Yankee tax" because he believes it unfairly singles out his team. In fact, the Yankees were the only team to pay a tax in each year of its existence, and only two other teams, the Boston Red Sox and the Los Angeles Angels, have ever paid the luxury tax.

The NBA's luxury tax is even stiffer. NBA teams pay a 100 percent tax ($1 of tax for every $1 their payroll exceeds the threshold). Computing the NBA threshold is similar to computing the salary cap. One takes 61 percent of the league's projected BRI, subtracts projected benefits paid to players, and adjusts for whether the previous season's BRI was greater or less than anticipated. Dividing this figure by the number of teams in the league (thirty) yields the threshold. In 2005/06, the threshold was $61.7 million, and six teams paid tax. The New York Knicks paid by far the highest tax ($37.2 million).[32] Neither the NFL nor the NHL has a luxury tax.

The effectiveness of a luxury tax is open to question. As we have seen, the NBA does very poorly with regard to most measures of competitive balance. In MLB a luxury tax that applies to only one team will naturally have a limited impact. Moreover, George Steinbrenner has openly stated that the luxury tax will not deter him from paying high salaries to attract star players to the Yankees.

Revenue Sharing

All four major North American leagues share revenue, but the degree and nature of revenue sharing varies considerably across leagues. All the leagues share revenue from league-negotiated broadcasts equally. The NFL's immense network contract (worth about $117 million annually to each team) virtually ensures that each NFL team will be profitable. By contrast, the NHL's minuscule contract with the Versus cable network adds little to team revenues. MLB and the NBA have network broadcast revenue that lies in between the NFL and the NHL. MLB's situation is complicated by the fact that some teams also have immense local media revenues, largely from cable companies. Until recently, these revenues were not shared at all.

The NFL shares more of its gate revenue than any other league. NFL teams keep only 60 percent of their home gate revenue, with the other 40 percent split equally among all other teams. Teams in the NBA keep 94 percent of their gate revenue, while NHL teams do not share any gate revenue.

Until recently, baseball did little to alter the immense differences in team revenues. In 2005, for example, *Forbes* reported that the New York Yankees had revenues of $277 million, while the Minnesota Twins had revenues of only $114 million. The 2002 CBA sought to bring a degree of revenue-sharing by having teams pay 34 percent of their net local revenue into a central pool, part of which is shared equally by all teams and part of which is paid only to teams with below-average net local revenue.

At first glance, revenue-sharing seems to be a good way to redistribute playing talent but not a good way to limit salaries. In fact, the opposite is true. To see why, first consider the advantages facing teams from large cities. Figure 8.3 shows a simple league in which there are two profit-maximizing teams: the New York Yankees and the Kansas City Royals. Because New York has more potential fans and a larger media market, the impact of one more win on the Yankees' revenue—its marginal revenue—is greater than the marginal revenue of the Royals. Figure 8.3 shows a simple version of the declining impact of performance on revenue in marginal revenue curves for the Yankees and Royals. The downward sloping curves show that winning one more game increases a team's revenue, but that each additional win adds less revenue than the previous win did. In effect, fans want their home team to win, but they become increasingly bored as the outcome becomes more predictable. In this simple example, the two curves are identical except for the fact that the Royals' marginal revenue curve lies below the Yankees'

FIGURE 8.3
Why Teams from Big Cities Win More Games

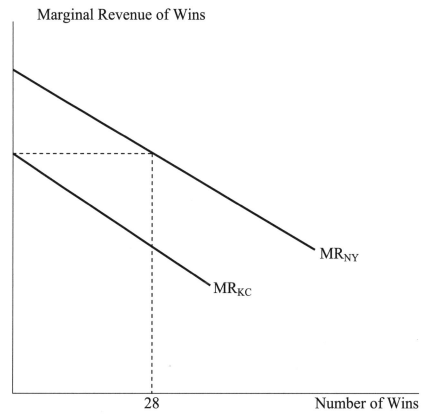

curve. This reflects the fact that an additional win generates less revenue in Kansas City than in New York.[33]

If players are free to move to the team that bids the most for their services and there is no revenue-sharing, the Yankees will outbid the Royals for talent as long as the marginal revenue of a win is greater for them than for the Royals, that is, as long as $MR_{NY} > MR_{KC}$. In this example, the marginal revenue for the Royals is less than the marginal revenue for the Yankees until the Yankees have already won twenty-eight games. In this simple example, that means that the Yankees will expect to average twenty-eight more wins than the Royals do.[34]

Let's now assume that both teams share all revenue equally, so the Yankees send half their revenue to the Royals, and vice versa. In this case, the two teams' revenues are equal, so it would appear that neither team has an advantage. If we let MR_{NY}^* be the Yankees' marginal revenue and MR_{KC}^* be the Royals' marginal revenue when the two teams share equally, then:

$$MR_{NY}^* = (1/2)^* MR_{NY} + (1/2)^* MR_{KC} = MR_{KC}^*$$

Because sharing revenues equally means that $MR_{NY}^* = MR_{KC}^*$, it appears that the two teams compete for talent on an equal basis. If the two teams maximize profits, however, this is not the case. While the MR curves for the two teams are equal, both teams' marginal revenue is maximized if they behave exactly as in Figure 8.3. As long as $MR_{NY} > MR_{KC}$, the two teams are better off if talent flows to the Yankees. Only when $MR_{NY} = MR_{KC}$—that is, when the Yankees have enough talent to be twenty-eight games better than the Royals—does it pay for the two teams to compete on an equal footing for talent. In other words, the distribution of talent remains skewed toward the Yankees.

While it does not affect where players go, revenue sharing does affect salaries. In this example, an additional win is now worth exactly half as much as it used to be, as are the players who generate those wins. Sharing revenues equally thus reduces the value of players to their teams and reduces the salaries that teams are willing to pay. This helps explain why NFL teams, which have by far the highest revenue streams but also share more of their revenue than any other league, pay relatively low salaries. It also clarifies why the MLBPA has opposed revenue sharing so vehemently for so long.

SOCCER ON TWO CONTINENTS

Both in Europe and the United States, soccer faces a very different economic climate than the four major North American sports. In the United States, Major League Soccer (MLS) is a new start-up, having been founded in 1993. MLS entered an already crowded field of spectator sports and has struggled to survive with a limited revenue stream. As a result, it has placed a premium on controlling costs.

The European Leagues are at the other end of the spectrum. Soccer is king in Europe, with no other sport generating nearly as much enthusiasm or revenue. Still, as good profit maximizers, soccer teams developed a method to limit player mobility and depress player costs.

MLS: The Single-Entity League

In the four major sports, the relationship between individual teams and the league is ambiguous. Economists and legal scholars disagree whether individual teams are competing firms—like Ford and General Motors—or complementary parts of one big producer—like Buick and Chevrolet, both divisions of General Motors. There is no question regarding the business model for MLS, which has kept a tight lid on costs by forming a single-entity league. In standard leagues, autonomous teams coordinate on schedules, rules, and the division of costs and benefits, but they compete with one another for players. In a single-entity league, the league's central office makes all decisions regarding resource allocation.[35]

While the single-entity structure has helped MLS to control costs, it has not been an unqualified success. MLS has been able to keep teams from bidding against one another for players, but it has been unable to keep its best players from taking better-paying jobs in other leagues. Low payrolls have thus come at the cost of a lower quality product. In addition, with all returns determined by the central office, the management of an individual team has little reason to engage in activities that benefit the league as a whole, such as marketing and community relations. In order to combat this problem, MLS has hit upon yet another unique resolution: two individuals, Phillip Anschutz and Lamar Hunt, own most of the teams. This takes centralization to yet another level, but the reliance on just a few investors also makes it highly unlikely that the single-entity league will serve as a model for future leagues.[36]

European Soccer and the Transfer System

Despite the sport's worldwide popularity, many top-level soccer teams are under great financial pressure. Low revenues in Latin America explain why the best Brazilian and Argentinean players compete in Europe. However, even some relatively wealthy European teams are struggling financially. One study found that only three teams in Italy's top league (Serie A) were financially stable.[37] Soccer teams are quick to claim that their problems are largely due to higher player costs that resulted from the 1991 Bosman ruling.

Prior to 1991, the mobility of soccer players worldwide was limited by transfer fees. Transfer fees served the same purpose as the Rozelle rule in the NFL. They were designed to compensate teams who lost players to free agency. If the team losing a player did not feel that it was receiving adequate compensation, it could prevent the player from leaving for another team.

In 1990 Jean-Marc Bosman, an obscure player with Liege, a second-tier Belgian soccer club, sought to move to the French team Dunkerque. Liege felt that Dunkerque's transfer offer was too low and blocked the move. Bosman then sued the Belgian soccer league before the European Court of Justice, claiming that the transfer system violated the European Union's antitrust laws. In 1995 the court ruled in Bosman's favor and struck down the transfer system. Today, teams may claim transfer fees only for players who are still under contract. Once a player's contract has ended, he is free to sign with another team.[38]

As with North American sports, the advent of free agency in European soccer has not had a clear impact on European soccer leagues. While teams in England and Italy have been severely pressed, teams in France and Germany are in no such financial difficulty. The relative prosperity in the latter two countries is mostly due to institutional arrangements that prevent extravagant payments to players. For example, France's national soccer association places tight limits on how much teams can borrow or spend. In Germany team officials must personally guarantee any loans that teams take out. This, in turn, discourages teams from going into debt to pay for star players.[39]

Tables 8.3 and 8.4 suggest that the Bosman ruling had little impact on the concentration of championships in European soccer. Table 8.3 shows the champions in the UEFA Champions League since 1985. The Champions League consists of thirty-two teams, sixteen of whom (the top teams from the most prestigious leagues) qualify automatically and sixteen of whom qualify via a playoff. These thirty-two teams then stage a tournament to determine the top professional club in Europe. Table 8.3 shows that the distribution of championships in the eleven years before Bosman is identical to the distribution in the eleven years since, with one team winning three times and eight teams winning once in each time period. (The HHI equals 0.140 in each time period.)

TABLE 8.3
European Champions Pre- and Post-Bosman Ruling

Pre-Bosman		Post-Bosman	
Year	Champion	Year	Champion
1985	Juventus	1996	Juventus
1986	Steaua	1997	Dortmund
1987	Porto	1998	Real Madrid
1988	PSV	1999	Manchester Utd.
1989	AC Milan	2000	Real Madrid
1990	AC Milan	2001	Bayern Munich
1991	Crvena Zvezda	2002	Real Madrid
1992	Barcelona	2003	AC Milan
1993	Marseilles	2004	Porto
1994	AC Milan	2005	Liverpool
1995	Ajax	2006	Barcelona

TABLE 8.4
Serie A Champions Pre– and Post–Bosman Ruling

	Pre-Bosman		Post-Bosman
1986	Juventus	1996	AC Milan
1987	Napoli	1997	Juventus
1988	AC Milan	1998	Juventus
1989	Internazionale Milan	1999	AC Milan
1990	Napoli	2000	Lazio
1991	Sampdoria	2001	AS Roma
1992	AC Milan	2002	Juventus
1993	AC Milan	2003	Juventus
1994	AC Milan	2004	AC Milan
1995	Juventus	2006[a]	Internazionale Milan

[a]The 2006 title was awarded to Internazionale Milan and the 2005 title was vacated due to a match-fixing scandal involving Juventus, the 2005 and 2006 Serie A champion.

Table 8.4 shows the distribution of championships for Italy's Serie A, the league that has experienced the most significant financial problems in the last several years.[40] The data for Italy are complicated by a match-fixing scandal involving Juventus, one of Serie A's dominant teams. One result of the scandal was Serie A's vacating the 2005 championship and declaring Internazionale Milan the 2006 champion. Using these data, the distribution of championships after the Bosman decision closely resembles the distribution prior to the Bosman decision. The HHI in the pre-Bosman period is 0.26, while the HHI in the post-Bosman period is 0.28. This latter figure could either overstate or understate the impact of the Bosman ruling. The HHI could overstate the impact of Bosman because the scandal also taints Juventus's other championships since 1996. If these were awarded to other clubs, the HHI might be lower. It could understate the impact if the increased cost of talent that resulted from the Bosman ruling led Juventus to engage in match-fixing as a cheaper way to win games. Still, using the HHI as the best available measure suggests that the Bosman ruling had little impact on the concentration of championships in Italy's Serie A.

CONCLUSION

In the wake of free agency, professional sports leagues have developed a variety of tools to limit the salaries they pay. Direct limits, such as the reserve clause, salary caps, single-entity leagues, and transfer fees appear to have been effective in reducing the average payroll as well as the spread between the teams with the highest and lowest payrolls. While salary caps are a possibility in European soccer leagues, the continuing objections of the MLBPA—still professional sport's strongest union—means that a salary cap is still unlikely in baseball. While it is still too early to evaluate the impact of MLB's attempt to limit salaries with a luxury tax, the limited nature of the tax and the apparent disregard of the teams most affected by it suggest that it will not be nearly as effective as a salary cap in restraining salaries.

Several of the restrictive measures—reserve clauses, transfer fees, and single-entity leagues—have been effective in restraining salaries but are not feasible business strategies. Courts in the United States and Europe clearly regard the reserve clause and transfer fees as violations of antitrust laws. No sports league will adopt them in the near future. While the courts have permitted single-entity leagues such as MLS to exist, none of the other major sports leagues are likely to move to a single-owner model any time in the near future.

While some restrictions have proven effective at restraining salaries, they have had less impact on competitive balance. I find no evidence that salary caps or free agency have had a discernible impact on the concentration of championships. These findings are consistent with the Coase theorem, which states that restrictions on the ability of players to sell their services freely do not affect the distribution of playing talent. In sum, restrictions make small market teams wealthier, but they do not necessarily make them better.

NOTES

1. See George B. Kirsch, *The Creation of American Team Sports: Baseball and Cricket, 1838–72* (Urbana: University of Illinois Press, 1989), 237.

2. See David J. Berri and Martin B. Schmidt, "Competitive Balance and Attendance: The Case of Major League Baseball," *Journal of Sports Economics* 2, no. 2 (2001): 145–167.

3. See Robert F. Burk, *Never Just a Game: Players, Owners, and American Baseball to 1920* (Chapel Hill: University of North Carolina Press, 1994), 97; Marvin Miller, *A Whole Different Ballgame* (New York: Birch Lane Press, 1991), 190–191.

4. Quotation from 1889 *Saint Louis Globe-Democrat* cited in Harold Seymour, *Baseball: The Early Years* (New York: Oxford University Press, 1960), 111.

5. Miller, *A Whole Different Ballgame,* 41.

6. Seymour, *Baseball,* 109. The National League is the oldest existing North American sports league.

7. The fascinating story of how the MLBPA outmaneuvered the owners is recounted in John Helyar, *Lords of the Realm* (New York: Villard Books, 1994), and Miller, *A Whole Different Ballgame.*

8. See, for example, Paul D. Staudohar, *Playing for Dollars: Labor Relations and the Sports Business* (Ithaca, N.Y.: ILR Press, 1996), 82–83.

9. *Forbes* defines operating income as "earnings before interest, taxes, depreciation, and amortization," often abbreviated EBITDA. See, for example, "NBA Team Valuations," Forbes.com, December 22, 2005, http://www.forbes.com/lists/2005/32/Income_1.html.

10. Data are not yet available for 2005/06, and the 2004/05 season was canceled due to the lockout of players by the owners.

11. For more on free agency in the NHL prior to the 2005 collective bargaining agreement, see Paul D. Staudohar, *Playing for Dollars: Labor Relations and the Sports Business* (Ithaca, N.Y.: ILR Press, 1996).

12. This is one of many ways to measure competitive balance. For a more complete description of various measures, see Michael Leeds and Peter von Allmen, *The Economics of Sports* (Boston: Addison-Wesley, 2005), 158–163.

13. The HHI was originally developed to determine the degree of monopoly in an industry. To see why, just replace the share of championships with a firm's market share of sales. One squares the share of championships because adding the shares always adds up to 1.0, no matter how much one team dominates.

14. Ronald Coase won the Nobel Memorial Prize in 1991 largely for this insight. The application to sports was first proposed by Simon Rottenberg, "The Baseball Players' Labor Market," *Journal of Political Economy* 64, no. 3 (June 1956): 242–258.

15. In fact, there are two complicating factors. First, the Coase theorem is based on profit-maximizing behavior, and there is evidence that George Steinbrenner, the Yankees' owner, is willing to sacrifice profits for victories. Second, the Texas Rangers, Rodriguez's old team, continue to pay a substantial portion of his salary.

16. The NFL rescinded the Dodgers franchise in 1946 when the team owner indicated that he planned to join the newly formed All American Football Conference. Football was the one sport at the time that largely drew its players from the college ranks.

17. Michael MacCambridge, *America's Game* (New York: Random House, 2004), 44.

18. For evidence of the perverse incentive posed by the draft, see Beck A. Taylor and Justin G. Trogdon, "Losing to Win: Tournament Incentives in the National Basketball Association," *Journal of Labor Economics* 20, no. 1 (January 2002): 23–41.

19. Salary data for the NBA can be found at *USA Today,* "USA Today Salaries Databases," at http://asp.usatoday.com/sports/basketball/nba/salaries/default.aspx (accessed August 15, 2006). Data for the other sports are available at analogous sites and can be accessed from this site.

20. See Staudohar, *Playing for Dollars,* 107–108. Staudohar provides an excellent history of the salary cap in the NFL and NBA.

21. The salary cap is described in the NBA's collective bargaining agreement, available at: National Basketball Players Association, "Collective Bargaining Agreement," http://www.nbpa.com/cba_articles.php (accessed November 2, 2006). A useful explanation of the cap can be found at Larry Coon, "NBA Salary Cap/Collective Bargaining Agreement FAQ," http://members.cox.net/lmcoon/salarycap.htm (accessed November 2, 2006).

22. Expansion teams actually have a somewhat lower salary cap in their first two years.

23. According to Coon, "NBA Salary Cap/Collective Bargaining Agreement FAQ," there are nine exceptions in total.

24. For rookies, the maximum is calculated as the greater of $9 million and 25 percent of the team cap. When computing the maximum individual salary, the NBA uses 48.04 percent of BRI to compute the team cap, not 51 percent. The maximum for players with seven years' experience is set at $11 million or 30 percent of the cap.

25. This percentage declines to 8 percent in the 2010/11 season.

26. The NFLPA had disbanded in order to allow its players to pursue antitrust lawsuits against the NFL and the modified Rozelle rule. As noted above, such lawsuits could not move forward as long as a collective bargaining framework existed.

27. The NFL's salary cap can be found in its CBA, which is available at National Football League Players Association, "CBA Complete," http://www.nflpa.org/CBA/CBA_Complete.aspx (2002); and the 2006 extension at National Football League Players Association, "CBA Extension," http://www.nflpa.org/CBA/CBA_Extension.aspx (2006).

28. Teams keep 60 percent of all ticket revenue from home games. The remaining 40 percent is shared equally with the other thirty-one teams.

29. If a player is released or traded, bonus payments that have not yet been counted are counted in the year in which the player was released. Because such payments go for players who are no longer with the team, they have come to be called "dead money."

30. Hockey's salary cap is too new for the HHI to have any meaning.

31. An interesting explanation for the heavy concentration of championships in basketball—the scarcity of skilled tall players—has recently been offered by David Berri, Stacey L. Brook, Aju Fenn, Bernd Frick, and Roberto Vicente-Mayoral, et al., "The Short Supply of Tall People: Explaining Competitive Imbalance in the National Basketball Association," *Journal of Economic Issues* 39, no. 3 (December 2005): 1029–1041.

32. See Coon, "NBA Salary Cap/Collective Bargaining Agreement FAQ." The other five teams were the Dallas Mavericks, Orlando Magic, Indiana Pacers, Memphis Grizzlies, and San Antonio Spurs.

33. This is a simplification of the framework spelled out in James Quirk and Rodney Fort, *Pay Dirt* (Princeton: Princeton University Press, 1992), 271–293.

34. Over a 162-game season, the Yankees would have a record of 95–67 while the Royals have a 67–95 record.

35. See Roger G. Noll, "The Organization of Sports Leagues," *Oxford Review of Economic Policy* 19, no. 4 (Winter 2003): 530.

36. Ibid., 541–542.

37. See Alessandro Baroncelli and Umberto Lago, "Italian Football," *Journal of Sports Economics* 7, no. 1 (February 2006): 13–28. The recent match-fixing scandal and subsequent demotion of Juventus might reduce that number to two: AC Milan and Inter Milan.

38. For a useful summary of the Bosman case, see Lindsey Valaine Briggs, "UEFA v. the European Community: Attempts of the Governing Body of European Soccer to Circumvent EU Freedom of Movement and Antidiscrimination Labor Law," *Chicago Journal of International Law* 6, no. 1 (Summer 2005): 439–454.

39. See Umberto Lago, Rob Simmons, and Stefan Szymanski, "The Financial Crisis in European Football," *Journal of Sports Economics* 7, no. 1 (February 2006): 3–12.

40. While I would have liked to include England's Premier League Champions, the Premier League has been in existence only since 1993, too short a period to make a meaningful comparison.

Nine

The Valuation of Nonmarket Benefits in Sport

Bruce K. Johnson

When Milwaukee lured the Braves from Boston in 1953 with the offer of a modern, taxpayer-financed baseball stadium, it set off a sort of gold rush. Before the Braves took up residence in Milwaukee's County Stadium, fifteen of sixteen Major League Baseball (MLB) teams played in privately owned stadiums. By 1991 twenty-one of twenty-six MLB teams had struck pay dirt in the form of publicly financed stadiums. The phenomenon was not limited to baseball teams, as fifty-six of the seventy-four teams in the National Football League (NFL), National Hockey League (NHL), and National Basketball Association (NBA) in 1991 also had gotten new, publicly funded buildings in which to play.[1]

Since 1991 most of the stadiums and arenas built in the boom from 1950 to 1980 have been replaced by newer, more elaborate, and much more expensive stadiums and arenas. The publicly announced subsidies for these buildings have been substantially more than half the total costs of the facilities, but taxpayers have in fact paid an average of 40 percent more than the announced subsidies.[2]

Taxpayer subsidies for sports have traditionally been justified by their allegedly large and positive impact on jobs and tax revenues. Such claims of sports-induced and stadium-driven prosperity have been repeatedly, unanimously, and conclusively refuted.[3] All impartial researchers agree that teams and stadiums do almost nothing to increase employment, income, or tax revenues for their host cities.

Although proponents of stadium subsidies almost never concede that the economic impacts they tout are overstated, they do say that even if critics are right and the impacts are nil, subsidies are still justified because the common rooting interest created by the home team provides intangible benefits such as civic pride and unity. In the words of one attorney, "It's what the janitor, valet parker, lawyer, and venture capitalist can all talk about when they are in an elevator together."[4] Sports fuel countless watercooler and backyard barbecue conversations, not to mention sports radio talk shows, fan weblogs, and Internet chat rooms that would not otherwise exist.

Sports certainly bring people together. In October 2004 the Red Sox brought 3.2 million people into the streets of Boston for a parade to mark the team's first World Series championship since 1918.[5] Pep rallies, parades, and celebrations mark high school, college, and professional victories in communities all around the country.

Many fans support their teams with nationalist fervor or religious devotion, pledging allegiance, for example, to the Red Sox Nation, or worshipping at the church of the Kentucky Wildcats. Sometimes, nationalism and religious devotion blend together. Citizens of Chicago Cubs Nation, for instance, supposedly possess moral clarity, the ability to distinguish good (Cubs) from evil (Cardinals).[6]

Even nonfans may take pride in their local teams. Having a team in one of the major leagues distinguishes a city as a "major-league" city. When Jacksonville, Florida, won an NFL expansion team in 1993, one politician said, "Jacksonville business leaders finally believe it is in the same league as the Charlottes, Tampas, and Atlantas of the world. . . . It's given us a new shot of self-esteem." When MLB considered eliminating the Minnesota Twins after the 2001 season, it was said that "fans and non-fans alike" would suffer "quality-of-life angst." When New Orleans lured the NBA Hornets away from Charlotte, a former mayor said, "New Orleans is truly back as a great city."[7]

Nonfans can also benefit if local teams improve racial and ethnic harmony. In the mid-1960s, many large American cities, riven by racial tensions, found themselves aflame. Riots erupted in Los Angeles, Philadelphia, Chicago, Washington, and elsewhere. Detroit's 1967 riots were among the worst. As the summer of 1968 heated up, many in Detroit braced themselves for a repeat of 1967, but a funny thing happened on the way to the riot—the Tigers, featuring stars both white and black, marched to the American League pennant and on to a dramatic comeback World Series victory over the St. Louis Cardinals. The Tigers have been credited with uniting the city, or at least distracting it from its problems, and sparing it another bloody riot.[8]

Nothing illustrates the importance of such intangibles to a community more than the collective emotional trauma inflicted upon Brooklyn when its beloved Dodgers moved to Los Angeles in 1957. The move of the NFL's Colts to Indianapolis in 1984 had a similarly powerful impact on Baltimore. When these teams moved, their abandoned cities experienced something akin to religious or national crises, which were chronicled in countless newspapers, books, and other media.

If teams are so valuable to the emotional and civic life of their communities, why do they leave? The problem is that teams cannot charge for civic pride and racial harmony. One need never purchase a ticket to be a fan, to take vicarious pride in the team's victories, or to enjoy a sense of camaraderie with fellow citizens. What fans don't pay for, teams don't profit from.

The Dodgers left Brooklyn for Los Angeles because they could make greater profits in California than in New York. But if the Dodgers had had a way to charge Brooklynites for the pleasure received when they discussed the team, read about it, or exulted in the civic pride it brought to the borough of Brooklyn, the Dodgers may well have stayed in Flatbush.

The move to Los Angeles may have been a case of market failure. Markets fail if they do not maximize the net benefits received by buyers and sellers. Markets fail in the case of monopolies. They fail if some costs are not reflected in prices, such as pollution costs. And they fail in the case of public goods. Civic pride, major-league status, racial harmony, and other sports intangibles are public goods. The term does not mean "good for the public." Rather, it distinguishes these intangibles from private goods.

Most goods and services are private goods because they are both excludable and rivalrous. A good is excludable if its producer can make people pay to consume it. Seats behind home plate are private goods produced by baseball teams. If you want to enjoy a game at the ballpark, you have to pay—otherwise, the team will exclude you.

The other essential feature of the seat at the ballpark is its rivalrous nature. In plain English, private goods get used up. If you sit in the seat, no one else can. That's why the New Testament miracle of loaves and fishes was a miracle—Jesus made the bread and fish nonrivalrous so they did not get used up.

The nonexcludability of public goods causes market failure. Because public goods are nonexcludable, firms cannot compel people to pay for them. Because people don't have to pay for them, firms have no incentive to produce them. If people want public goods, government usually has to pay for them. Take, for example, tornado sirens. Throughout the Midwest and the South, sirens warn people to take cover whenever a tornado approaches. Sirens are nonexcludable—anyone in the area can hear them, whether they pay or not. No private firm could make a profit in such a market, so governments levy taxes to pay for sirens.

Like tornado warnings, sports public goods are not excludable. Boston Red Sox and Green Bay Packers fans never have to buy a ticket to feel proud, connected, and joyful when their teams take the field. The religious fervor experienced by fans may be stoked simply by reading a box score or a fan weblog.

Teams produce public goods only as unintended byproducts. Staging games so that tickets can be sold leads indirectly to major-league identity and civic pride. If a team can make a profit from tickets, concessions, broadcast rights, and other private goods, it will stay in town. But if team owners think the team can make more profits elsewhere, they will either move to another city or ask the host city to build a stadium that can generate more revenue.

In other words, the value of public goods does not enter into the calculus of profit-maximizing team owners except to the extent that owners think they can use them to extract a better stadium deal from their host cities. As a result, the total benefits produced by the team, consisting of profits and the value of public goods, may actually fall if the owner moves to a more profitable location. Although it is impossible to say whether total benefits produced by the Dodgers rose or fell when they moved to Los Angeles in 1957, Brooklyn suffered a significant loss of public goods. Otherwise, the move would have been uncontroversial and forgotten long ago, instead of remaining one of the most famous betrayals in sports history.

Perhaps only once has the value of sports public goods been invoked to block a team's relocation. In October 1998 the Pittsburgh Penguins of the NHL declared Chapter 11 bankruptcy. The NHL considered two options: disbanding the franchise or selling it to the highest bidder. If sold, the Penguins would most likely have moved. Before the NHL could act, however, Federal bankruptcy judge Bernard Markovitz issued an injunction against moving the Penguins.

> The Penguins are as much a part of the warp and woof [*sic*] of this community as are its other professional sports teams, museums, parks, theaters and ethnic neighborhoods. As important as [the creditors'] interests are, they may have to give way when the interest of the community at large so dictates. In this case, it so dictates.[9]

Markovitz ruled, in essence, that the team's value in Pittsburgh, including profits and public goods, exceeded the profits the Penguins could make in another city. Moving the team based on profits alone would thus be a market failure and would make Pittsburgh worse off. Soon after the injunction, the NHL sold the Penguins to a group of local investors for less than they were worth on the open market.

Just how much were the Penguins' public goods worth to Pittsburgh? Judge Markovitz never said. At the time, sports economists weren't able to say much either. Unfortunately, sports economists have devoted so much effort to refuting outlandish claims about jobs and taxes that until recently they nearly ignored sports public goods.[10]

They have nearly ignored the value of sports public goods in part because it is hard to measure them. Hard, but, as it turns out, not impossible. Economists use two approaches: the measurement of compensating wage and rent differentials, and contingent valuation method (CVM) surveys.

COMPENSATING DIFFERENTIALS

Compensating differentials in wages and rents indirectly reflect the value of public goods and other factors that affect the quality of life in an area. Imagine two otherwise identical cities except that one has fabulous weather and the other has awful weather. If wages and rents were equal in the two cities, the lousy-weather city would empty out as everyone moved to the fair-weather city. But rents would fall and wages would rise as landlords and employers tried to entice people to stay in the lousy-weather city. In the fair-weather city, wages would fall as new workers flooded the labor market and rents would rise with housing demand. The rent and wage differentials arising between the cities would stem the migration between them. Those who most value good weather would tolerate lower wages and higher rents. Those for whom weather is less important would choose higher wages and lower rents.

Weather is an environmental amenity available to all who live in an area. Environmental amenities can be private goods, such as fine restaurants, museums, and seats in an NFL stadium, or they can be public goods such as weather, natural beauty, and NFL-inspired civic pride. Cities with more and better environmental amenities will tend to have lower wages and higher rents than otherwise similar cities with fewer and worse amenities. As an example, the median home price in 2006 in San Diego, a city with famously fabulous year-round weather and gorgeous ocean views, was about $602,000. In Buffalo, the archetypal example of a city with harsh winters and no ocean views, the median home price was about $98,000.[11] Perhaps houses in San Diego are bigger, or perhaps construction costs are higher in San Diego than in Buffalo, but environmental amenities probably account for much of the difference in prices.

By carefully controlling for environmental amenities across cities, economists have been able to estimate what people are willing to pay in the form of higher rents and lower wages for another day of sunny weather per year, one less rainy day per year, or one less inch of snow per year. Rappaport and Wilkerson note that the typical stadium subsides have been about the same size as the estimated net present value associated with an extra day of nice weather each year for the next thirty years, "so if the contribution to quality of life from hosting a major league team is at least as great as the contribution from one extra day per year of pleasant weather, then the public outlays on sports stadiums and arenas may be justified."[12]

But nearly all major-league sports teams locate in areas with high levels of population and employment. "This makes it impossible to distinguish between variations in wages and house prices that are due to the presence of a sports team and those that are due to the high population and employment."[13] Bigger cities also tend to have more cultural environmental amenities than do smaller cities, including large concentrations and varieties of restaurants, shopping opportunities, music, theater, and museums. These can contribute to quality of life, complicating the business of disentangling the effects of sports teams from the other amenities on rents and wages.

Swindell and Rosentraub found that "museums" and "music" contributed as much to civic pride in Indianapolis as did the NFL Colts and NBA Pacers. Schwester surveyed residents of Cleveland and Baltimore and found that sizable percentages believed their new baseball stadiums contributed to civic pride. Groothuis, Johnson, and Whitehead found similar results in a survey of the Pittsburgh metropolitan area. They asked whether ten different local amenities were "very important," "important," or "not important" to civic pride. The four lowest-ranking contributors to civic pride were the three major-league sports teams and an annual regatta. Others, such as the Carnegie Museum, the zoo, and the Carnegie Science Center contributed much more to civic pride.[14]

Despite the difficulty of disentangling the effects of various amenities from sports teams, Carlino and Coulson attempted to measure the compensating rent differentials between cities that host NFL teams and those that do not. Using data on monthly rent from 7,275 apartments scattered across the sixty largest metropolitan areas, including all the NFL cities, they concluded that the people in NFL cities paid rents averaging 8 percent more than those in non-NFL cities. If the higher rents truly represent the value people place on football teams, and nothing else, then people are willing to pay more than $139 million per year for a team. Assuming the $139 million in benefits occur each year forever and using an annual interest rate of 5 percent, the effect of an NFL team is to increase property values in its host city by $2.78 billion. The estimate applies only to central cities, not the metropolitan areas as whole—if suburban rents also exhibit compensating differentials, the value could be much higher still. In contrast, the market value of an NFL team is about $1 billion. If these estimates are correct, then, even the profits of the most lucrative NFL teams account for well under half of the total value of the teams.[15]

But these estimates have come under severe criticism. The most damaging comes from Coates, Humphreys, and Zimbalist, who carefully examined the data used by Carlino and Coulson. Six apartments among the 7,275 had monthly rents reported as $0 and twenty had monthly rents reported at less than $20. These are almost certainly mistakes in the data. If these twenty-six apartments are dropped from the sample, the rent differential between NFL cities and non-NFL cities disappears.[16]

Even if the differential were not due to data errors, it remains an open question as to whether wage and rent differentials were caused by NFL teams or by other big-city amenities. As of yet, the jury is still out. The study of compensating differentials has not been able to add much insight into the value of sports public goods.

CONTINGENT VALUATION METHOD

There's an old joke about an economist and an engineer stranded on a desert island with nothing to eat but canned peas, and no way to open the cans. The engineer proposes a complicated scheme involving an explosion and calculating the subsequent trajectory of the flying peas. The economist says, "Let's assume we have a can opener." In the same spirit, economists who want to measure the value of public goods have said, "Let's assume we have a market." Fortunately, if properly conceived, imaginary markets are more useful than imaginary can openers.

Imaginary markets are the key to contingent valuation method (CVM) surveys, widely used by environmental economists to measure the value of public goods. Johnson and Whitehead first used CVM for sports.[17] The idea is straightforward. Respondents are presented with a hypothetical market in which they can pay for a specified improvement in a public good or pay to avoid a specified loss of a public good. Their willingness to pay is contingent upon the hypothetical scenarios and markets described to them, hence the name "contingent valuation method."[18]

Here's a sports example from a survey in Jacksonville, Florida, in the spring of 2002.

> Professional football teams often move to new cities. Since 1984, National Football League teams have left Baltimore, St. Louis, Oakland, Houston, Cleveland, and Los Angeles (twice).
>
> Consider the following situation. Within the next 10 years the owners of the Jaguars decide to sell the team. The new owners want to move the team to another city, such as Los Angeles, where they could make higher profits.
>
> Suppose the city of Jacksonville was able to buy a majority of the team. If the city owned a majority of the team the Jaguars would never leave Jacksonville.

Large sums of money from Duval County taxpayers would be needed to buy a majority of the team. It has been estimated that it would take annual tax payments of $40 for the next 20 years from all Duval County households to buy a majority of the team. Your total payment would be $800.[19]

The tax payments mentioned will vary from respondent to respondent, as will the number of years over which the payments will be required.

After presenting the hypothetical scenario, the survey asks whether respondents would be willing to pay the higher taxes. Some surveys ask a discrete-choice question about willingness to pay: "Would you be willing to pay the annual tax payments of TAX for the next T years out of your own household budget so the city of Jacksonville could buy a majority of the Jaguars?" TAX could take any one of several randomly assigned values; in the Jacksonville survey, the values were $5, $10, $20, or $40. The number of years T was 10 in half the surveys, 20 in the other half. Respondents were given three choices: "Yes," "No," and "I don't know."

Some CVM surveys follow the discrete-choice question with a second question in a so-called payment-card format. For instance, the Jacksonville survey asked, "What is the highest annual tax payment you would be willing to pay for the next T years out of your own household budget to keep the Jaguars in Jacksonville?" Respondents were given the following choices: "zero," "between $0.01 and $4.99," "between $5 and $9.99," "between $10 and $19.99," "between $20 and $39.99," "between $40 and $75," and "more than $75."

Both discrete-choice and payment-card responses can be used to estimate willingness to pay. The estimates from the two questions should be similar. If not, people were either confused or not taking the survey seriously.

To illustrate the economic theory behind CVM analysis, consider the following example. Imagine that Jane spends her income to achieve a certain target level of utility, or satisfaction, from her consumption of goods and services, including the goods produced by her local sports team. If the team should leave, Jane's utility will fall. To return to her original utility level, she will have to consume more of other goods and services than before. She may have to spend, for instance, $30 more per year on other goods and service to replace the utility she got from the team. The $30 is her annual willingness to pay to keep the team in town.

In addition to asking willingness to pay, CVM surveys ask about the consumption of private and public goods. In sports CVM surveys, the private goods consist of attendance at games—how many games do you attend each year? The public goods, to be discussed in more detail below, include such things as civic pride, reading about the team, and discussing the team with others. The precise public goods asked about vary from survey to survey.

By correlating the willingness-to-pay responses with the responses about private and public goods consumption, household willingness to pay can be broken into two components: the willingness to pay for private goods and the willingness to pay for public goods. Willingness to pay can also be correlated to such personal and demographic characteristics as sex, age, race, income, and education.

Several sports CVM surveys covering a fairly diverse set of scenarios have been conducted. Surveys have asked the willingness to pay for public goods produced by teams in each of the four major leagues in North America, a college basketball arena, a minor-league baseball team, amateur sports and recreation programs, and the Summer Olympics. Though few in number, there are enough sports CVM surveys that we can start to generalize about the value of sports public goods and to answer the question of whether they justify the enormous public subsidies granted to sports.

Table 9.1 summarizes the estimated willingness to pay results of the different surveys. The first column names the team or project and the year in which the survey was conducted. The second column contains the discount rate used to convert annual willingness to pay to present discounted value. The third column lists the present discounted values of the total willingness to pay, including private and public goods, while the fourth column lists the present discounted willingness to pay for public goods alone. Both columns 3 and 4 show the results in dollars of 2006 purchasing power. Columns 5 and 6 show the survey results in dollars of whatever year the survey was conducted in.

Without exception, the CVM estimates of willingness to pay for public goods for North American major-league sports fall far short of the public subsidies typically provided to build new arenas and stadiums. These results suggest that most cities would be better off bidding farewell to their teams rather than bidding for new stadiums despite the fact that survey respondents frequently consume and enjoy sports public goods, as shown in Table 9.2. Sizable percentages regularly read about and discuss their local teams, consider themselves fans, and believe their team improves the quality of life.

The following section describes the studies listed in Table 9.1 and Table 9.2 in greater detail, with those about major league teams considered first.

Pittsburgh Penguins

The first CVM study to estimate the value of public goods produced by a major-league sports team focused on the NHL's Pittsburgh Penguins.[20] In 2000 Johnson, Groothuis, and Whitehead mailed surveys to people throughout the Pittsburgh metropolitan area. The survey presented a hypothetical

TABLE 9.1
Willingness to Pay for Sports Teams

Team	Type of sport	Year of Survey	Discount rate (%)	Willingness to pay, 2006		Willingness to pay at time of survey	
				Total	For Public Goods	Total	For Public Goods
Pittsburgh Penguins	NHL	2000	8	$77,232	$56,573	$65,969	$48,323
Jacksonville Jaguars	NFL	2002	7	$40,114	$27,786	$35,796	$24,795
Jacksonville	NBA	2002	7	$29,245	$20,966	$26,097	$18,709
Minnesota Vikings	NFL	2003	NA	$105,889	NA	$96,645	NA
Portland	MLB	2003	6.25	$81,034	$60,441	$73,960	$55,164
University of Kentucky	NCAA basketball	1997	8	$9,140	$2,760	$7,277	$2,197
Lexington, Ky.	Minor-league baseball	1997	8	$8,868	$891	$7,060	$709
London	Olympics	2004	5	NA	$3,849,259	NA	$3,597,438
Alberta	Amateur sports	2006	6	$188,828	NA	$188,828	NA

Sources: Bruce K. Johnson, Peter A. Groothuis, and John C. Whitehead, "The Value of Public Goods Generated by a Major League Sports Team: The CVM Approach," *Journal of Sports Economics* 2, no. 1 (February 2001): 6–21; Bruce K. Johnson, Michael J. Mondello, and John C. Whitehead, "The Value of Public Goods Generated by a National Football League Team," *Journal of Sport Management* 21, no. 1 (January 2007): 123–136; Aju Fenn and John R. Crooker, "The Willingness to Pay for a New Vikings Stadium Under Threat of Relocation or Sale," working paper, Colorado College, 2005; Charles Santo, "Beyond the Economic Catalyst Debate: Can Consumption Benefits Justify a Municipal Stadium Investment?" *Journal of Urban Affairs* (forthcoming); Bruce K. Johnson and John C. Whitehead, "Value of Public Goods from Sports Stadiums: The CVM Approach," *Contemporary Economic Policy* 18, no. 1 (January 2000): 48–58; Giles Atkinson, Susana Mourato, and Stefan Szymanski, "Quantifying the 'Un-quantifiable': Valuing the Intangible Impacts of Hosting the Summer Olympic Games," *Urban Studies* (forthcoming); Bruce K. Johnson, John C. Whitehead, Daniel Mason, and Gordon J. Walker, "Willingness to Pay for Amateur Sport and Recreation Programs," working paper, Department of Economics, Appalachian State University, 2007, http://econpapers.repec.org/paper/aplwpaper/.

Note: As measured by CVM surveys. All values expressed in terms of thousands of 2006 US$.

TABLE 9.2
Public Good Consumption: Percentage of Respondents Responding "Yes"

Team	Read[a]	Discuss[b]	Fan[c]	Quality of Life[d]
Pittsburgh Penguins	44%	33%	72%	42%
Minnesota Vikings	41	54	18[e]	NA
Jacksonville Jaguars	38	36	79	64
Kentucky Wildcats	72	72	89	49

[a]Percentage of respondents who read about the team at least several times per week.
[b]Percentage of respondents who discuss the team with others at least several times per week.
[c]Percentage of respondents who consider themselves to be at least casual fans of the team.
[d]Percentage of respondents who believe the team improves the local quality of life at least slightly.
[e]The figure for the Vikings is the percentage who consider themselves "die-hard" fans.

scenario in which the city of Pittsburgh would buy the team to keep it from leaving. Discrete-choice and payment-card questions asked about willingness to pay higher annual taxes to keep the Penguins in town.

The survey asked people about the Penguins public goods they consumed. Of the respondents, 44 percent said they read about the Penguins a few days per week or more often, 33 percent discussed them at least as often as a few days a week, 72 percent identified themselves as casual or "die-hard" fans, and 42 percent thought the quality of life would fall if the Penguins left. As for private goods consumed, 39 percent of the sample attended an average of 4.5 games, while 61 percent attended no games in the 1999–2000 season.

Although 72 percent identified themselves as fans, only 51.5 percent were willing to pay higher taxes to keep the Penguins in town. Among those willing to pay, both private and public goods affected the amount. People who went to games were willing to pay more than nonattenders, everything else equal. Attenders were willing to pay $2.88 plus $.32 per game. For example, someone who went to one game would be willing to pay about $3.10 per year, while someone attending ten games would pay $6.08.

Consumption of public goods affected willingness to pay even more than attendance did. Reading about the Penguins, discussing them, being a fan, or believing they improve the quality of life each raised willingness to pay by $2.31 per year. Together, all four increased annual willingness to pay by $9.24. The excitement of experiencing a championship mattered, too. Those who lived in Pittsburgh during the Stanley Cup championship years of 1991 and 1992 were willing to pay $4.47 more per year to keep the Penguins.

While some households were willing to pay a lot and others were willing to pay nothing, the average Pittsburgh household in 2000 was willing to pay a total of $5.57 per year to keep the Penguins in town, including $4.08 for public goods. For the 947,500 households in metropolitan Pittsburgh, the total willingness to pay for Penguins public goods came to $3,865,800 per year.

At an interest rate of 8 percent, $3.866 million per year could finance a lump sum payment of $48.3 million. This is the maximum subsidy that could be justified by the value of public goods, far less than the total development costs of recently built NHL arenas. Nashville's Gaylord Entertainment Center cost $155 million in 1997, the Raleigh Sports Arena cost $160 million in 1999, and the Nationwide Arena in Columbus cost $152 million in 2000. In 2006 the Penguins asked for a new arena costing $290 million.[21] Adjusted for inflation, the estimated Pittsburgh willingness to pay in 2007 is now $56.6 billion, about one-fifth the cost of their proposed arena.

Jacksonville Jaguars

The Pittsburgh results immediately drew criticism. Rappaport and Wilkerson noted that the Penguins play the least popular major-league sport, implying that baseball, football, and basketball produce more valuable public goods. They also suggest that since the Penguins are just one of three major-league teams in Pittsburgh, the low willingness to pay may merely reflect the diminishing marginal value of sports teams.[22] In other words, if your football and baseball teams already produce the usual array of public goods, a hockey team probably doesn't add much value. The world would think of Pittsburgh as a major-league city whether it has a hockey team or not.

Partly in response to this criticism, Johnson, Mondello, and Whitehead set out to estimate the value of public goods produced by the NFL Jaguars, the only major-league team in Jacksonville, Florida. As the forty-sixth largest metropolitan area in the United States, and the second smallest city among those represented in the NFL, NBA, or MLB, few would consider Jacksonville without the Jaguars to be a major-league city. Certainly that was the case when the NFL awarded the Jaguars to Jacksonville in 1993. Mike Littwin of the *Baltimore Sun* wrote, "But Jacksonville? . . . Was the NFL looking for a small, dumpy city with no TV market, no sports history and a decrepit stadium?" Bernie Miklasz of the *St. Louis Post-Dispatch* said, "This had to be a joke, right. . . . Do they have cable TV in Jacksonville yet?"[23]

As in Pittsburgh, the Jacksonville survey asked how much people would be willing to pay in higher taxes to keep their team from moving away. People were asked questions about game attendance and about public goods that fans consume, such as reading about and discussing the team. Unlike the Pittsburgh survey, the Jacksonville survey also asked two questions about public goods that benefit nonfans: "Do you think having the Jaguars in town puts Jacksonville 'on the map,' just like other 'major league' cities?"

"Do you think having the Jaguars in town helps improve relations among whites, African-Americans, Hispanics, and other groups?" About three-fourths believed the Jaguars put Jacksonville on the map, while 43 percent gave the Jaguars credit for improving relations among different racial and ethnic groups.

Despite widespread consumption of Jaguars public goods, only 46 percent said they would be willing to pay anything at all to keep the Jaguars in town. Among those willing to pay, each game attended increased total willingness to pay by $11.91 over a twenty-year period. But public goods had even larger effects. Watching games on TV, reading about the team, discussing them, and wearing team clothing each increased willingness to pay by $42.61 over a twenty-year period. Those who believe the Jaguars make Jacksonville a major-league city were willing to pay $127.12 more to keep them in town, while those who thought the team improves racial and ethnic relations were willing to pay $58.62 more.

All told, the average Jacksonville household was willing to pay a total of $148.36 spread over twenty years to keep the Jaguars in town. Of this, $102.82 was for public goods. Discounting future payments at 7 percent per year, the 426,584 households in the Jacksonville metropolitan area were willing to pay $35.8 million, of which about $24.8 million was for public goods.

Jacksonville had to pledge to upgrade Municipal Stadium, built in 1946, to NFL standards before the NFL agreed to award it a franchise. The initial subsidy to what is now called Alltel Stadium came to $121 million. Subsequent improvements raised the total to $166 million and additional payments have raised the total subsidy to $207 million.[24] In light of the CVM estimates, Jacksonville appears to have made a lousy bargain. The willingness to pay to retain the Jaguars—and by extension, major-league status—amounts to a small fraction of the subsidy required to attract the team in the first place.

Some might consider these results surprising. The NFL is by far the most popular professional league in the United States, and survey respondents overwhelmingly named football as their favorite sport. The Jaguars, unlike the Penguins, confer major-league status on their host city, yet the value of public goods produced by the Jaguars falls far short of those produced by the Penguins. One reason is that Pittsburgh is more than twice as populous as Jacksonville. Even so, the per capita willingness to pay for the Jaguars is a bit lower than for the Penguins, so even if Jacksonville was the same size as Pittsburgh, the total value of Jaguars public goods would still fall short of the value of Penguins public goods. The mystery remains. Why is the value of major-league status in Jacksonville so low?

To test the hypothesis that additional teams have declining marginal value, the Jacksonville survey also contained a hypothetical scenario about attracting an NBA team. Would an NBA team be worth less since the Jaguars have already vaulted the city into major-league ranks and given people something to talk about?

About 38 percent of respondents were willing to pay to get an NBA team. The Jacksonville metro area was willing to pay a total net present value of $26.1 million. The value of public goods accounted for $18.7 million of the total. This is less than the figure for the Jaguars, consistent with the hypothesis of declining marginal value of teams. However, it may simply be that football, the favorite sport of most Jacksonville respondents, is inherently more valuable than basketball in Jacksonville.

Compare $18.7 million to the cost of recently built NBA arenas: Miami— $263 million in 1999, Toronto—$216 million in 1999, and Dallas—$380 million in 2001.[25] An NBA team would be an even worse investment for Jacksonville taxpayers than were the Jaguars.

Minnesota Vikings

Both the Minnesota Twins baseball team and the Minnesota Vikings football team play in the Hubert H. Humphrey Metrodome in Minneapolis, and both have been asking for new stadiums for years. Both teams have threatened to move to other cities unless they get significant taxpayer support to build new stadiums.

In this environment in 2003, Fenn and Crooker conducted a CVM survey to ascertain the willingness to pay for a new stadium for the Vikings.[26] They asked people if they would be willing to pay a one-time, lump-sum amount for a new stadium and, if so, how much. They included questions about public goods consumed by fans. Of the respondents, 41 percent claimed to read about the team regularly and 54 percent said they talked about them often. Only 11 percent thought a new stadium would help the Vikings win a Super Bowl. They also asked about public goods that appeal to nonfans and 44 percent thought a new stadium would enhance the area's prestige.

Consumption of public goods strongly affected willingness to pay. Regularly reading or talking about the team each increased willingness to pay by $41.15. People who believed a new stadium would enhance the area's prestige were willing to pay $83.90 more, and those who thought it would help bring a Super Bowl championship to the Vikings were willing to pay $79.85.

Perhaps the most important difference between this survey and other major-league sport CVM surveys is that it was given throughout Minnesota, not just the Twin Cities metropolitan area. Since they are called the

"Minnesota Vikings," people throughout the state may share in civic pride and other public goods. That seems to be the case. Rural Minnesotans' willingness to pay did not differ from that of Twin Cities residents.

The average Minnesota household was willing to pay a lump sum of $148.36 to build a new football stadium. The statewide total of $96.6 million was split almost evenly between the Twin Cities and the rest of the state. Fenn and Crooker do not break the total into willingness to pay for public and private goods, but, as in Pittsburgh and Jacksonville, even the total willingness to pay falls far short of the estimated cost for a new stadium.

Jeffrey Owen also conducted a statewide survey asking Minnesotans about their willingness to pay for the Vikings, as well as the Minnesota Twins and Timberwolves. He also asked Michiganders about their willingness to pay for the Detroit Tigers, Lions, Pistons, and Red Wings. The results are broadly consistent with those of the other studies reported in this chapter, that willingness to pay is typically less than the cost of a new stadium or arena. He also found that most respondents were unwilling to pay so much as a penny for their teams.[27]

While Owen's conclusions were in broad agreement with those in the other surveys discussed in this chapter, he nevertheless estimated a willingness to pay for the Vikings of $218 million to $544 million, compared to Fenn and Crooker's $97 million. Owen's estimates for the other also teams tend to be higher—not quite in the same ballpark—than estimates from other studies of other major-league teams discussed in this chapter. This suggests the explanation may be in the design of Owen's surveys.

It does not appear that Owen's surveys corrected for hypothetical bias, a tendency of some to overstate their willingness to pay in CVM surveys. Typically, many of those who say they favor higher taxes also say, if asked, that they are not sure they would in fact vote for higher taxes in a real election. Since they may not really support higher taxes, willingness to pay estimates will be inflated.

Portland, Oregon

In an unprecedented move, MLB bought the Montreal Expos in 2002 and made it known they would probably move the team to another, more profitable city. Over the next two years, MLB considered moving the Expos to Las Vegas, Portland, or Washington, D.C. Extracting a promise from the D.C. city council to fully finance a new stadium, the Expos moved to Washington after the 2004 season and became the Nationals.[28]

In 2003, when Portland was still a contender, Charles Santo surveyed people in Portland, asking their willingness to pay higher taxes for a thirty-year period for a new stadium that would attract a baseball team.[29] As in the Pittsburgh and Jacksonville surveys, respondents were given discrete-choice and payment-card questions to elicit their willingness to pay.

To measure public goods consumption, Santo asked whether they would regularly read about the team and talk about it, and whether they think it would improve Portland's national reputation and make it a better place to live. Consumption of each of these four public goods increased annual willingness to pay by about $4.41. Private good consumption also affected willingness to pay—each game they thought they would attend increased annual willingness to pay by about $.41 per year.

The Portland survey contained several innovations that shed light on the issue of stadium subsidies. Some people hate taxes and are willing to pay less for their public goods simply because they are financed by taxes. Tax-averse respondents were willing to pay $6.44 per year less than were otherwise identical people who don't hate taxes. People who think Portland has more important things to spend money on were willing to pay $7.10 less per year.

The survey also asked if building a baseball stadium would improve Portland's economy. If they agreed, as did 69 percent, they were willing to pay $6.73 more per year. Though stadium projects have minimal effects on employment and income, the general public seems unaware of this. This phenomenon has been called "stadium illusion," and it appears widespread in Portland.[30] According to the old adage, "ignorance is bliss." That might be an exaggeration of what Portlanders would experience, however, as bliss would almost surely be valued at more than $6.73 per year.

The survey shows an annual willingness to pay for public and private goods of $9.68 per household in the three-county metropolitan area. The thirty-year net present value for all 570,000 households, discounting at 6.25 percent, is about $74 million, of which about $55.2 million is for public goods. This is far below the cost of constructing a MLB stadium—the stadium Washington, D.C., agreed to build is projected to cost $611 million.[31]

No matter the sport, no matter whether to keep a team or attract a new one, none of the CVM surveys about major-league sports has found public goods valuable enough to justify subsidies typically given to stadiums and arenas. Granted, all of the cities surveyed have been fairly small, much smaller than cities such as Chicago, Los Angeles, or New York. But even much larger cities with similar per capita willingness to pay would be unable to justify paying the full cost of a new basketball arena or outdoor stadium. The Chicago metropolitan area is about nine times as large as Jacksonville. If Chicagoans have the same discounted per capita willingness to pay for football public goods as do Jacksonvillians, the aggregate willingness to pay in Chicago would be about $225 million. Given that Chicago hosts four other major-league teams, however, that probably overstates the value Chicago places on their NFL Bears. Yet the 2003 renovation of city-owned Soldier Field, home of the Bears, cost $632 million.[32]

Lexington, Kentucky

A few months after the University of Kentucky (UK) Wildcats won their sixth National Collegiate Athletic Association (NCAA) basketball championship in 1996, the coach, with support from the university and private donors, proposed a $100-million arena to generate more income, provide more seats for fans, and have better practice facilities for the team. The coach said it would make UK more competitive. Although it would be built with private money, the plan would have imposed large costs on taxpayers in Lexington, the team's host city. They own UK's current arena, subsidize its operating costs, and will be paying off construction debt until 2016. The loss of their major tenant would have increased the tax revenue needed to pay debt and operating costs.

Also in 1996, Lexington was one of the largest metro areas in the United States without a professional baseball team. The Southern League said it would move a team to Lexington if the city built a stadium for $10 to $12 million. The mayor initially backed the idea, but changed her mind and killed the project. In 1997 stadium proponents unsuccessfully asked the state to pay instead.

The Lexington survey presented hypothetical scenarios for each project.[33] The basketball scenario allowed the valuation of an improvement in an existing public good, while the baseball scenario allowed the valuation of a public good that did not yet exist.

Lexington households were willing to pay a net present value of just $7.28 million for a new arena, discounted at 8 percent for forty years. Five million dollars of this was for private goods—people thought it would be easier to get UK tickets.

Perhaps because UK had won the national championship in 1996, had narrowly lost the 1997 NCAA title game in overtime just a few weeks before the survey, and would go on to win the 1998 NCAA title, most respondents did not think a new arena would make UK more competitive. Nor did the Wildcats pose a threat to move away if they did not get a new arena. The simplest interpretation of the UK results is that people do not want to pay for something that produces no benefits.

Lexingtonians were even less willing to pay for a minor-league baseball stadium. The aggregate net present value of willingness to pay was less than $7.1 million, of which 90 percent was for attending games. People did not seem to think that minor-league baseball would produce valuable public goods, an attitude apparently shared by residents of Indianapolis. In a non-CVM survey, they said that minor-league baseball and hockey contributed far less to their sense of civic pride than did their major-league teams, their museums, and their music.[34]

An interesting footnote to the Lexington survey: After both requests for a publicly financed baseball stadium were rejected, an entrepreneur built a stadium with private funds. Total cost of the stadium was about the same as the survey's estimated willingness to pay for minor-league baseball private goods, that is, tickets. The team that moved in has drawn well and the stadium appears to be a success.

Alberta, Canada, Amateur Sports and Recreation

Most sports CVM surveys have focused on professional and big-time college spectator sports. But for many people, participatory sports provide benefits, whether as athletes, coaches, referees, or parents. The province of Alberta, Canada, subsidizes scores of amateur sport and recreation programs throughout the province, encompassing at least 105 different sport and recreational activities from Alpine skiing to hockey to water polo.

While amateur sports do not confer major-league status on a community, they may produce other public goods and promote civic pride and unity. They may enhance the quality of life even for nonparticipants. For instance, organized sports may keep adolescents under adult supervision and off the street.

To determine willingness to pay for these programs, researchers surveyed 967 Alberta households in April 2006.[35] The households were evenly divided among the two major cities of Calgary and Edmonton and the rest of the province, reflecting the distribution of the Albertan population. The hypothetical scenario said the Alberta government was considering proposals to expand amateur sport and recreation programs, funded by increases in the provincial income tax. Respondents were told that the rise in income taxes would be $10, $25, or $50 per year—each person was quoted just one figure—which would be enough to raise participation rates in sport and recreation programs by either 2 percent or 10 percent. Because the tax and participation rates were mixed and matched, six different combinations were presented to respondents.

Next, respondents were asked whether they would vote for a referendum to raise income taxes.

The survey asked a series of questions about their participation as a player, official, volunteer, or parent of a player with Alberta sport and recreation programs. Nearly 66 percent said they participated in the previous twelve months, suggesting that the Alberta population is broadly involved in provincially sponsored sport and recreation activities.

Albertans were willing to pay CDN$18.32 per household per year to expand participation rates in sport and recreation programs by 2 to 10 percent. Aggregated over all Alberta households and discounted at 6 percent, the present value of the willingness to pay for the small increase in participation rates is CDN$214,246,293, or about US$188.8 million, far exceeding any CVM estimates for professional sports in the United States.

How could willingness to pay to avoid total loss of a high-profile major-league team be so far below that for a small increase in the provision of amateur, participatory sport and recreation programs? Several possible explanations exist. First, the Alberta programs directly involve many more people than does a major-league team. Second, the experience of playing, coaching, or organizing a sporting activity may be more intense and satisfying than is passively watching a professional game played by strangers, even if they do represent your hometown. Third, pro sports offer few options, perhaps imperfectly matching the preferences of many fans. If you aren't a football fan in Jacksonville, too bad—it's the only major-league option you have. With 105 sport and recreation activities, Albertans have a good chance of finding one that closely matches their preferences.

The Alberta results raise other questions. Do the quality-of-life benefits from active, participatory sports generally exceed those of passive, spectator sports? Would the large public subsidies provided to professional sports in the United States be better spent on amateur, participatory sports? Do Americans have the same willingness to pay as Canadians for amateur sports and do Canadians have the same willingness to pay as Americans for professional sports?

London Olympics

In 2005 the International Olympic Committee awarded the 2012 Olympic Games to London after an intense bidding competition among London, Paris, New York, Madrid, and Moscow. The IOC insisted that the host governments would have to underwrite the entire cost of staging the Games, ensuring that a sizable public subsidy would be required of whatever city and nation won the Games. During 2004 Atkinson, Mourato, and Szymanski surveyed people in London, Manchester, and Glasgow about their willingness to pay to attract the Games to London in 2012.[36] Their survey focused on the intangible costs and benefits of holding the games. The intangible benefits, or public goods, included national pride and unity;

improving awareness of disability, since the Olympics would be followed by a twelve-day Paralympics; motivating and inspiring children to exercise; new facilities that would be useful after the Games; environmental improvements as a result of environmental regeneration to be undertaken in preparing the Olympic venues; promoting healthy living; and boosting knowledge and understanding of cultural diversity. They also asked about intangible costs, including crowding and congestion, increased risk of petty theft, increased risk of terrorism, local disruption during construction, transport delays during the Games, and excessive media coverage.

Taking all the intangible costs and benefits into consideration, London households had an average willingness to pay of £22, or about $43.40 per year for ten years in 2006 (after correcting for inflation and converting to U.S. dollars),. Manchester households were willing to pay £12 per year and Glasgow households £11 per year. Aggregating over all London households and discounting at 5 percent yields a total willingness to pay in London of £480 million. Extrapolating the Manchester and Glasgow willingness to pay estimates to the rest of the United Kingdom yields an aggregate discounted total willingness to pay of £1,472 million in the rest of the country, for a total of £1,952 million, or about US$3,849 million.

The willingness to pay for the Olympics dwarfs any sports willingness to pay estimates in North America. Why the big difference? There are several. First and most important is the sheer scale involved. Major-league sports teams produce their public goods on a local or state level. Jacksonville has 426,000 households. The United Kingdom has more than 24 million households. Second, the Olympics are a unique sporting event, focusing world attention on the host in a way no professional sports team can. The Olympic host dominates the attention of the sporting world for the two weeks of the competition and enjoys significant attention for months and years leading up to the Games. The Olympic host also enjoys a status far more rarified than that of a mere major-league city. An Olympic city is one of a handful in any given generation. Jacksonville, in contrast, competes for attention with twenty-nine other NFL cities and forty-six other cities with at least one team in one of the four major professional sports leagues. And unlike the Olympics, interest in American sports does not extend much beyond the United States and Canada.

Even though the willingness to pay for the 2012 Games is of an Olympian magnitude, it nevertheless falls far short of the subsidies British taxpayers will likely end up providing for the London Games. The projected cost of hosting the Olympics had more than trebled to £9.3 billion from the time London was awarded the Games in 2005 by March 2006.[37]

WHAT DOES IT MEAN?

The estimates of the willingness to pay for sports public goods listed in Table 9.1 are calculated using discount rates ranging from 5 percent to 8 percent. These rates were chosen in part to reflect market interest rates faced by state and local governments at the time of the surveys. They are also roughly in line—in the ballpark at least—with the 2 and 7 percent discount rates required by the Congressional Budget Office and the Office of Management and Budget for cost-benefit analyses of federal government programs.

Regardless of federal requirements or prevailing market rates faced by state and local government, the discount rates used in the Table 9.1 studies may be lower than those actually used by the respondents. Since lower discount rates result in higher present values, the total willingness to pay figures in Table 9.1 may be overstated.

When consumers borrow to pay for such things as vacations or home appliances, they typically pay much higher rates than those paid by municipal and state governments. If a consumer finances a vacation by borrowing on a credit card with a 15 percent interest rate, and if she pays it off in one year, she will end up paying about $1,150 one year from now for each $1,000 she spends on her vacation today. But if she could finance the vacation at a rate of 5 percent, she would only have to pay about $1,050 next year.

The design of the Jacksonville survey allows researchers to calculate the discount rate applied by respondents to sports public goods received in the future.[38] Some respondents were asked to pay for ten years while others were asked to pay for twenty years. By comparing the willingness to pay over ten years and the willingness to pay over twenty years, the interest rate implicitly used by consumers can be calculated. For Jacksonvillians willing to pay for football public goods, the annual interest rate turns out to be 12 percent, similar to credit-card rates. The basketball rate of 28 percent is similar to market rates offered by finance companies to high-risk borrowers.

The point is, if the appropriate discount rate is 28 percent, or even 12 percent, instead of 7 or 8 percent, the net present values of the public goods will be much lower than the estimates in Table 9.1, further weakening the case for large subsidies to sports teams. To take the case of the Pittsburgh Penguins, if a discount rate of 12 percent had been used to calculate the present value of public goods, the willingness to pay would drop from $48.3 million to $32.2 million. The only estimate in Table 9.1 that would not be affected if, in fact, higher discount rates are appropriate, is that for the Minnesota Vikings; respondents were asked how much they would be willing to pay in a one-time only, up-front payment, so no discounting was necessary.

The CVM results, even if not overstated, represent something of a mystery. Sports dominate the nation's attention as few other things do—almost every major daily newspaper has a sports section, local newscasts devote 25 or 30 percent of their time to sports, and with the exception of a papal visit, it's hard to think of anything else besides a World Series or Super Bowl championship that can attract millions to a parade. So why are the estimated values of sports public goods so low? Why, if people care so much about sports, are they not willing to pay more for the civic pride, the thrill of victory, and the pleasure of reading about and discussing the home team?

Perhaps the obliteration of distance by the Internet and satellite and cable TV has made civic pride and bonding with neighbors less important than it once was. Go to any MLB ballpark and you'll see people wearing Atlanta Braves and Chicago Cubs caps and shirts, teams whose cable superstations make it possible for millions of fans far from Atlanta and Chicago to follow the teams. And baseball is widely thought to be the most parochial of sports, with the strongest ties between local teams and local fans. One recent example may be seen in Detroit, where the success of the MLB Tigers in 2006 may have boosted civic pride more than recent successes by the Detroit hockey and basketball teams.[39]

The bond between NFL teams and their host cities may be less strong than those between MLB teams and host cities. The NFL has succeeded so spectacularly in part because it has marketed itself as a national entity and because it has marketed its star players.[40] During the 2006/07 season, the Pittsburgh Steelers were the most popular team in the NFL, thanks to their 2006 Super Bowl championship and their talented, attractive players. But their home is Pittsburgh, just the twentieth largest metropolitan area. The third most-popular team that year was the Colts, who play in Indianapolis. The Colts rose from among the least-popular teams to one of the most popular despite playing in the twenty-ninth largest metropolitan area, largely on the shoulders of Peyton Manning, their star quarterback who led them to a Super Bowl championship in 2007.[41]

Some psychologists have found that people feel a sense of personal accomplishment when "their" team wins.[42] But in an age when cable TV and the Internet make it possible for fans to follow any team they want, there is no particular reason why someone must stick with the local team. If you feel better backing a winner than a loser, and if the local team is a loser, why suffer?

Fantasy football and Rotisserie league baseball give a monetary incentive to fans to follow, identify with, and cheer for nonlocal players. This would further diminish the bonds between teams and their local fans, and presumably lower their willingness to pay for them. If much of the enjoyment derived from sports is independent of team location, the willingness to pay for a local team will understate the value of sports.

Still, it is easy to find evidence that local sports teams produce valuable public goods—take, for example, the 3.2 million delirious fans celebrating in the streets of Boston after the 2004 World Series. How many of them would have preferred one more sunny day rather than the Red Sox victory? Another example is the sentiment expressed by the University of Louisville fan who said, the day after Louisville's football team won the Orange Bowl in 2007, that it was "the most important day of my life, aside from my daughter being born." The boost in morale the Tigers gave to Detroit by winning the 2006 American League pennant is another case in point.[43] So the question becomes, how can this dramatic, if anecdotal, evidence of extremely valuable sports public goods be reconciled with the low estimates produced by the CVM studies discussed in this chapter?

One possible explanation is that the most dramatic and obvious examples of sports public goods arise from the winning of a major championship. None of the CVM studies conducted thus far have involved a championship team. The Pittsburgh study does, however, provide some support for the claim that championships matter. Among respondents who were willing to pay something to keep the Penguins in town, those who lived in Pittsburgh during the Penguins' Stanley Cup championship seasons in 1991 and were willing to pay $4.47 per year more than were those who had not experienced the championships. Remember, the survey was taken eight years after the second championship. Had the survey been taken in 1991 or 1992, it is plausible that the willingness to pay responses would have been much higher. Likewise, respondents who thought a new stadium would help the Vikings win a Super Bowl were willing to pay much more for a stadium than were those who did not think it would help them win.

Another possible explanation for the apparent discrepancy between low CVM willingness to pay estimates and the jubilation evident on the streets of Boston in October 2004 is that all the CVM studies conducted thus far have concerned teams that are much younger than the Red Sox. The Pittsburgh Penguins began play in 1976, the Jacksonville Jaguars in 1995, and the Minnesota Vikings in 1961. Other CVM studies covered teams that did not even exist: an MLB team in Portland, an NBA team in Jacksonville. Much of the Red Sox public goods value, judging from newspaper and media accounts, comes from the team's ability to bind children to parents and grandparents through the sharing of common childhood experiences. The parents and grandparents in Jacksonville have no childhood experience with the Jaguars to share with their children and grandchildren. It will be decades before the Jaguars can unite the generations in the same way the Red Sox and other old teams can.

While the estimated values of public goods from sports is small, it is possible that a CVM study of a very old team or of a team winning a major championship might produce a much larger estimate. However, conducting a CVM study of the Boston Red Sox, for instance, or of the New York Yankees would be hard. The teams enjoy two of the most lucrative local markets in sports. They would be unlikely to find another market as profitable, and so do not represent a credible threat to move. Even though both teams have asked local taxpayers for a new stadium, they have never threatened to leave. A CVM survey positing a hypothetical move away from Boston or New York might produce results similar to those in the UK Wildcats survey—people unwilling to pay for something they don't consider plausible.

This might explain why, despite the Red Sox's requests for public funding for a new stadium, none has been forthcoming. Nor were the New York Yankees and the New York Mets able to pry open the public purse to fund new baseball stadiums. The Yankees' and Mets' new buildings are being financed virtually entirely with private money.[44] This does not mean Yankees and Mets public goods are worthless. It may merely reflect New Yorkers' confidence that either team would be mad to give up its lucrative New York markets for a subsidized stadium in a smaller, poorer place. The experience of the Red Sox, Yankees, and Mets is consistent with Owen's model predicting that subsidies are more likely in smaller cities, since teams in bigger markets are profitable and competitive without subsidies.[45]

Despite the potential difficulties, a CVM study of an old team or a championship team might yield much higher estimates of sports public goods than any studies thus far. So too might CVM studies of major sporting events such as the Kentucky Derby, the Indianapolis 500, and the Masters golf tournament. As major events that help identify their host cities to the rest of the world, they may plausibly generate highly valuable civic pride benefits for local residents. The difficulty in designing a CVM study is in devising a plausible scenario in which the events might relocate. But whatever their problems in Louisville or Indianapolis might be, moving the Kentucky Derby to, say, New York or the Indianapolis 500 to Las Vegas is not plausible. They would cease to be the same events if they were removed from their traditional venues and renamed.

Contingent valuation method surveys have thus far shown that the typical subsidies granted to professional teams and stadiums cannot be justified on the basis of public goods and market failure. The value of sports public goods typically fall far short of the value of subsidies granted. Even the 2012 Olympics, which will produce the most valuable public goods thus far measured, will cost billions more than the estimated public goods produced.

Amateur, participatory sports may be much more deserving of subsidy than are professional sports. Nevertheless, it is possible that in some cases sports public goods could justify a new stadium. Perhaps the most likely case would involve a subsidy enabling a team to win a championship. But the results of CVM studies thus far suggest that in the vast majority of cases, subsidies are bad deals for the taxpayers footing the bills.

NOTES

1. James Quirk and Rodney D. Fort, *Pay Dirt: The Business of Professional Team Sports* (Princeton, N.J.: Princeton University Press, 1992), 131.

2. Judith Grant Long, "Full Count: The Real Cost of Public Funding for Major League Sports Facilities," *Journal of Sports Economics* 6, no. 2 (May 2005): 119.

3. See, for instance, John Siegfried and Andrew Zimbalist, "The Economics of Sports Facilities and Their Communities," *Journal of Economic Perspectives* 14, no. 3 (Summer 2000): 95–114; Roger G. Noll and Andrew Zimbalist, "The Economic Impact of Sports Teams and Facilities," in *Sports, Jobs, and Taxes: The Economic Impact of Sports Teams and Stadiums,* ed. Roger G. Noll and Andrew Zimbalist, 55–91 (Washington, D.C.: Brookings Institution Press, 1997); Dennis Coates and Brad R. Humphreys, "The Growth Effects of Sports Franchises, Stadia, and Arenas," *Journal of Policy Analysis and Management* 18, no. 4 (Fall 1999): 601–624.

4. Darren Rovell, "What's the Lease You Can Do?" ESPN.com, September 19, 2002, http://sports.espn.go.com/espn/print?id=1434048&type=story.

5. Brian MacQuarrie, "Thank You: Millions Turn Out to Salute Red Sox for a Season to Remember," *Boston Globe*, October 31, 2004, http://www.boston.com/sports/baseball/redsox/articles/2004/10/31/thank_you_boston_globe (accessed August 8, 2006).

6. A Web site devoted to the Red Sox Nation is www.redsox.nation.com (accessed August 8, 2006). John Feinstein, "Pitino's Head Was Uneasy Before He Wore the Crown," in "1997 Final Four," supplement to *Wall Street Journal*, March 28, 1997, 6+; Lonnie Wheeler, *Blue Yonder: Kentucky, the United State of Basketball* (Wilmington, Ohio: Orange Frazer Press, 1998); Rafael D. Martinez, "On Being a Cubs Fan," http://www.spiritwatch.org/gocubsgo1.htm (accessed March 3, 2008).

7. Mike Williams, "NFL Team Boosts Jacksonville's Image," *Atlanta Constitution,* December 12, 1993, H6; Charles Laszewski, "Baseball Gives Prestige to Host Cities/Teamless Towns Yearn for Big-League Status," *St. Paul Pioneer Press*, November 11, 2001, A1; John Reid, "We Did It!" *New Orleans Times-Picayune,* May 11, 2001, A1.

8. John J. Miller, "City on Fire," *National Review,* July 30, 2002 (retrieved through Lexis-Nexis Academic).

9. "Penguins Must Stay in Pittsburgh: Judge," *Montreal Gazette,* March 27, 1999, G2.

10. Jeffrey Owen, "The Stadium Game: Cities versus Teams," *Journal of Sports Economics* 4, no. 3 (August 2003): 187.

11. National Association of Realtors, "Median Sales Prices of Existing Single-family Homes for Metropolitan Areas," Realtor.org, 2007, http://www.realtor.org/Research.nsf/files/MSAPRICESF.pdf/$FILE/MSAPRICESF.pdf (accessed February 28, 2007).

12. Jordan Rappaport and Chad Wilkerson, "What Are the Benefits of Hosting a Major League Sports Franchise?" *Federal Reserve Bank of Kansas City Economic Review* (First quarter 2001): 73.

13. Ibid., 74.

14. David Swindell and Mark S. Rosentraub, "Who Benefits from the Presence of Professional Sports Teams? The Implications of Public Funding of Stadiums and Arenas," *Public Administration Review* 58, no. 1 (January/February 1998): 15; Richard W. Schwester, "An Examination of the Public Good Externalities of Professional Athletic Venues: Justifications for Public Financing?" *Public Budgeting and Finance* (Fall 2007): 89–109; Peter A. Groothuis, Bruce K. Johnson, and John C. Whitehead, "Public Funding of Professional Sports Stadiums: Public Choice or Civic Pride?" *Eastern Economic Journal* 30, no. 4 (Fall 2004): 521.

15. G. Carlino and N. E. Coulson, "Compensating Differentials and the Social Benefits of the NFL," *Journal of Urban Economics* 56, no. 1 (2004): 25–50.

16. Dennis Coates, Brad R. Humphreys, and Andrew Zimbalist, "Compensating Differentials and the Social Benefits of the NFL: A Comment," *Journal of Urban Economics* 60, no. 1 (2006): 124–131.

17. Bruce K. Johnson and John C. Whitehead, "Value of Public Goods from Sports Stadiums: The CVM Approach," *Contemporary Economic Policy* 18, no. 1 (January 2000): 48–58.

18. R. C. Mitchell and R. T. Carson, *Using Surveys to Value Public Goods: The Contingent Valuation Method* (Washington, D.C.: Resources for the Future, 1989), 2–3.

19. Bruce K. Johnson, Michael J. Mondello, and John C. Whitehead, "The Value of Public Goods Generated by a National Football League Team," *Journal of Sport Management* 21, no. 1 (January 2007): 123–136.

20. Bruce K. Johnson, Peter A. Groothuis, and John C. Whitehead, "The Value of Public Goods Generated by a Major League Sports Team: The CVM Approach," *Journal of Sports Economics* 2, no. 1 (February 2001): 6–21.

21. Long, "Full Count," 124–125; Shelly Anderson, "Penguins's Sale Reaches Crucial Stage," *Pittsburgh Post-Gazette*, July 11, 2006, http://www.post-gazette.com/pg/pp/06192/704885stm (accessed December 19, 2006).

22. Rappaport and Wilkerson, "Benefits of Hosting a Franchise," 73.

23. Johnson, Mondello, and Whitehead, "The Value of Public Goods Generated by a National Football League Team"; "What the Columnists Are Saying," *USA Today,* December 2, 1993, C3.

24. Long, "Full Count," 123.

25. Ibid., 123–124.

26. Aju Fenn and John R. Crooker, "The Willingness to Pay for a New Vikings Stadium under Threat of Relocation or Sale," working paper, Colorado College, 2005.

27. Jeffrey Owen, "The Intangible Benefits of Sports Teams," *Public Finance and Management* 6, no. 3 (2006): 321–345.

28. Lori Montgomery and Thomas Heath, "Baseball's Coming Back to Washington," *Washington Post,* September 30, 2004, A1.

29. Charles Santo, "Beyond the Economic Catalyst Debate: Can Consumption Benefits Justify a Municipal Stadium Investment?" *Journal of Urban Affairs* (forthcoming).

30. Johnson and Whitehead, "Value of Public Goods from Sports Stadiums," 52.

31. Thomas Heath, "With New Stadium, Name of Game Is Money," *Washington Post*, November 28, 2006, E1.

32. Steven A. Reiss, "Soldier Field," *The Electronic Encyclopedia of Chicago,* Chicago Historical Society, 2005, http://www.encyclopedia.chicagohistory.org/pages/1165.html (accessed February 28, 2007).

33. Johnson and Whitehead, "Value of Public Goods from Sports Stadiums."

34. Swindell and Rosentraub, "Who Benefits from the Presence of Professional Sports Teams?" 16.

35. Bruce K. Johnson, John C. Whitehead, Daniel Mason, and Gordon J. Walker, "Willingness to Pay for Amateur Sport and Recreation Programs," working paper, Department of Economics, Appalachian State University, 2007, http://econpapers.repec.org/paper/aplwpaper.

36. Giles Atkinson, Susana Mourato, and Stefan Szymanski, "Quantifying the 'Unquantifiable': Valuing the Intangible Impacts of Hosting the Summer Olympic Games," *Urban Studies* (forthcoming).

37. Brendan Carlin and David Bond, "Olympics Budget Trebles to £9.3 Billion," *Daily Telegraph,* March 16, 2006, http://www.telegraph.co.uk/news/main.jhtml?xml=/news/2007/03/16/nolym16.xml (accessed March 16, 2007).

38. Bruce K. Johnson, Michael J. Mondello, and John C. Whitehead, "Contingent Valuation of Sports: Temporal Embedding and Ordering Effects," *Journal of Sports Economics* 7, no. 3 (August 2006): 267–288.

39. Peter Slevin, "Tigers Give City a Reason to Roar: Detroit's Stunning March to the World Series Lifts Beleaguered Residents," *Washington Post,* October 18, 2006, A3.

40. Eric Leifer, *Making the Majors: The Transformation of Team Sports in America* (Cambridge: Harvard University Press, 1995), 127–135.

41. Vito Stellino, "Trailing in the Polls: Nationally, Jaguars not America's—or Anyone's—Team," *Florida Times-Union,* October 15, 2006, http://www.jacksonville.com/tu-online/stories/101506/jag_5594484.shtml (accessed October 16, 2006).

42. C. M. End, B. Dietz-Uhler, and E. A. Harrick, "Identifying with Winners: A Reexamination of Sport Fans' Tendency to BIRG," *Journal of Applied Social Psychology* 32, no. 5 (May 2002): 1017–1030.

43. Katya Cengel, "Fans Soak Up Thrill of Big-Time Postseason Game," *Louisville Courier-Journal,* January 3, 2007, A4; Slevin, "Tigers Give City a Reason to Roar."

44. "Future American League Ballparks: N.Y. Yankees," *Ballparks by Munsey and Suppes,* Ballparks.com, http://www.ballparks.com/baseball/american/nyybpk.htm (accessed February 28, 2007); "Future National League Ballparks: Citifield," *Ballparks by Munsey and Suppes,* Ballparks.com, http://www.ballparks.com/baseball/national/nymbpk.htm (accessed February 28, 2007).

45. Owen, "Stadium Game," 183.

Ten

Facility Finance: Measurement, Trends, and Analysis

Andrew Zimbalist and Judith Grant Long

Conventional wisdom has it that the public share of stadium and arena construction costs has been falling in recent years. Many have attributed this perceived decrease in part to the emergence of the academic literature in the 1990s, finding that one cannot expect that a new team or sport facility by itself would promote economic development in an area.[1] We find that the conventional wisdom is incorrect.

Measuring sports facility costs is rarely as straightforward as the public authorities, team owners, and newspapers would have us believe. Not only is this measurement issue difficult, it is also important. The ongoing public debate about the appropriateness of public subsidies depends critically on our ability to accurately measure the underlying costs.

In this paper, we use both the available reported cost data as well as adjusted cost data and find that trends in public financing are considerably more complex than traditionally thought. We proceed first by discussing issues in the measurement of costs, then by elaborating the methodology we employ for our estimates, next by expositing our results, and lastly by offering an interpretation for our findings.

ISSUES OF MEASUREMENT

There are numerous measurement conundrums and pitfalls that complicate the assessment of overall and public costs of sports facilities. First, and most obviously, publicly released figures may apply to initial, intermediate, or final cost estimates. Because bells and whistles are often added after the original design or political approval, because of mistakes in the a priori cost estimation, and because cost overruns can easily run at 30 percent or more of budgeted expenditures, it is important that final costs be measured consistently.

Second, public figures often refer to building costs alone; less often they can also include land and infrastructure. Land costs estimated at market value can produce widely different interpretations, or its value may be erroneously recorded at the "write-down" or discounted amount. Infrastructure is easier to value if publicly provided, yet it presents attribution issues, since it often includes on- and off-site improvements, such as nonadjacent roads, utility upgrades, public transportation improvements, or environmental remediation. Released figures rarely include opportunity costs.

Third, identifying what does and what does not constitute a public subsidy can be tricky, to say the least. Consider the following. The project to build a new Yankee Stadium in the Bronx is estimated to cost approximately $1.035 billion; of this, public expenditures for infrastructure come to $235 million. The latter is for park space, public sports facilities (e.g., ball fields, tennis courts) and parking. Some of the public sports facilities will replace existing facilities, but some will be incremental. Should the spending on the incremental facilities be considered a subsidy to the Yankees? A large share of the "public spending" will be on new parking garages, but the government has put out a request for proposal (RFP) to private construction companies to build and operate the garages. Revenue from the garages will accrue to the company that wins the contract, not to the Yankees. Should the garage construction spending be counted as a public investment? Further, the city made $5 million in rent credits available each to the Yankees and the Mets toward the planning of their new stadiums that the city could then recover under certain conditions; how should this benefit or the land value be reckoned?

The new Yankees, Mets, and Nets facilities projects reportedly will all benefit from sales-tax exemption on construction materials and none of the teams will pay property or possessory interest tax. Some commentators consider these provisions to be public subsidies. Perhaps, but in four of the five boroughs of New York City (other than Manhattan) new construction projects receive these benefits. That is, they are generally "as of right" or available to all builders; should they be considered a subsidy?

Or consider, for instance, the proposed new ballpark in Washington, D.C. It is projected (before overruns, which are the public's responsibility) that the facility will cost $611 million. A bond will be issued for this amount, which will be financed as follows: $5.5 million rent payments by the team, roughly $12.5 million from taxes on tickets, concessions, and merchandise at the ballpark, and roughly $24 million from new business taxes. What is the public share? It depends entirely on how one treats the taxes from stadium revenue. If one assumes conservatively that 50 percent of these taxes are passed on to the consumer, then the annual public cost is $24 million plus $6.25 million or $30.25 million, 72 percent of capital costs. If one assumes that the team passes along none of the stadium taxes, then the public share would be 57 percent; or, assuming that all of the taxes are passed on, the public share would be 87 percent. To say the least, there is some subjectivity involved here.[2]

Adding a relatively new twist to the subsidy story, team owners are also pursuing the right to develop land adjacent to their new facility. Sometimes the owners must buy this land, but they typically do so on preferential terms and usually they receive tax preferences as well. Other team owners benefit from zoning variances. How should these subsidies be evaluated?

Many teams enjoy financing schemes that enable the use of tax-exempt bonds for the private contribution to facility construction. This exemption amounts to a subsidy from the federal government and is generally not counted as part of the public subsidy, but given that some of the debt issues amount to hundreds of millions of dollars it is conceivable that they could affect a municipality's bond rating and, hence, cost of capital. Notionally, these too are subsidies, but they have never, to our knowledge, been included. Nor do we include them.

Lastly, and importantly, it is problematic to assess the public burden in sports facility projects by only considering the construction costs. When teams and municipalities agree on a new stadium or arena, the deal often includes not only construction costs, but also an ongoing operating agreement (e.g., a lease in the case of a publicly-owned facility). The terms of the operating agreement are likely to include: annual rent payments, sharing arrangements pertaining to facility revenues from sport and nonsport events (parking, concessions, premium seating, signage, local media, etc.), tax privileges, and operating, maintenance, and improvement costs. Thus, there is an entire package that defines the local government's financial relationship to a sports facility and to consider any part of that package in isolation of the other parts can yield misleading results.

For instance, the Metrodome in Minneapolis was built in 1982 for $84 million (in 1982 dollars) with 100 percent public funding; however, the domed stadium housed both the Twins and the Vikings and each team had leases that were very favorable to the city. The outcome was that after considering the substantial revenue streams that flowed back to the city from the Metrodome, the city not only received back its initial investment, but in present value terms received a return of 94 percent on its initial capital outlay. This trade-off between initial public outlays and revenue/cost obligations going forward became sharper after the 1986 Tax Reform Act, to be discussed below.

In theory, each of the issues above could be resolved by gathering enough detailed information on each facility deal. The problem is that full information is not usually available and that studying trends in facility finance involves dozens of distinct projects, with over 230 major league stadiums and arenas built since 1870 for franchises still operating today, 104 facilities in-use at 2006, and another 10 in the discussion stage. Given the complexity of each individual deal, details and nuances invariably escape the grasp of even the most careful analysts.[3]

METHODOLOGY

While we do not have sufficiently detailed information to adjust for all of the factors alluded to above, we have gathered enough data to allow us to begin to consider the entire financing and operating packages of in-use facilities. Because our information on entire packages is incomplete, we present two sets of results: on capital costs (building, land, and infrastructure) and on total cost (capital and operating).

Data Description

Data are drawn from the population of over 230 facilities that were built for "big four" (Major League Baseball [MLB], National Football League [NFL], National Basketball Association [NBA], National Hockey League [NHL]) franchises, and where those franchises are still in operation today. The first data set, "public capital cost" includes capital cost data for 160 major league sports facilities opened between 1950 and 2006 for franchises still in operation at 2006, as well as 7 facilities due to open between 2007 and 2010 (see Table 10.1).[4] The second data set, "total public cost" includes public capital and operating cost data for all 82 facilities opened between 1990 and 2006 (see Table 10.2). The data analyzed are restricted to this time period since these facilities are still in-use and current operating data is available; and where the public participates in revenue sharing, current agreements and leases are available. While public operating cost data is available for some facilities built prior to 1990, including many opened during the 1980s, and a smaller number opened in earlier decades, it is only available for those with active leases. We chose not to include these data. We do include all facility renovations over $50 million (nominal) in both populations.[5]

TABLE 10.1
Public Subsidies for Major League Sports Facilities, by Decade (In Million US$)

	1950–59	1960–69	1970–79	1980–89	1980–84	1985–89	1990–99	1990–94	1995–99	2000–06	2007–10	2000–10
All Facilities												
Facilities opened	10	27	27	14	6	8	53	15	38	29	7	36
Average capital cost	43	148	237	195	168	211	258	233	263	386	619	428
Median capital cost	45	149	161	176	176	150	254	251	257	403	569	436
Average public capital cost	29	90	194	116	143	100	152	155	151	251	237	248
Median public capital cost	38	75	136	96	112	67	111	186	105	247	198	240
Simple average public share	70%	79%	89%	65%	87%	48%	58%	59%	58%	68%	42%	63%
Median public share	100%	100%	100%	82%	100%	38%	74%	82%	73%	74%	27%	72%
Weighted average public share	68%	61%	82%	60%	85%	47%	59%	67%	57%	65%	38%	58%
Stadiums												
Total facilities opened	6	13	16	4	2	2	22	5	17	21	6	27
Average capital cost	48	137	328	320	167	473	298	297	298	431	628	475
Median capital cost	45	156	225	203	167	473	297	279	313	427	576	455
Average public capital cost	31	114	260	149	104	193	233	281	219	267	272	268
Median public capital cost	38	134	225	104	104	193	252	279	245	254	270	254
Simple average public share	67%	87%	87%	46%	62%	29%	79%	95%	74%	63%	48%	59%
Median public share	100%	100%	100%	57%	62%	29%	93%	95%	86%	70%	49%	70%
Weighted avg. Pub. Share	65%	84%	79%	46%	62%	41%	78%	95%	73%	62%	43%	57%

(continued)

TABLE 10.1 (*continued*)

	1950–59	1960–69	1970–79	1980–89	1980–84	1985–89	1990–99	1990–94	1995–99	2000–06	2007–10	2000–10
Arenas												
Total facilities opened	4	14	11	10	4	6	31	10	21	8	1	9
Average capital cost	45	162	105	139	169	124	228	219	232	238	558	274
Median capital cost	45	94	82	120	190	109	220	230	213	204	558	210
Average public capital cost	30	57	98	102	169	69	93	93	93	171	27	155
Median public capital cost	30	36	82	90	190	67	69	49	74	181	558	164
Simple average public share	67%	71%	91%	72%	100%	54%	43%	41%	44%	75%	5%	68%
Median public share	100%	100%	100%	100%	100%	62%	24%	31%	23%	92%	5%	85%
Weighted avg. Pub. Share	68%	35%	93%	73%	100%	55%	41%	42%	40%	72%	5%	57%

Note: Includes capital costs only (building, land, infrastructure). All facilities in-use for big four major-league sports, 1990–2006.

TABLE 10.2
Public Cost and Share, Including Capital and Operating Costs
(In Million US$)

	1990–94	1995–99	2000–2006
All Facilities			
Facilities opened	15	38	29
Average capital cost	233	263	386
Median capital cost	247	238	403
Average total public cost	164	161	280
Median total public cost	158	149	249
Simple average public share	65%	61%	75%
Median public share	72%	67%	82%
Weighted average public share	68%	65%	75%
Stadiums			
Facilities opened	5	17	21
Average capital cost	297	298	431
Median capital cost	279	313	427
Average total public cost	281	227	319
Median total public cost	294	213	316
Simple average public share	94%	78%	75%
Median public share	95%	93%	82%
Weighted average public share	95%	88%	74%
Arenas			
Facilities opened	10	21	8
Average capital cost	219	232	238
Median capital cost	230	213	204
Average total public cost	99	101	171
Median total public cost	62	102	203
Simple average public share	49%	45%	73%
Median public share	41%	39%	76%
Weighted average public share	47%	43%	72%

Note: Facilities in-use at 2006, opened from 1990 to 2006. Capital cost includes building, land, and infrastructure. Total public cost includes public capital costs, and ongoing public costs including estimated lease-based expenses (net of revenues), and foregone property taxes.

Public Cost and Public Share Models

Public subsidies are estimated and analyzed using three measures, "public capital cost," "total public cost" and "public share."[6] "Public capital cost" estimates the present value of all reported public expenditures for building, land, and infrastructure, adjusted to 2006 using the consumer price index (Equation 1).

(1) PV_{2006} Public Capital Cost $(\$) = PV_{2006}$ Public Building Cost $+ PV_{2006}$ Public Land Cost $+ PV_{2006}$ Public Infrastructure Cost

"Total public cost" includes "public capital cost" as well as estimates of the present value of all ongoing annual public expenses (maintenance, capital improvements, and municipal services), minus the present value of the sum of all ongoing annual public revenues (base rent, ticket surcharges, and shares of revenues from gate, premium seating, concessions, advertising, naming rights, parking, other major league tenants, and other tenants), based on lease terms in effect in 2006, discounted to 2006 based on an average lease duration of thirty years, and foregone property taxes estimated at 1 percent of replacement value, incurred over a thirty-year lease and discounted to 2006 (Equation 2). The discount rate is set at 7 percent, and is intended to reflect the public cost of capital for a term similar to the life of the project.

(2) PV_{2006} Total Public Cost (\$) = PV_{2006} Public Capital Cost + PV_{2006} Net Annual Public Cost + PV_{2006} Foregone Property Taxes

(3) PV_{2006} Net Annual Public Cost (\$) = PV_{2006} Public Revenues − PV_{2006} Public Expenses

where

(4) PV_{2006} Public Revenues (\$) = PV_{2006} Base Rent + PV_{2006} Ticket Surcharges + PV_{2006} Share of Total Facility Revenues + PV_{2006} Share of Gate + PV_{2006} Share of Premium Seating + PV_{2006} Share of Concessions + PV_{2006} Share of Advertising + PV_{2006} Share of Naming Rights + PV_{2006} Share of Parking + PV_{2006} Share of Other ML Tenant Revenues + PV_{2006} Share of Other ML Revenues + PV_{2006} Share of Non-ML Revenues

and where

(5) PV_{2006} Public Expenses (\$) = PV_{2006} Share of Maintenance + PV_{2006} Share of Capital Improvements + PV_{2006} Municipal Services Expenses + PV_{2006} Share of Other Expenses

Public cost outcomes across locations and facility types are compared by measuring the share of total costs paid by the public sector ("public share") relative to that paid by the private sector. Public share is calculated for both capital cost and total cost data, referred to as "Public share, capital cost" (Equation 6) and "Public share, total cost" (Equation 7).

(6) Public Share, Capital Cost (%) = PV_{2006} Public Capital Cost / PV_{2006} Capital Cost

(7) Public Share, Total Cost (%) = PV_{20001} Total Public Cost / PV_{2006} Capital Cost

where

(8) PV_{2006} Capital Cost (\$) = PV_{2006} Total Cost Building + PV_{2006} Total Cost Land + PV_{2006} Total Cost Infrastructure

There are two important caveats to the use of the public share measure "public share, total cost." First, the numerator includes both capital and the present value of annual net operating costs, whereas the denominator includes only capital costs. The distinction arises from the overall objective of accounting for those instances where public participants earn net income from facility operations that are intended to either directly or indirectly service any publicly issued development debt, sometimes referred to as "lease givebacks." Our public share formula takes into account the degree to which facilities "pay for themselves" from the public sector perspective. Consequently the second caveat: public share outcomes can fall outside the range of 0–100 percent. Public shares less than 0 percent indicate that the public sector has more than offset its initial investment through annual revenues. Conversely, public shares greater than 100 percent indicate that the public sector has not paid back any of the upfront capital costs through facility operations and instead is continuing to pay out additional subsidies year after year.

Data Sources

Capital cost data builds on earlier work by Long and includes new data for facilities opened between 2002 and 2006, as well as facilities under construction and in the discussion phase.[7] Capital cost data is cross-referenced from different sources, including academic case studies, industry publications, general-interest publications, and Lexis/Nexis searches of major newspapers and periodicals for each facility.[8] Total public cost data, including annual public revenue and expense data is cross-referenced from industry publications and selected academic studies.[9]

RESULTS

Table 10.1 presents our results on the long-term trend in capital expenditures (building, land, and infrastructure) and the associated public share. As expected, the average and median facility capital costs rise steadily from the 1950s to the first decade of the twenty-first century. In 2006 dollars, the average facility capital cost increases tenfold from $43 million during the 1950s to $428 million during 2000–2010. Less expectedly, however, the average and median public capital cost was actually lower during the 1980s and 1990s than during the 1970s.[10] The public share in capital costs rises from the 1950s through the 1970s if a simple average is considered, but falls from the 1950s to the 1960s before rising again in the 1970s if a weighted average is used.[11] The public share then falls in the 1980s and again in the 1990s in all three measures (simple average, median, and weighted average). The public share in capital costs, however, does not continue to fall during 2000–2010: it basically stagnates using either the weighted average (going from 59% in the 1990s to 58% during 2000–2010) or the median (going from 74% to 72%), but it increases modestly (from 58% to 63%) using the simple average. This somewhat surprising result—that the downward trend in the public share from the 1970s through the 1990s is halted or reversed in the 2000s—will be interpreted in the next section.

The capital cost of stadium (as opposed to arena) construction trends upward through the 1970s, as does the public capital contribution, but these patterns are interrupted in the 1980s. In consequence, the weighted average public share of stadium capital costs rises from 65 percent during the 1950s, to 79 percent in the 1970s, before falling to 46 percent in the 1980s, rising to 78 percent in the 1990s, and falling again to 62 percent during 2000–2006.[12] The public shares for arena construction display an even more erratic pattern, again rising from 35 percent in the 1960s, to 93 percent in the 1970s, then falling to 73 percent in the 1980s, and to 41 percent in the 1990s, before rising to 72 percent during 2000–2006.

The public share in arena capital and total costs, however, is consistently below that for stadiums. Since arenas can be used 200 to 350 days a year, and sometimes twice in one day, arenas can be a cost-effective private investment. The same is rarely true for stadiums which are used less than thirty days a year in the case of football facilities and less than one hundred days a year in the case of baseball stadiums. For these reasons, private capital is more forthcoming for arenas than for stadiums, particularly arenas that host more than one major-league team.[13]

Table 10.2 shows our results when both capital and operating public costs (total public costs) are included. Data limitations restrict these results to the 1990–2006 period. For most measures, when net operating costs are included, the public share goes up. For instance, the weighted average public share of total costs exceeds that of capital costs for all facilities by 1 percentage point for 1990–1994, by 8 percentage points for 1995–1999 and by 10 percentage points for 2000–2006. This means that on average the public sector spends more on the operation of the sports facilities than it receives back, raising the overall public subsidy.

The average total public contribution per facility decreases slightly from $164 million during 1990–1994 to $161 million during 1995–1999, but then increases sharply to $280 million during 2000–2006. The sharp increase during 2000–2006 holds for both stadiums and arenas, and runs counter to prevailing notions of an ongoing diminution in the public contribution.

The public share in total costs also decreases for all facilities, stadiums and arenas between 1990–1994 and 1995–1999, but then increases rapidly during 2000–2006. The weighted average total public share during 2000–2006 was 75 percent for all facilities, 75 percent for stadiums, and 72 percent for arenas.

We include data on the median expenditures and shares to elucidate whether outliers are distorting our average results. Not only are the medians not suggestive of such distortion, but the consideration of individual facilities prior to the 2000s reinforces this view.[14] For stadiums, there are three significant outliers during 2000–2006: AT&T in San Francisco, Gillette in Foxboro, new Busch in St. Louis, each funded overwhelmingly with private funds that lead to the drop in the public share for stadiums, though not the share for all facilities (stadiums and arenas) together. For the period 2007–2010, the three planned facilities in New York for the Nets, Mets, and Yankees, each costing in excess of $600 million and more than 75 percent privately financed drop both the stadium and arena shares.

ANALYSIS OF RESULTS

Our finding of a stagnant or upward share in the public contribution to facility financing since 2000 deviates from the general perception. This perception—of a falling public share—has been explained by a variety of causal factors.

Dennis Howard and John Crompton offer four explanations for this trend.[15] First, the Deficit Reduction Act of 1984 (DEFRA) prohibited the use of tax-exempt bonds to finance the construction of luxury boxes. While this act may have been modestly related to the growing private share, it is unlikely to have caused a break in 1985 since facilities under construction at the time were grandfathered. Further, the act may be seen as a mediating factor, itself the result of a growing wariness about public financing subsidies to privately owned sports teams.

Second, the tax reform act of 1986 provided *inter alia* that stadium revenues could not contribute more than 10 percent of facility debt service for the financing to benefit from tax-exempt debt. The provisions of this act too were grandfathered and many loopholes were identified by teams, municipalities, and the investment bankers who counseled them. The most prominent loophole enabled teams to make upfront contributions to construction costs instead of paying higher rent or sharing more stadium revenues with the public coffers. Many teams made deals with concessions companies wherein the companies made upfront payments for concession rights and lowered the share of sales revenue shared with the team. The team used this upfront money to help finance its capital contribution. Similarly, teams sold naming rights, pouring rights, permanent seat licenses, and long-term suite leases to raise initial capital for construction. Thus, the 1986 act incentivized teams to substitute lower rent (and stadium revenue-sharing) payments for higher initial contributions to facility capital costs.

Other things being equal, then, the act would lower the public share in capital costs but have no impact on the public share in total costs.

Our data set does not permit us to analyze years prior to 1990 for total costs, but the capital cost data in Table 10.1 is consistent with this expectation. Public contributions to facility capital costs drop appreciably after 1985. It is difficult to attribute this dropoff, however, to the 1986 tax reform act since facilities under construction at the time were grandfathered. It is likely that the trend in the late 1980s had to do more critical attitudes toward public stadium subsidies at the time.

Third, Howard and Crompton argue that the lower public or higher private share is a product of the fact that new sports facilities provided such enhanced revenues from premium seating, signage, catering, and concessions that team owners could afford to make larger contributions.

Fourth, Howard and Crompton posit that the inauguration of President Reagan in 1981 coincided with a new ideology that favored a smaller government involvement in the economy. It would not be surprising if this attitude extended to the sports industry, especially in the context of growing fiscal problems in the 2000s. Yet Howard and Crompton also suggest that more critical attitudes toward facility subsidies flowed from the growing academic literature that found the lack of an economic impact from sports teams and facilities. This literature did not emerge until the early 1990s and did not gain wide recognition until the end of the decade.

Our results do not support the contention of a significant impact of this literature. The public capital share for all facilities between the 1980s and 1990s remains basically the same, and then rises significantly after 2000. (The share falls between 1990–1994 and 1995–1999, but it is problematic to attribute this drop to the academic literature because most of the financing for the deals between 1995 and 1999 was put in place during 1993–1996—before the academic literature gained prominence.) The public share in total costs displays a similar pattern, falling modestly from 1990–1994 (68%) to 1995–1999 (65%), but then rising sharply to 75 percent during 2000–2006.[16]

This pattern becomes more striking when it is recalled that the since the late 1990s both the NFL and MLB have had subsidy programs to help teams contribute to stadium construction expenses. The NFL's G3 program has, in essence, provided league grants of between $50 million to $150 million (in proportion to the size of a team's market) to help fund an owners' private contribution to stadium costs.[17]

Since the introduction of its revenue sharing program in 1997, MLB has also subsidized the private team contribution to stadium construction. In MLB, teams share revenue based on their "net local revenue," or their local revenue minus their stadium capital and operating expenses. Between 2002 and 2006 the top half of teams (in terms of revenues) faced an effective marginal tax rate of approximately 39 percent, so every dollar a team spent on building or renovating its stadium essentially was refunded by MLB by 39 cents, that is, the team's revenue-sharing obligation was reduced by 39 cents. Thus, for instance, under the 2002–2006 system, the Yankees' $800-million investment in their new stadium would lead to an annual reduction in the team's revenue-sharing of approximately $21 million per year over each of the forty years of the lease.[18] Using a discount rate of 7 percent, the present value of this revenue-sharing reduction is $280 million—nearly double the size of the NFL stadium support maximum or roughly 35 percent of the Yankees' total investment to the stadium.[19]

While these substantial league subventions augment the team's upfront capital contributions and would be expected, other things equal, to lower the public share of initial stadium investment, they may also lead to the team paying lower rent and sharing less stadium revenue. In the case of the Yankees' new stadium, for instance, the team will pay no rent to New York City.

The question then remains: why does the public share in facility finance reverse its trend and begin to rise after 2000? One possible answer is that the leagues are using their monopoly power more effectively. As urban populations and incomes have continued to grow, the big three leagues in the United States have not increased the number of franchises commensurately. The last expansion in MLB was in 1998, while the NBA and NFL each have only added one franchise since 1995. MLB even waived the contraction flag in 2001 and 2002, threatening to eliminate teams in several cities if they did not build new publicly financed stadiums.[20]

Another, albeit related, possible explanation is that demand for the major spectator sports is growing rapidly. This growth is in part a function of rising incomes and an increasing fan base, but it may also be a product of an increase in the nonpecuniary benefits from professional sports. As U.S. culture has become less cohesive, the integrating and identifying role of sports becomes more central. Accordingly, as fans grow more intense, their willingness to support public subsidies to attract a new or retain an existing team increases. Even if a sports team cannot be counted on to generate new jobs or higher incomes, it can yield a variety of important benefits that are not directly registered in the marketplace in the form of consumer surplus, externalities, and public goods. The median public total cost to build a sports facility during 2000–2006 was $249 million. This amounts to approximately $20 million a year of debt service over thirty years. For an urban area that has a population of two million, this subsidy amounts to a meager $10 per person per year. Given the small tax burden per capita, the popularity of sports teams, the large amount of money that is dedicated to the lobbying effort to get new facilities approved, and the powerful political and business forces that line up behind a new facility, it is perhaps not so surprising that on average the public share of financing has been maintained at such a high level.

Confounding the interpretation of trends is the presence of special factors and idiosyncrasies that affect each facility deal. These special factors become more important during quinquennia or decades when the number of new facilities is small, for example, 1980–1984 when only six facilities (including two stadiums) were built. Since large cities have more bargaining leverage than small cities, other things equal, we expect to observe lower public shares in large cities. Indeed, for the sixty years (1950–2010) and 167 facilities covered in our data set, the simple average public share in capital costs is 77 percent for cities with below median population and 61 percent for cities with above median population.[21] Hence, we would expect that periods when a disproportionate share of new facilities is being built in small cities would exhibit higher public shares.[22] However, the flattening or reversal of the trend toward smaller public shares after the 1990s does not appear to be affected by this factor. The percent of facilities opened in cities with above median population was 49 percent in the 1990s and 53 percent in the 2000s.[23] If anything, this slight increase would lead to the expectation of a drop in the public share between these two decades.

Another anomaly appears in the 2000s as the public capital share for arenas rises above that for stadiums by ten percentage points. One of the reasons for this is that, unlike the 1990s when there were eleven joint NBA/NHL arenas, during 2000–2006 there were six solo NBA arenas, three solo NHL arenas, and no joint arenas. When an arena has only one top-level professional team it is more difficult for a private investor to achieve a positive return; this compels the team to seek a larger public contribution.

The local idiosyncrasies of politicians, political culture, the personalities of team owners, the relationships between politicians and team owners, the fiscal situation and real estate market, among other conditions, will also affect the terms of facility deals. It would be difficult to conclude, for instance, that, absent the fawning behavior of D.C. mayor Anthony Williams, Washington, D.C., could not have bargained a more favorable stadium deal with Major League Baseball. As the nation's capital and eighth-largest media market, the Washington market was in a strong position to negotiate with MLB. This position was enhanced by the absence of concrete stadium proposals from any other city and MLB's desperately needing to move the Expos whose Montreal market had been despoiled. Had Rudy Giuliani remained as New York City mayor, rather than being replaced by Michael Bloomberg, it is likely that the Yankees, Mets, and Nets would have received substantially more public subsidies for their new facilities. Such subjective factors will undermine any attempts to identify the systemic forces that underlie trends in facility financing.

CONCLUSION

We have presented comprehensive summary data for capital and total costs for all professional sport facilities built since the 1950s. Most of our evidence accords with conventional views about the public contribution and the public share over time. We find, however, that the trend toward a downward public share that began in the 1980s does not continue into the 2000s. Because facility financing deals are generally set two to three years prior to the opening of the building and because the academic literature finding that a city cannot expect a positive economic contribution from a new facility (or a new team) does not become extant until the late 1990s, it is problematic to attribute a significant financial impact to this literature. It is, of course, possible that absent this literature the average public share would have risen further in the 2000s. The end of the downward trend in the public share seems to be attributable to the growing popularity of sports, the growth of U.S. cities, and the ongoing monopoly power of sports leagues, as well as idiosyncratic factors.

NOTES

Copyright © 2006, *International Journal of Sport Finance*, Volume 1, Issue 4, November 2006. Morgantown, West Virginia: Fitness Information Technology, International Center for Performance Excellence (ICPE), School of Physical Education, West Virginia University. Used with permission. www.fitinfotech.com.

1. This literature did not become publicly prominent until the late 1990s after the Washington, D.C.–based Brookings Institution Press published *Sports, Jobs, and Taxes* in 1997.

2. We assume that 50 percent of the taxes are passed on by the team to the consumer for our estimate of the public capital share of the new Washington Nationals' stadium.

3. For example, earlier work by Long ("Full Count: The Real Cost of Public Funding for Major League Sports Facilities," *Journal of Sports Economics* 6, no. 2 [2005]: 119–143; "Full Count: The Real Cost of Public Funding for Major League Sports Facilities and Why Some Cities Pay More to Play," Ph.D. diss., Harvard University, 2002) comes closest to achieving comprehensive and consistent measures across all facilities, including both capital and operating costs, while still acknowledging that on a case-by-case basis, significant subsidies remain uncounted.

4. We only include facilities that have received political approval in the data set for 2007–2010. Thus, we exclude the proposed $542-million arena in Sacramento, for which the team owners are slated to contribute only 11 percent of the building and land costs. This project was voted down in the November 2006 elections.

5. For facilities opened between 2002 and 2006, public capital cost and public operating cost data was gathered based largely on secondary sources, rather than the primary record research and verification that characterizes data for facilities opened by 2001, presented in Long ("Full Count" [2002]) and reproduced for this analysis. Forthcoming work by Long will present updated primary source data.

6. A modified form of these measures was developed by Long (ibid.) and based in part on the small number of financial analyses within the broader literature on the economics of sports facilities. B. A. Okner, "Subsidies of Stadiums and Arenas," in *Government and the Sports Business* (Washington, D.C.: Brookings Institution Press, 1974); J. Quirk and R. D. Fort, *Pay Dirt: The Business of Professional Team Sports* (Princeton, N.J.: Princeton University Press, 1997); D. Baim, *The Sports Stadium as a Municipal Investment* (Westport, Conn.: Greenwood Press, 1994); M. S. Rosentraub, *Major League Losers: The Real Cost of Sports and Who's Paying for It* (New York: Basic Books, 1997).

7. Long, "Full Count" (2002).

8. Baim, *Sports Stadium as a Municipal Investment;* R. Noll and A. Zimbalist, eds., *Sports, Jobs, and Taxes* (Washington, D.C.: Brookings Institution Press, 1997); Quirk and Fort, *Pay Dirt;* Rosentraub, *Major League Losers;* and R. Keating, *Sports Pork: The Costly Relationship between Major League Sports and Government* (Washington, D.C.: The Cato Institute, 1999), 339; M. J. Greenberg, *The Stadium Game* (Milwaukee, Wis.: National Sports Law Institute, Marquette University, 2000); M. Gershman, *Diamonds: The Evolution of the Ballpark* (Boston: Houghton Mifflin, 1993); M. Benson, *Ballparks of North America: A Comprehensive Historical Reference to Baseball Grounds, Yards, and Stadium, 1845 to Present* (Jefferson, N.C.: McFarland, 1989); P. Lowry, *Green Cathedrals: The Ultimate Celebration of All 27 Major League, Negro Ballparks, Past and Present* (Boston: Addison-Wesley, 1992).

9. *Inside the Ownership of Professional Sports Teams* (Chicago: Team Marketing Report, Inc., 2000); *Stadium Revenue Agreements* (Chicago: Team Marketing Report, 2005); Greenberg, *The Stadium Game;* Petersen, 1996; Long, "Full Count" (2002); K. C. Forsythe, "The Stadium Game Pittsburgh Style: Observations on the Latest Rounds of Publicly Financed Sports Stadia in Steeltown, USA; and Comparisons with 28 Other Major League Teams," *Marquette Law Review* 10, no. 2 (2000): 237; M. Danielson, *Home Team: Professional Sports and the American Metropolis* (Princeton, N.J.: Princeton University Press, 1997); Noll and Zimbalist, eds., *Sports, Jobs, and Taxes;* Rosentraub, *Major League Losers.*

10. These observed trends are not affected when we omit renovations from our data. Again, we only include renovations over $50 million in current dollars. The number of such renovations by decade is: 1950s, 0; 1960s, 0; 1970s, 2; 1980s, 0; 1990s, 8; 2000s, 3.

11. The simple average takes the mean of the public shares for each facility during the decade. The weighted average sums all public capital costs over the decade and divides all public and private capital costs over the decade, weighting facilities according to how much they cost.

12. The drop in the public share after 2000 is affected by some notable outliers: AT&T Stadium in San Francisco, Gillette Stadium in Foxboro, new Busch Stadium in St. Louis. Since these outliers are all for stadiums, the public shares for arenas rises after 2000 as does the overall share for both arenas and stadiums.

13. The only exception to this pattern is for 2000–2006 when the public share in capital (but not total) costs is higher for arenas than for stadiums (72% to 62%). This exception appears to be the product of a small sample and idiosyncratic circumstances which are discussed below.

14. The most significant outliers in our data set prior to the 2000s are the following. Madison Square Garden from the 1960s cost $774 million in 2006 dollars and was entirely privately financed. Part of the deal, however, made the privately -owned Garden exempt from city property taxes, which today provides a benefit of approximately $10 million annually to Cablevision Corporation. Montreal's Olympic Stadium from the 1970s at $1.9 billion in 2006 dollars and New Orleans' Superdome from 1975 at $613 million were each 100 percent publicly funded and among the first forays into domed roofs. In the 1980s Toronto's SkyDome (or, presently, Rogers Centre), at $716 million in 2006 U.S. dollars, was the first retractable roof facility. Lastly, when we run our data excluding renovations, all of the observed trends remain.

15. D. Howard and J. Crompton, *Financing Sport,* 2nd ed. (Morgantown: West Virginia University Press, 2005).

16. In the case of stadiums alone, however, the weighted average public capital (total) share does fall from 73 (88) percent during 1995–1999 to 62 (75) percent during 2000–2006. As noted above, this drop owes to the overwhelmingly privately funded stadiums in San Francisco, Foxboro, and St. Louis. Yet, for stadiums alone the public share rises sharply from the 1980s to the 1990s. Notably, our data set includes virtually identical numbers of MLB and NFL stadiums being built in the 1980s, 1990s, and 2000s. The breakdown for the NBA and NFL is a bit more complex and is discussed in the text.

17. The G3 transfer is referred to by the league as a loan, but the reality is that the team "pays back" this loan over time from its 34 percent sharing of club-seat premiums and the latter sharing takes place with or without a G3 transfer. Hence, the loan is really a grant. The G3 program was formalized in 1999, but existed on an informal, ad hoc basis earlier in the 1990s as well.

18. An independent city agency will issue a bond for the $800 million (actually more, to cover expenses), which will be paid off over forty years, the term of the Yankees' lease. The Yankees will cover annual debt service on this tax-exempt bond via payment in lieu of taxes (PILOT) payments. If amortization and interest amounts to 7 percent annually, then the Yankees annual capital costs would be $56 million. With a marginal tax rate of 39 percent, the annual reduction in the Yankees revenue sharing obligation (which exceeded $75 million in 2005) would be around $21 million. This number is derived from the terms of the collective bargaining agreement that expired in December of 2006. The new collective bargaining agreement will yield a different computation but the same principle will operate.

19. In both the NFL and MLB, the teams expect to generate a sufficient amount of extra revenues from their new facilities that in net terms the leagues will benefit.

20. In contrast, it would be hard to argue that the NHL has strengthened its monopoly power in recent years. The league expanded by one team in 1999–2000 and by two more in 2000–2001; moreover, it grew five teams earlier in the 1990s.

21. For cities below median population, the median public share in capital costs is 94 percent and the weighted average public share is 75 percent. For cities above median

populations, the median public share in capital costs is 81 percent and the weighted average is 53 percent.

22. Of course, it is also possible that some team owners will not perceive a large advantage to being in a big city if it means having to share the market with several professional teams from other sports and with a richer array of other cultural activities. In these instances, the expectation would not necessarily be for a lower public share.

23. The percent of facilities opened with above median population basically stays constant between 1995–1999 (47%) and 2000–2006 (48%). Median population is defined for DMA households (Nielsen's media market measure) in 2005–2006. The same cutoff is used for each period.

Eleven

Salary Arbitration in Major League Baseball

John Fizel

Even though salary arbitration has been in effect in Major League Baseball (MLB) since 1974, the process has been overshadowed by free agency and has remained one of baseball's misunderstood elements. Even owners and players have conflicting perspectives about the arbitration process. For example, arbitration results in salary increases for all arbitration-eligible players. It does not matter if the player negotiates a settlement prior to arbitration, wins an arbitration case, or loses an arbitration case. This apparent win-win situation for players lies at the heart of the animosity that owners feel toward arbitration and explains why owners have often targeted arbitration as the single greatest factor in baseball's mushrooming costs. However, the salaries resulting from arbitration often fall short of players' market value. Players are typically undercompensated for their contribution to revenues of their respective clubs. Also, owners and players frequently accuse arbitrators of ignoring the merits of arbitration cases in an attempt to balance the wins of players and owners and provide an appearance of impartiality. Despite these divergent perspectives, the salary arbitration process has gone largely unchanged since its inception in 1974.

The purpose of this chapter is to improve the understanding of salary arbitration by explaining how it works and showing that salary arbitration has been a viable, albeit imperfect, method for resolving salary disputes in MLB.

ARBITRATION GUIDELINES

Prior to 1974, MLB players had little to no bargaining power in salary negotiations. Once a player was drafted by a team, he could negotiate with only that team. Even if he did not sign a contract, the "reserve clause" pro-hibited him from selling his services to any team other than the one that drafted him. A player became perpetually tied to that team unless that team traded the rights to a player for the rights to a player or players from another team or if the contract of the player was sold to another team. The restrictions on player mobility granted monopsony power to team owners, which meant that clubs could unilaterally decide what to pay players. Conse-quently, players, on average, were paid only 15 percent of their market value.[1]

During this period players were left with the choice of accepting the club's salary offer or hold out, hoping absence from the field could be used for leverage to earn some extra dollars. Holdouts sometimes worked but usu-ally took time in sacrificed playing time to gain an additional few thousands of dollars from the owners. Then came the most celebrated holdout of the time when in 1966 baseball's finest pitchers, Don Drysdale and Sandy Kou-fax of the Los Angeles Dodgers, stood together in their contract demands. They sought $1 million over three years to be split between them. Koufax explained that he had joined forces with Drysdale seeking "bargaining power." Dodger owner Walter O'Malley declared that he would not yield to mere ballplayers. Eventually the parties compromised with Koufax signing a one-year contract for $125,000 and Drysdale for $110,000 becoming the highest-paid players of the time.

The next attack on the reserve clause came through litigation. In 1970 Curt Flood was traded from the St. Louis Cardinals to the Philadelphia Phillies, but refused to report to the Phillies. He requested free agency to negotiate his own contract, was refused, and filed suit under the Sherman Act claiming restraint of trade. The case eventually went to the Supreme Court and in 1971 the Court ruled in the favor of the owners, declaring that baseball's reserve system enjoyed an exemption from antitrust laws, a precedent set some fifty years earlier. Justice Thurgood Marshall, in the dis-senting opinion, did point out that the emergence of collective bargaining in baseball could dramatically change the legal status of the reserve clause over time.

In spring training of 1972, the assault on the reserve clause continued with a players' strike. Then spring training for the 1973 season was delayed by labor-management negotiations and another strike over the reserve clause seemed imminent. Owners' concerns over the possibility of increased player bargaining power through effective labor organization and orchestrated cooperation among players multiplied. In March 1973 owners proposed to players a plan that would prohibit all holdouts by players who reached an impasse in contract negotiations and would require instead the use of salary arbitration. The players' union quickly agreed to implement arbitration beginning in 1974.

The advent of arbitration prompted yet another labor market change. Andy Messersmith and Dave McNally played the 1975 season without a contract and asked to be declared free agents at the end of the season. They claimed that the reserve clause under the existing baseball contract was only a one-year renewal option, and that playing for one year without a contract fulfilled their obligations. Peter Seitz, an independent arbitrator, ruled in favor of the players. Quickly, the owners appealed Seitz's ruling in the federal courts but the initial ruling was upheld and then again upheld on appeal. The decision in March 1976 was followed by a player lockout that provided time for a new collective bargaining agreement (CBA) to be formulated and passed.

The baseball labor market looked then much like it looks today. Players with more than six years of service and not currently under contract with a team can opt for free agency. Under free agency players operate in a competitive market where all teams have the option to bid for a player's services. Second, players with between three and six years of service continue under the umbrella of the "reserve clause" but are given the option to settle salary disputes through arbitration when their contracts expire. Recent CBAs also allowed players known as "super-twos" to file for arbitration. "Super-twos" are players with two full years of service, plus at least an extra eighty-six days of service. These players are then ranked in descending order based on the extra days of service, with the top 17 percent earning the title of "super-two." Another class of arbitration-eligible players includes free agents with six or more years of service. In this instance, the team has the option of offering arbitration. A team must offer arbitration in order to get compensation in the form of draft picks should the free agent player sign with another team. If the player accepts arbitration, he is no longer considered a free agent and becomes bound to his current team. If the player refuses arbitration, as most players do, he is a free agent who can sign with any team including his current team. When free agents accept arbitration, the cases usually end in a prehearing salary agreement as arbitration has been avoided in every instance since 1991 except for two 2007 cases involving Tony Graffanino of Milwaukee and Todd Walker of San Diego. Nevertheless, the primary players in arbitration have three to six years of service and the "super-twos." Players with less than three years of service, minus the "super-twos," are still subject to the "reserve clause" and lack leverage in any salary negotiations.

After a player files for arbitration (in early January), both the player and the club submit final salary figures for how much they believe the player contract should be worth (mid-January), followed by the scheduling of a hearing (early to mid-February) before the arbitrator(s). From 1974 to 1997 hearings were held and adjudicated by a single arbitrator. Beginning in 1998, baseball phased in a system of using panels of three arbitrators rather than single arbitrators. In 1998 half of the cases were heard by panels, which increased to three-quarters in 1999, and by 2000 all cases were addressed by panels.

Major League Baseball's Players Association (MLBPA) and the owners' Player Relations Committee (PRC) jointly select a roster of arbitrators and assign them to particular hearing dates and sites. Both the MLBPA and PRC may veto the choice of an arbitrator deemed unfair. Arbitrators have no idea which players' cases they have been assigned but players and agents do know the assigned arbitrators. Salary negotiations may continue up to the scheduled hearing. If a settlement is reached prior to a hearing, the case is withdrawn from arbitration. If no settlement is reached prior to the hearing, the case and the submitted salary figures go to arbitration. And, if the case goes to arbitration, the arbitrator panel's salary decision is limited to either the player's salary request or the owner's salary offer. There can be no compromise between these salary figures. This is called "final-offer arbitration."

CONDUCTING A HEARING

Suppose that a player demands $2 million and his team offers him $1 million as part of the final salary submission in the arbitration system. Both player and team know that the arbitrator(s) must decide which position—the player's or the team's—is closer to the real market value of the player. In the decision-making process the arbitrators can consider the following criteria in deciding the case: player performance during the past season, length and consistency of player performance, salaries of comparable players, prior player salary, special player characteristics such as public appeal, leadership, or physical/mental defects, and the team's on-field success and attendance. Also, the salaries of players in arbitration hearings must be evaluated relative to comparable players in terms of position, performance, and years of service. Arbitrators may examine salaries of only those players who have no more than one additional year of service. Other factors including market size, financial position of player and team, negotiating costs, and offers made in prior negotiations are specifically precluded from arbitrator decision-making.

As you might guess, salary arbitration hearings become a battle of statistics. Player performance is personalized, garnished, chopped, and diced. Anything that cannot be converted into numerical terms seems to play no role. Each side has one hour to use its huge pile of numbers to make its claims.

In the player's case, emphasis is given to the strength of his performance and his awards and special achievements. Emphasis may also be placed on performance relative to highly paid, comparable players. The objective is to build a case that supports a salary higher than the midpoint between the two salary offers ($1.5 million). If the player and his representatives can successfully make a case for $1.7 million, then the market value of $1.7 million will be closer to the player salary demand of $2 million than the salary offer of $1 million made by the team. The arbitrators will be expected to select the more reasonable salary submission, or the player salary demand, in their final decision. The challenge of the team is to point out limitations in the performance of the player without personally offending the player. This "delicate" strategy may highlight good but not outstanding performance, limited awards, and comparisons to players in the same service class with comparable performance but relatively low salaries. The ultimate goal is to build a case that supports a salary lower that the midpoint of the final salary offers. After a break to review the arguments of the case, each side has one-half hour to provide counterclaims and rebuttal. Arbitrators then have twenty-four hours to digest the onslaught of data and make a decision.

THE NEGOTIATION PROCESS: SALARY OFFERS AND ARBITRATION ACTIVITY

The final offer aspect of the arbitration process was designed to promote bargaining efforts that encourage the teams and the players to resolve their salary differences without resorting to an arbitration hearing. Let's continue the use of the hypothetical case presented above to see how the process works.

Suppose again a player demands $2 million and his team offers him $1 million in salary arbitration. It is the strategic advantage of each party that its final offer be closer to the player's real market value because then that party's final offer should prevail in arbitration. Although the opinion regarding a fair salary is unknown, it is predictable. The exchangeability hypothesis states that arbitrators will use the arbitration-eligible facts of the case to form an opinion that will preserve an image of impartiality and protect their future employability.[2] Suppose that the player is able to make the case at his hearing that the market value of his contract is worth $1.7 million. Because the player's offer is nearer to the real market value, the rational arbitrator, under the exchangeability hypothesis, is expected to select $2 million, the player's offer, in his final decision.

But suppose that the player had been less reasonable in his salary request and opted to submit a salary of $2.5 million. If he now made the case that his contract was worth $1.7 million he might not win the arbitration hearing. The midpoint between the salaries submitted by player and team is $1.75 million ($2,500,000 + $1,000,000/2). Since the market value is below the midpoint, the arbitrator would now be expected to select the team salary offer. The inflated salary request by the player insured that he would lose in final-offer arbitration and have to accept the team's salary offer. Reducing the incentive for such unreasonable salary offers reduces the submitted salary differences between the bargaining parties, increasing the likelihood of negotiated settlements.

Lest we forget, negotiations between player and team can continue between the time of final salary submissions and the hearing date. The reasonable salary offers presented for possible arbitration may be the impetus for additional concessions that result in a negotiated settlement prior to arbitration. Clearly there are good reasons for such dispute settlements. The product of salary arbitration is a single-year contract at the arbitrator-defined salary. If they settle, the parties can be creative in designing the compensation package, including bonuses, special stipulations such as no-trade clauses, or multiyear contracts. Also, arbitration may strain the relationship between player and team as the team inevitably diminishes the accomplishments of the player during the hearing. Settlements can foster rather than rupture the parties' relationships.

Has final-offer arbitration successfully promoted negotiation? The answer includes two dimensions: salary convergence and arbitration activity.

Final-offer arbitration should promote a convergence of final salary positions, given that unreasonable salary proposals have less chance of acceptance in this no-compromise environment. Cognizant of this risk, each party will make compromises in order to submit what that party believes to be a reasonable salary offer. Salary compromises should result in a narrowing of final-offer positions.

The data in Table 11.1 provide two methods of addressing salary-offer convergence. Analysts commonly offer comparisons that focus on the dollar differences between the player salary request and the team salary offer as indicated by "average spread." A quick glance at these figures suggests that final-offer arbitration fails miserably because the current differences in salary offers are significantly larger, not smaller, than the average spread in the early years of arbitration. Although average spread values provide some insight into salary offer convergence or divergence, this measure ignores time-related factors such as inflation, changes in team revenues, and changes in local and national media contracts, all of which alter the market value of a player over time and mask the true differences between salary submissions. What is needed is a measure of salary differences that captures the factors both the players and owners perceive to have changed the value of player contracts.

TABLE 11.1
Salary Positions for Arbitration Eligible Players

Year	Arbitration		Negotiation	
	Average Spread	Relative Spread	Average Spread	Relative Spread
1974	9,623	1.20	NA	NA
1975	15,322	1.21	NA	NA
1978*	25,000	1.29	NA	NA
1979	19,375	1.39	NA	NA
1980	51,903	1.44	NA	NA
1981	87,422	1.47	NA	NA
1982	123,045	1.53	NA	NA
1983	124,817	1.48	NA	NA
1984	123,400	1.43	NA	NA
1985	163,000	1.43	NA	NA
1986	162,286	1.44	107,145	1.36
1987	163,654	1.29	104,160	1.27
1988	151,169	1.28	143,370	1.31
1989	212,833	1.35	149,576	1.30
1990	339,583	1.49	247,491	1.39
1991	557,500	1.51	361,198	1.43
1992	675,250	1.61	514,892	1.50
1993	1,660,560	1.63	225,000	1.36
1994	610,625	1.48	650,000	1.17
1995	834,375	1.59	NA	NA
1996	551,000	1.51	564,415	1.50
1997	681,800	1.55	651,721	1.50
1998	540,625	1.63	709,962	1.58
1999	952,273	1.50	784,444	1.47
2000	615,000	1.42	493,462	1.37
2001	789,643	1.45	682,200	1.39
2002	720,000	1.37	645,540	1.42
2003	640,000	1.20	564,800	1.30
2004	1,000,714	1.46	980,000	1.37
2005	253,333	1.27	864,868	1.41
2006	391,670	1.29	749,000	1.32
2007	596,790	1.42	792,000	1.32
Average	**432,612**	**1.43**	**523,107**	**1.38**

*There was no salary arbitration 1976–1977.
Sources: Data from the *Sporting News Official Baseball Guide* (various issues) and the Doug Pappas' Business of Baseball for SABR Web site, http://roadsidephotos.sabr.org/baseball/data.htm.
Key: "Arbitration" includes players that went to arbitration in a given year; "Negotiation" includes players that negotiated a salary settlement prior to their arbitration hearing; "Average Spread" is the average difference of the player offer and owner offer in dollars; "Relative Spread" is the average ratio of the player offer to the owner offer; NA = data not available; 1995 is poststrike data which is not comparable to other years.

One alternative is "relative spread" (player's final offer ÷ team's final offer). The relative spread of 1.42 for arbitration cases in 2007 indicates that player salary requests were, on average, 42 percent higher than the team's salary offer. Salary positions show little convergence or divergence using relative spread; yet, three of the most recent five years have low relative spreads indicating some salary convergence. Historically, convergence was only seen in the years when there was no free agency (1974–1975) or when free agency was ineffective due to owner collusion (1987–1989). Perhaps the recent initiation of arbitrator panels has resulted in better salary decisions or decisions more representative of player market value that, in turn, has prompted players and/or teams to make more salary concessions as they opt for arbitration.

Average spread and relative spread can also be calculated using the player and team salary offers for those players that file for arbitration and submit final salary offers but negotiate a settlement with the team prior to the arbitration hearing. Similar to the outcomes for arbitration cases, average spread fluctuates widely whereas relative spread is comparatively stable. Also, and not unexpectedly, both average and relative spread are greater for cases that go to arbitration than those that result in a settlement. The greater divergence in salary offers for arbitration cases is indicative of a situation where one party or the other fails to correctly gauge the market value of a player, or the personalities or egos of one party or the other cause one not make concessions consistent with the market value of the player. Without appropriate compromise, arbitration ensues.

Whereas the data on salary convergence did not definitively indicate that final-offer arbitration successfully promotes negotiation, the data in Table 11.2 concerning actual arbitration activities does. In the thirty-four-year history of salary arbitration, approximately two-thirds of all players eligible for arbitration have filed to use the system. However, the rate of filing has increased dramatically since the inception of arbitration. In the first five years of salary arbitration the average filing rate was 20 percent; then the rate climbed to 39 percent for the next five years and to 69 percent for the following five years. Since 1990, the filing rate has always been well above 80 percent except for the strike years of 1994 and 1999. Clearly "players feel it is necessary to have the threat of going to arbitration in order to force their teams to negotiate with them in good faith."[3]

Once players file for arbitration, good faith negotiation seems to follow. Each year, on average, there have been approximately fifteen arbitration cases, signifying that only one of every five players who file for arbitration actually end up in arbitration. Or, in other words, approximately 80 percent of all players who file for arbitration settle their contract disputes without

TABLE 11.2
Cases Filed for Arbitration and Cases Heard at Arbitration

Year	Arbitration Eligible	Cases Filed	Percent File	Arbitration Cases	Percent Arbitration
1974	500	53	11	29	55
1975	500	38	8	16	42
1978	97	16	16	9	56
1979	110	40	36	12	30
1980	201	65	32	26	40
1981	210	96	46	21	22
1982	163	103	63	23	22
1983	197	88	45	30	34
1984	192	80	42	10	13
1985	192	98	51	13	13
1986	227 (295)	159	70	35	22
1987	135 (163)	109	81	26	24
1988	156 (149)	111	71	18	16
1989	190	136	72	12	9
1990	197	162	82	24	15
1991	191 (180)	159	83	17	11
1992	158	157	99	20	13
1993	132	118	89	18	15
1994	119	80	67	16	20
1995	58	58	100	8	14
1996	80	76	95	10	13
1997	103	80	78	5	6
1998	99	81	82	8	10
1999	87	62	71	11	18
2000	110	90	82	10	11
2001	112	102	91	14	14
2002	110	93	85	5	5
2003	83	72	87	7	10
2004	77	65	84	7	11
2005	108	89	82	3	3
2006	120	100	83	6	6
2007	125	106	85	7	7
Total	**5139**	**2942**	**57**	**476**	**16.00**
Average	**160.59**	**91.94**	**68**	**14.88**	**18.75**

Sources: All data prior to 1986 is from various issues of the *Sporting News Official Baseball Guide* and all other data from 1986 forward is either from the Major League Baseball Players' Association or *USA Today*. Conflicting data in 1986–1988 and 1991 are indicated with the early reports in parentheses. Percentages calculated using data outside parentheses. Percent File = Cases filed as percent of arbitration eligible. Percent Arbitration = Arbitration cases as percent of cases filed.

the use of arbitration. The results are more dramatic in recent years. In the last six years an average of only six hearings per year are employed and only an average of 7 percent of filers invoke arbitration. In the last three years, those averages drop to five and 5 percent, respectively.

When there is no compromise between salary offers and the arbitrators must select one of the party's offers, the fear that the other party's offer may be perceived as more reasonable promotes sincere, intensive, and effective negotiation. Compromises during negotiations lead to high settlement rates and infrequent use of arbitration. As a result, a generation of players, owners, and fans have never seen, heard, or spoken the word "holdout"—a path taken by Babe Ruth, Joe DiMaggio, Mickey Mantle, Sandy Koufax, and others so that they could get more money or make a point about the reserve clause system. Each spring as organizations open training camp, virtually every player in camp will have signed a contract for the upcoming season.

ARBITRATION OUTCOMES

Teams have done extremely well in salary arbitration although owners regularly complain about the results of the process. A total of 476 cases have been heard in salary arbitration since 1974. The teams triumphed in 273 (57%); the players in 203 (43%). As Table 11.3 shows, the players won more cases than the owners in only six of the thirty-two arbitration years (1979, 1980, 1981, 1989, 1990, and 1996). The arbitration outcomes for 2007 represent the eleventh straight year that the majority of decisions went in favor of the teams. These findings may indicate that players and agents misread the market more often than owners and their representatives. Alternatively, the outcomes may show that some arbitrators are reluctant to award players increasingly high salaries. However, the latter of these implies that the arbitrator is not operating rationally in terms of making impartial decisions to foster employment in future arbitration cases.

The arbitration system also includes the outcomes for negotiated contracts and the salary outcomes from contracts generated by both arbitration decisions and negotiated outcomes. The 2007 arbitration results provide a good example of the diverse outcomes possible under the arbitration system. In 2007 106 players filed for arbitration, with fifty of these players agreeing to contracts with their teams before players and teams exchanged final salary offers. Of the remaining fifty-six players, only seven went to arbitration with the arbitrators selecting the team salary offer in four of the cases. The other forty-nine players exchanged salary offers but settled before the scheduled hearing. Their outcomes include: twenty-three players signed one-year contracts for a salary below the midpoint of the two submitted salary offers,

TABLE 11.3
Arbitration Outcomes—Who Wins?

Year	Cases Arbitration	Player Wins	Player Win (%)
1974	29	13	44.83
1975	16	6	37.50
1978	9	2	22.22
1979	12	8	66.67
1980	26	15	57.69
1981	21	11	52.38
1982	23	8	34.78
1983	30	13	43.33
1984	10	4	40.00
1985	13	6	46.15
1986	35	15	42.86
1987	26	10	38.46
1988	18	7	38.89
1989	12	7	58.33
1990	24	14	58.33
1991	17	6	35.29
1992	20	9	45.00
1993	18	6	33.33
1994	16	6	37.50
1995	8	2	25.00
1996	10	7	70.00
1997	5	1	20.00
1998	8	3	37.50
1999	11	2	18.18
2000	10	4	40.00
2001	14	6	42.86
2002	5	1	20.00
2003	7	2	28.57
2004	7	3	42.86
2005	3	1	33.33
2006	6	2	33.33
2007	7	4	42.86
Total	**476**	**203**	**42.65**

Sources: All data prior to 1986 is from various issues of the *Sporting News Official Baseball Guide* and all other data from 1986 forward is either from the Major League Baseball Players' Association or *USA Today*.

twelve players signed at the midpoint, four signed above the midpoint, and ten players signed multiyear contracts. Ignoring the multiyear contracts, the data show that 85 percent of the players lost in that four of seven arbitration cases and thirty-five of thirty-nine negotiated contracts result in players receiving salaries for the upcoming season that are below the midpoint of the two salary offers. This result is typical of outcomes since 2000.

TABLE 11.4
Salary Outcomes—Who Wins?

Year	Negotiated Settlements	Arbitration Winners	Arbitration Losers
1984	75	174	46
1985	72	91	30
1986	54	145	40
1987	33	72	14
1988	65	44	65
1989	71	120	19
1990	96	141	110
1991	107	114	61
1992	102	135	74
1993	110	174	54
1998	122	580	82
1999	142	517	87
2000	103	98	62
2001	94	188	285
2002	93	449	224
2003	66	120	70
2004	96	554	450
2005	91	507	115
2006	94	108	68
2007	99	332	72

Sources: Data from the *Sporting News Official Baseball Guide* (various issues) and the Doug Pappas' Business of Baseball for SABR Web site, http://roadsidephotos.sabr.org/baseball/data.htm.
Note: Figures are average percentage increase in salary per player from previous season.

Salary outcomes suggest a different story. The data in Table 11.4, from the ten seasons prior to the last baseball strike in 1994 and the most recent ten seasons, indicate that players always win. Despite most players receiving contracts with salaries below the midpoint of the offers, the one-year salary increase received through the arbitration process is significant. Salaries escalate most for players who have won an arbitration hearing, but gains are also received by players that negotiate a contract prior to arbitration, and even by those who go to arbitration and lose. These gains were modest (14%, 19%) in the years of owner collusion (1987–1989), astronomical (> 300%) in six of the most recent ten years for arbitration winners. The largest of these outcomes is often due to the involvement of a small number of players, one of whom was instrumental in causing the enormous salary change. For example, Kyle Lohse had his salary increase from $395,000 to $2.4 million in 2005, A.J. Pierzynski's salary went from $365,000 to $3.5 million in 2004, and Eric Gagne saw his salary explode to $5 million from $550,000 in

2004. Avoiding arbitration through negotiation can also be expensive. In 2005 Adam Dunn received a raise from $445,000 to $4.6 million and Jason Jennings's earnings went from $340,000 to $3.5 million. Yet, the average increase in the arbitration process has never been less than 60 percent. The tag of "loser" applied to players in arbitration seems inappropriate when receiving salary increments of this magnitude. No wonder baseball management believes there is no downside risk for players—even losers win big!

A review of the unique MLB labor market provides a perspective for understanding these salary figures. Players with less than three years of service, who are subject to the reserve clause, have little bargaining power in salary negotiations. Normally these players receive minimum or near-minimum salaries regardless of their performance. Players with three to six years of service and the super-two can opt for arbitration. For the first time, these players have power to negotiate a pay for performance contract or allow arbitrators to determine an appropriate salary for a given performance level. Not surprisingly, arbitration winners and losers receive large salary increases. Salary escalation is likely to have occurred with any movement from a monopsonistic (all power with owners) to a more competitive labor market (power shared with players through threat of arbitration). After a player has completed six years of service he is eligible to become a free agent. As a free agent the player can sell his services to any major-league team. Both the threat of becoming a free agent and actually entering free agency can allow the player to test his market value. Not surprisingly, much higher salaries are paid to the free agents.

The salary of comparable players is one criterion arbitrators can use in making their decisions. This criterion requires that the arbitrator, as well as the agents for each of the bargaining parties, evaluate performance and salaries on reserve clause, arbitration-eligible, and free-agent players. Yet, only players with one additional year of experience can be included in the list of comparable players. This caveat creates the situation where arbitration-eligible players with five to six years of service can be compared to free agents but arbitration-eligible players with three to four years of service cannot. Comprehensive analyses of arbitration salary results show that all players eligible for arbitration receive higher salaries than reserve clause players but those in the early years of arbitration eligibility receive lower compensation than those in the last year of arbitration eligibility. The players in the last year of arbitration sign contracts comparable in value to free agents.

The use of "comparables" permits the effects of a competitive labor market to percolate through salary negotiations for arbitration-eligible players although they still operate under the umbrella of the reserve clause. Thus, arbitration removes artificially low salaries rather than introducing artificially high salaries. While the competitive effect is complete for players in the last year of arbitration who reach the competitive salaries of free agents for comparable performance, it is incomplete for other arbitration-eligible players who, on average, fall short of free-agent salaries for comparable performance.

CONCLUSION

Final-offer arbitration is an imperfect yet viable method of resolving baseball salary conflicts. The risks involved in final-offer arbitration have successfully motivated players and teams to engage in productive negotiations so that most arbitration cases are settled without the use of arbitrators. Fewer than one in ten arbitration filings currently require arbitration decisions. The protocol and restrictions implicit in the system eliminate costs normally associated with disputes of such a magnitude, enabling the business of baseball to operate without interruption. Perhaps the biggest winners are the fans who know their favorite players will be in uniform when spring training games begin.

Final-offer arbitration has been less successful in motivating submissions of convergent final salary figures. The ratio of player salary demand to team salary offers has remained relatively stable over time. However, if conventional arbitration had been used in lieu of final-offer arbitration, it is likely that arbitrators would have been forced to select from much more unreasonable salary demands and fewer disputes would have been settled prior to arbitration.

Final-offer arbitration has a mixed impact on salaries. At first glance arbitration appears to be a source of exorbitant salaries. However, upon closer examination, it is clear that the escalating salaries of arbitration eligible players are likely to occur under any system that is more competitive than the monopsonistic or reserve-clause system players face in the years prior to gaining arbitration eligibility. Additionally, final-offer arbitration provides a unique method of allowing teams to retain player control for six years (under the reserve clause) and allowing players to receive market-influence salaries three years prior to the advent of free agency while enhancing the quality of dispute resolution.

Final-offer salary arbitration has taken heat from baseball fans, players, and team owners, yet it is an effective tool that offers benefits to each of these stakeholders. Final-offer arbitration is likely to remain a part of baseball for some time to come.

NOTES

1. G. Scully, "Pay and Performance in Major League Baseball," *American Economic Review* 64, no. 6 (1974): 431–450.

2. O. Ashenfelter, "Arbitration and the Negotiation Process," *American Economic Review* 77, no. 2 (1987): 342–347.

3. J. Dworkin, "Salary Arbitration in Baseball: An Impartial Assessment after Ten Years," *Arbitration Journal* 41 (March 1986): 63–69.

About the Editors and Contributors

Brad R. Humphreys is the Chair in the Economics of Gaming and an associate professor in the Department of Economics at the University of Alberta in Edmonton, Alberta, Canada. He holds a Ph.D. in economics from the Johns Hopkins University. He was previously an associate professor at the University of Illinois at Urbana-Champaign and the University of Maryland, Baltimore County. His research on the economic impact of professional sports, the economic determinants of participation in physical activity, and competitive balance in sports leagues has been published in scholarly journals, including the *Journal of Urban Economics,* the *Journal of Policy Analysis and Management*, the *Journal of Economic Behavior and Organization*, the *Journal of Sports Economics*, and *Contemporary Economic Policy*. His research has been featured in numerous media outlets, including *Sports Illustrated*, the *Wall Street Journal*, and *USA Today*. In 2007 he testified before the U.S. Congress on the financing and economic impact of professional sports facilities.

Dennis R. Howard is the Philip H. Knight Professor of Business at the Lundquist College of Business, University of Oregon. He joined the Lundquist College in 1997 after serving six years as the director of the Graduate Program in Sport Management at Ohio State University. He has published numerous articles on the marketing, financing, and management of sports in such journals as the *Journal of Sport Management, Marketing Management*, and *Sport Marketing Quarterly*, and is coauthor of the textbook *Financing Sport*. He is the founder and editor of the *International Journal of Sport Finance*.

Xia Feng is a Ph.D. candidate in the Department of Agricultural and Consumer Economics, Regional Economics, and Public Policy (REAP) at the University of Illinois at Urbana-Champaign. She received both her bachelor's and master's degrees in economics in China. Her research areas concentrate on regional economics modeling and policies, applications of spatial econometrics and spatial exploratory data analysis skills in various topics (including regional economic growth, environmental and health problems, and determinants of housing values), and evaluation of the economic impact of sports facilities and franchises.

John Fizel is the director of Penn State University's on-line MBA program, the *iMBA*. He holds a Ph.D. in economics from Michigan State University. He has edited *Handbook of Sports Economics Research* and coedited *International Sports Economics Comparisons, Economics of College Sports* (each with Rodney Fort), *Baseball Economics,* and *Sports Economics* (each with Elizabeth Gustafson and Lawrence Hadley). He has also contributed chapters on competitive balance in *Stee-rike Four! What's Wrong with the Business of Baseball?* and "The College Sports Industry" (with Randall Bennett) in *The Structure of American Industry.* His research papers, on a variety of sports economics topics, have been published in prominent economic journals and featured in numerous media outlets including the *Wall Street Journal,* the *New York Times,* the *Washington Post,* and CNN. He also has an ongoing research agenda in applied microeconomic topics that currently focuses on on-line reverse auctions.

Bernd Frick is professor of organizational and media economics in the Department of Management and Economics at the University of Paderborn, Germany. Before taking his current position, he was professor of personnel and organizational economics at the University of Greifswald (1995–2001) and professor of organizational economics and leadership at Witten/Herdecke University (2001–2007). His research on the economics of professional sports, incentive-compatible remuneration systems, and mandated codetermination has been published in a number of scholarly journals, including *Kyklos, Scottish Journal of Political Economy, Eastern Economic Journal, Journal of Sports Economics, Oxford Review of Economic Policy, Applied Economics, Industrial Relations, Contemporary Economic Policy, Journal of Economic Issues, British Journal of Industrial Relations, Labour*, and *International Journal of Human Resource Management.* His research has been presented and discussed on a number of German TV and radio shows. He once was a competitive long-distance runner with personal bests of 33:25 (10 k), 1:12:46 (half marathon), and 2:39:46 (marathon). Now, at the age of forty-eight, he is a slightly less motivated yet still enthusiastic jogger.

David Haber is an associate at MZ Sports LLC. He joined the firm in 2004 and provides financial and operational advisory services to the firm's clients. In the past three years, he has advised on fourteen acquisitions of sports properties, including five closed acquisitions: the Washington Nationals, Cleveland Cavaliers, Anaheim Mighty Ducks, Seattle Supersonics, and Portland Beavers. He graduated magna cum laude from the Wharton School of the University of Pennsylvania in 2004, where he received a B.S. in economics with a triple major in finance, marketing, and decision processes. Prior to joining MZ Sports, he worked at Bear, Stearns and Co. as a summer analyst in the fixed income sales, trading, and research division. Additionally, he has developed a background in a variety of disciplines within the sports industry, through positions with the Sydney Olympic Broadcasting Organization, Worldwide Entertainment and Sports, and *The Sporting News*.

Bruce K. Johnson is the James Graham Brown Professor of Economics at Centre College in Danville, Kentucky. His research on the economics of sports has appeared in journals including *Contemporary Economic Policy*, *Eastern Economic Journal*, *Journal of Sports Economics*, and *Journal of Sport Management*. His research has been reported on in media outlets including the *Washington Post* and *Business Week*, and he is regularly sought out by reporters from newspapers coast to coast for his insights on sports economics. He has also been a contributing columnist for the Lexington, Kentucky, *Herald-Leader* and has written numerous op-ed articles on the economics of current events, including sports, for newspapers including *USA Today*, the *Boston Globe*, the *Atlanta Constitution*, the *Minneapolis Star Tribune*, and the *Cincinnati Enquirer*. He holds a Ph.D. in economics from the University of Virginia.

Michael Leeds is an associate professor in the Department of Economics at Temple University. While trained as a labor economist, he is best known for his teaching and research in sports economics. His research has appeared in such journals as *Contemporary Economic Policy*, *Economic Inquiry*, and *Journal of Sports Economics*. Along with Peter von Allmen, he is coauthor of *The Economics of Sports* and a principles of economics textbook. His recent research includes work on how participation in athletics affects the accumulation of human capital and on the economic value of naming-rights purchases. From 1994 to 2006 he served as director of the honors program in the Fox School of Business at Temple University. He is currently an assistant dean at Temple's Japan Campus.

Judith Grant Long is an assistant professor of urban planning at the Harvard University Graduate School of Design. Her research interests focus on physical planning and development finance, with particular attention to the growing role of sports, tourism, and cultural infrastructure in cities.

Jon H. Oram is a partner in Proskauer Rose LLP's corporate department and a member of the firm's sports practice group. He has a broad-based transactional practice with a particular emphasis on the representation of professional sports leagues, teams, stadiums, and arenas, as well as the banks and other financial institutions that provide capital to sports properties and their owners. Among his clients are the National Basketball Association, National Hockey League, Major League Soccer, Philadelphia Eagles, New York Jets, New York Yankees, New Jersey Devils, JPMorgan Chase Bank, and numerous other leagues, teams, facilities, and financial institutions. He was recently recognized by Chambers USA as one of the nation's leading individuals in the field of sports law. He received his J.D. from Yale Law School in 1999, where he was an essays editor for the *Yale Law Journal*, and he graduated from Stanford University in 1996 with a bachelor's degree in public policy and a master's degree in education. He and his wife, Lisa Rubin, live in Manhattan.

Daniel A. Rascher received his Ph.D. in economics from the University of California at Berkeley. He is director of academic programs and associate professor for the Sport Management Program at the University of San Francisco, where he also teaches courses in sports economics and finance and sports business research methods. Prior to joining the University of San Francisco, he was an assistant professor at the University of Massachusetts, Amherst. He has authored articles for academic and professional journals and book chapters in the sport management and economics fields, and he has been interviewed hundreds of times by the media for his opinion on various aspects of the business of sports. He has testified as an expert in state court and in a number of arbitration proceedings, and has provided public testimony numerous times to local and state governments. He serves on the editorial boards of the *Journal of Sport Management*, *Sport Management Review*, *International Journal of Sport Finance*, and the *Journal of the Quantitative Analysis of Sports*. He is also founder and president of SportsEconomics, LLC, a consulting firm dedicated to bringing economic and financial analysis to the sports industry.

Bradley I. Ruskin is a senior partner in Proskauer Rose LLP's litigation and dispute resolution department and co-head of the firm's sports practice. He has also served two terms on the firm's executive committee. He has extensive experience successfully litigating for, as well as providing counseling and advice to, the leaders in today's sports industry. His sports clients include the National Hockey League, Major League Soccer, National Basketball Association, Association of Tennis Professionals, and World Tennis Association. Additionally, he has represented ownership groups and clubs in each of the major U.S. sports, including the Florida Marlins, New York Jets, Philadelphia

Eagles, and New Jersey Devils. He has handled multiple high-profile issues such as the right of a sports league to control and regulate expansion opportunities, relocation policies, scheduling, eligibility requirements, and the domestic and international telecasts of their games via broadcast, cable, and satellite; the legality of certain rules relating to player movement (including from Russia) and player discipline; valuation issues; the scope of rights of first refusal; the right of teams to sell personal seat licenses; the right of a league to reduce the number of its member clubs; the rights of leagues or teams in antidoping cases; the rights of leagues as licensors of intellectual property, including in bankruptcy proceedings; along with many other significant matters both in the sports world and in the media, communications, and finance worlds. He has been named as one of the nation's top sports practitioners by several national and international publications. He received his J.D. in 1981 from New York University School of Law and graduated with honors from Brown University in 1978. He also has served as the chair of numerous Bar Association committees, has taught a graduate-school class at NYU's Tisch School, and is a frequently published author of articles.

Rob Simmons is a senior lecturer in economics in the Department of Economics at Lancaster University Management School, United Kingdom. His Ph.D. is from University of Leeds. Simmons's research interests include economics of sports, labor and personnel economics, and economics of gambling. Recent journal outlets include *Economic Inquiry, International Journal of Forecasting, Journal of Sports Economics,* and *Southern Economic Journal.* Simmons is a qualified Football Association referee and long-time supporter of Manchester City FC.

Brian P. Soebbing is a Ph.D. candidate at the University of Alberta. His main research interest is the study of competitive balance in professional sports leagues and in college sports. Other interests include pay and performance, coaching performance, and the strategic decisions of sports leagues. He received his bachelor's degree from Saint Louis University and his master's from the University of Illinois at Urbana-Champaign.

Mitchell Ziets is the president and CEO of MZ Sports LLC, a boutique investment banking firm catering to the sports industry. Over the past nineteen years, he has advised on a number of sports facilities and franchise acquisitions. His client roster includes some of the nation's most well-known sports facilities including Oriole Park at Camden Yards, Dodgers Stadium, Miller Park, Paul Brown Stadium, Giants Stadium, the Georgia Dome, Lincoln Financial Field, and Petco Park. In addition, he has advised on thirty acquisitions of sports properties and has successfully closed six acquisitions over the past three years: the Washington Nationals, Los Angeles Dodgers, Cleveland Cavaliers, Anaheim Mighty Ducks, Seattle Supersonics, and Georgia Force. He received an M.S. in operations research from the University of California, Berkeley, and is a graduate of the Wharton School of the University of Pennsylvania, where he received a B.S. in economics with a double major in operations research and actuarial science. He is a board member of the Philadelphia Sports Congress. In 2000 he was selected as one of the "Top Forty under Forty" leaders in the Philadelphia region by the *Philadelphia Business Journal* and as one of the "Top Forty under Forty Sports Executives" by the *Sports Business Journal*.

Andrew Zimbalist is the Robert A. Woods Professor of Economics at Smith College, where he has been in the Economics Department since 1974. He received his B.A. from the University of Wisconsin, Madison, in 1969 and his M.A. and Ph.D. from Harvard University in 1972 and 1974, respectively. He has consulted in Latin America for the United Nations Development Program, the U.S. Agency for International Development, numerous companies, and has consulted in the sports industry for players' associations, cities, companies, and leagues. He has published seventeen books and several dozen articles, including *Baseball and Billions* (1992), *Sports, Jobs and Taxes* (1997), *Unpaid Professionals: Commercialism and Conflict in Big-Time College Sports* (1999), *The Economics of Sport*, 2 vols. (2001), *May the Best Team Win: Baseball Economics and Public Policy* (2003), *National Pastime: How Americans Play Baseball and the Rest of the World Plays Soccer* (with Stefan Szymanski) (2005), *In the Best Interests of Baseball? The Revolutionary Reign of Bud Selig* (2006), and *The Bottom Line: Observations and Arguments on the Sports Business* (2006).

Index